D0685438

COMPLETE
FRENCH
THE BASICS

Written by
CarolAnn D'Annunzio

Edited by
Zvjezdana Vrzić, Ph.D.

Published in the United States by Living Language, an imprint of Random House, Inc.

www.livinglanguage.com

Editor: Zvjezdana Vrzić, Ph.D.
Production Editor: Lisbeth Dyer
Production Manager: Thomas Marshall
Interior Design: Sophie Ye Chin

First Edition

ISBN: 978-1-4000-2409-4

Library of Congress Cataloging-in-Publication Data available upon request.

This book is available at special discounts for bulk purchases for sales promotions or premiums. Special editions, including personalized covers, excerpts of existing books, and corporate imprints, can be created in large quantities for special needs. For more information, write to Special Markets/Premium Sales, 1745 Broadway, MD 6-2, New York, New York 10019 or e-mail specialmarkets@randomhouse.com.

PRINTED IN THE UNITED STATES OF AMERICA

10 9 8 7 6 5 4 3 2 1

DEDICATION
I would like to dedicate this book to my husband and best friend, Paul Sonnenberg, who has been my biggest fan, supporting me in all of my endeavors, especially in the writing of this course.

ACKNOWLEDGMENTS
Thanks to the Living Language team: Tom Russell, Nicole Benhabib, Christopher Warnasch, Zvjezdana Vrzić, Suzanne McQuade, Shaina Malkin, Elham Shabahat, Sophie Chin, Denise DeGennaro, Linda Schmidt, Alison Skrabek, Lisbeth Dyer, and Tom Marshall. Special thanks to Brigitte Dewever for reviewing the book.

The author would like to thank her former student Christopher Warnasch, his Living Language team, and her editor, Zvjezdana Vrzić. Special thanks to Frances and Rick Gonzalez, Agnieszka Leesch, Dana Salmon, and Joseph Porretta.

COURSE OUTLINE

—————— How to use this course ——————

Welcome to *Complete French: The Basics*! We know you're ready to jump right in and start learning French, but before you do, you may want to spend some time familiarizing yourself with the structure of this course. This will make it easier for you to find your way around and will really help you get the most out of this course.

UNITS AND LESSONS

Complete French: The Basics is made up of ten *Units,* each with its own topic, from talking about yourself and making introductions to asking directions and going shopping. Each Unit is divided into four *Lessons*:

1. *Words,* featuring the essential vocabulary based on each Unit's topic;

2. *Phrases,* bringing words together into more complex structures and introducing a few idiomatic expressions;

3. *Sentences,* expanding on the vocabulary and phrases from previous lessons, using the grammar you've learned to form complete sentences; and

4. *Conversations,* highlighting how everything works together in a realistic conversational dialogue.

The lessons each comprise the following sections:

WORD LIST/PHRASE LIST/SENTENCE GROUP/CONVERSATION

Every lesson will begin with a list of words, phrases, or sentences, or a dialogue (conversation). The grammar and exercises will be based on these lists or dialogues, so it is important to spend as much time as possible reading and rereading these before getting into the heart of the lesson.

NOTES
A brief section may appear after the list or dialogue to expand on any intricacies in the language or culture.

NUTS & BOLTS
This is the nitty-gritty of each lesson, where we explain the grammar of the language, the nuts and bolts that hold the pieces together. Pay close attention to these sections; this is where you'll get the most out of the language and learn what you need to know to become truly proficient in French.

PRACTICE
It's important to practice what you've learned on a regular basis. You'll encounter practice sections throughout each lesson; take your time to complete these exercises before moving on to the next section. How well you do on each practice exercise will determine whether or not you need to review a particular grammar point before you move on.

TIP!
In order to enhance your experience, we offer you several tips for learning French throughout the course. This could be a tip on a specific grammar point, additional vocabulary related to the lesson topic, or a tip on language learning in general. For more language learning tips, you can also refer to the *Language learning tips* section that follows this introduction.

CULTURE NOTES AND LANGUAGE LINKS
Becoming familiar with the culture of French-speaking countries is nearly as essential to language learning as grammar. These sections allow you to get to know these cultures better through facts about French-speaking countries and other bits of cultural information. We've also included the addresses for various websites you can visit on the internet to learn more about a particular country or custom.

DISCOVERY ACTIVITY

Discovery activities are another chance for you to put your new language to use. They will often require you to go out into the world and interact with other French speakers or simply to use the resources around your own home to practice your French.

UNIT ESSENTIALS

Finally, each Unit ends with a review of the most essential vocabulary and phrases, the essentials. Make sure you're familiar with these phrases, as well as their structure, before moving on to the next Unit.

The coursebook also contains *Supplemental vocabulary lists, Internet resources,* and *Summary of French grammar* sections to be used for further reference.

LEARNER'S DICTIONARY

If you've purchased this book as a part of the complete audio package, you also received a learner's dictionary with more than 20,000 of the most frequently used French words, phrases, and idiomatic expressions. Use it as a reference any time you're stuck for words in the exercises and discovery activities, or as a supplemental study aid.

AUDIO

This course works best when used along with its accompanying audio, which features key vocabulary, example sentences, and dialogues from the course. This audio can be used along with the book, or on the go for hands-free practice.

And that's it—the basics! To get even more out of this course, you may wish to read the *Language learning tips* section that follows this introduction. If you're confident that you know all you need to know to get started and you wish to head straight to Unit 1, you can always come back to this section for tips on enhancing your learning experience.

Good luck!

If you're not sure about the best way to learn a new language, take a moment to read this section. It includes lots of helpful tips and practical advice on studying languages in general, improving vocabulary, mastering grammar, using audio, doing exercises, and expanding your learning experience. All of this will make learning more effective and more fun.

GENERAL TIPS

Let's start with some general points to keep in mind about learning a new language.

1. FIND YOUR PACE

The most important thing to keep in mind is that you should always proceed at your own pace. Don't feel pressured into thinking that you only have one chance to digest information before moving on to new material. Read and listen to parts of lessons or entire lessons as many times as it takes to make you feel comfortable with the material. Regular repetition is the key to learning any new language, so don't be afraid to cover material again, and again, and again!

2. TAKE NOTES

Use a notebook or start a language journal so you can have something to take with you. Each lesson contains material that you'll learn much more quickly and effectively if you write it down or rephrase it in your own words once you've understood it. That includes vocabulary, grammar points and examples, expressions from dialogues, and anything else that you find noteworthy. Take your notes with you to review wherever you have time to kill—on the bus or train, waiting at the airport, while dinner is cooking—or whenever you can find the time. Remember, practice (and lots of review!) makes perfect when it comes to learning languages.

3. Make a regular commitment

Make time for your new language. The concept of "hours of exposure" is key to learning a language. When you expose yourself to a new language frequently, you'll pick it up more easily. On the other hand, the longer the intervals between your exposure to a language, the more you'll forget. It's best to set time aside regularly for yourself. Imagine that you're enrolled in a class that takes place at certain regular times during the week, and set that time aside. Or use your lunch break. It's better to spend shorter amounts of time several days a week than a large chunk of time once or twice a week. In other words, spending thirty or forty minutes on Monday, Tuesday, Wednesday, Friday, and Sunday will be more effective than spending two and a half or three hours just on Saturday.

4. Don't have unrealistic expectations

Don't expect to start speaking a new language as if it were your native language. It's certainly possible for adults to learn new languages with amazing fluency, but that's not a realistic immediate goal for most people. Instead, make a commitment to become "functional" in a new language, and start to set small goals: getting by in most daily activities, talking about yourself and asking about others, following TV and movies, reading a newspaper, expressing your ideas in basic language, and learning creative strategies for getting the most out of what you already know in the language you're learning. Functional doesn't mean perfectly native-fluent, but it's still a great accomplishment!

5. Don't get hung up on pronunciation

"Losing the accent" is one of the most challenging parts of learning a language. If you think about celebrities, scientists, or political figures whose native language isn't English, they probably have a pretty recognizable accent. But that hasn't kept them from becoming celebrities, scientists, or political figures. Very young children are able to learn the sounds of any language in the world, and they can reproduce them perfectly. That's part of the process of learning a native language. In an adult, or even in an older child, this ability has diminished, so if you agonize over sounding like a native speaker in your new language, you're just setting yourself up for disappointment. That's not to say that you can't learn pronunciation well. Even adults can get pretty far through mimicking the sounds that they hear. So, listen carefully to the audio several times. Listening is a very important part of this process: you can't reproduce a sound until you learn to distinguish the sound. Then mimic what you hear. Don't be afraid of sounding strange. Just keep at it, and soon enough, you'll develop good pronunciation.

6. DON'T BE SHY
Learning a new language inevitably involves speaking out loud, and it involves making mistakes before you get better. Don't be afraid of sounding strange, awkward, or silly. You won't; you'll impress people with your attempts. The more you speak, and the more you interact, the faster you'll learn to correct the mistakes you do make.

TIPS ON LEARNING VOCABULARY
You obviously need to learn new words in order to speak a new language. Even though that may seem straightforward compared with learning how to actually put those words together in sentences, it's really not as simple as it appears. Memorizing words is difficult, even just in the short term, but long term memorization takes a lot of practice and repetition. You won't learn vocabulary simply by reading through the vocabulary lists once or twice. You need to practice.

There are a few different ways to "lodge" a word in your memory, and some methods may work better for you than others. The best thing to do is to try a few different methods until you feel that one is right for you. Here are a few suggestions and pointers.

I. AUDIO REPETITION
Fix your eye on the written form of a word, and listen to the audio several times. Remind yourself of the English translation as you do this.

2. Spoken repetition

Say a word several times aloud, keeping your eye on the written word as you hear yourself speak it. It's not a race—don't rush to blurt out the word over and over again so fast that you're distorting its pronunciation. Just repeat it, slowly and naturally, being careful to pronounce it as well as you can. And run your eye over the shape of the word each time you say it. You'll be stimulating two of your senses at once that way—hearing and sight—so you'll double the impact on your memory.

3. Written repetition

Write a word over and over again across a page, speaking it slowly and carefully each time you write it. Don't be afraid to fill up entire sheets of paper with your new vocabulary words.

4. Flash cards

Flash cards may seem like child's play, but they're effective. Cut out small pieces of paper (no need to spend a lot of money on index cards), and write the English word on one side and the new word on the other. Just this act alone will put a few words in your mind. Then read through your deck of cards. First go from the target (new) language into English—that's easier. Turn the target language side face-up, read each card, and guess at its meaning. Once you've guessed, turn the card over to see if you're right. If you are, set the card aside in your "learned" pile. If you're wrong, repeat the word and its meaning, and then put it at the bottom of your "to learn" pile. Continue until you've moved all of the cards into your "learned" pile.

Once you've completed the whole deck from your target language into English, turn the deck over and try to go from English into your target language. You'll see that this is harder, but also a better test of whether or not you've really mastered a word.

5. Mnemonics

A mnemonic is a device or a trick to trigger your memory, like "King Phillip Came Over From Great Spain," which you may have learned in high school biology to remember that species are classified into kingdom, phylum, class, order, family, genus, and species. Mnemonics work well for vocabulary, too. When you hear and read a new word, look to see if it sounds like anything—a place, a name, a nonsense phrase, etc. Then, form an image of that place or person or even nonsense scenario in your head. Imagine it as you say and read the new word. Remember that the more sense triggers you have—hearing, reading, writing, speaking, imagining a crazy image—the better you'll remember.

6. Groups
Vocabulary should be learned in small and logically connected groups whenever possible. Most of the vocabulary lists in this course are already organized this way. Don't try to tackle a whole list at once. Choose your method—repeating a word out loud, writing it across a page, etc.—and practice with a small group of words.

7. Practice
Don't just learn a word out of context and leave it hanging there. Go back and practice it in the context provided in this course. If the word appears in a dialogue, read it in the full sentence and call to mind an image of that sentence. If possible, substitute other vocabulary words into the same sentence structure ("John goes to the *library*" instead of "John goes to the *store*"). As you advance through the course, try writing your own simple examples of words in context.

8. Come back to it
This is the key to learning vocabulary—not just holding it temporarily in your short term memory, but making it stick in your long term memory. Go back over old lists, old decks of flash cards you made, or old example sentences. Listen to the vocabulary audio from previous lessons. Pull up the crazy mnemonic devices that you created at some point earlier in your studies. And always be on the lookout for old words appearing again throughout the course.

TIPS ON USING AUDIO

The audio in this course not only lets you hear how native speakers pronounce the words you're learning; it also serves as a second kind of input to your learning experience. The printed words serve as visual input, and the audio serves as *auditory* input. There are a few different strategies that you can use to get the most out of the audio. First, use the audio while you're looking at a word or sentence. Listen to it a few times along with the visual input of seeing the material. Then, look away and just listen to the audio on its own. You can also use the audio from previously studied lessons as a way to review. Put the audio on your computer or an MP3 player and take it along with you in your car, on the train, while you walk, while you jog, or anywhere you spend your free time. Remember that the more exposure you have to and contact you have with your target language, the better you'll learn it.

TIPS ON USING CONVERSATIONS

The conversations, or dialogues, in this book are a great way to see language in action, as it's actually used by people in realistic situations. To get the most out of a dialogue as a language student, think of it as a cycle rather than a linear passage. First read through the dialogue once in the target language to get the gist. Don't agonize over the details just yet. Then, go back and read through it a second time, but focus on individual sentences. Look for new words or new constructions. Challenge yourself to figure out what they mean from the context of the conversation. After all, that's something you'll be doing a lot of in the real world, so it's a good skill to develop! Once you've worked out the details, read the dialogue again from start to finish. Now that you're very familiar with the dialogue, turn on the audio and listen to it as you read. Don't try to repeat yet; just listen and read along. This will build your listening comprehension. Then, go back and listen again, but this time, pause to repeat the phrases or sentences that you're hearing and reading. This will build your spoken proficiency and pronunciation. Now listen again without the aid of the printed dialogue. By this point, you'll know many of the lines inside and out, and any new vocabulary or constructions will be very familiar.

TIPS ON DOING EXERCISES
The exercises are meant to give you a chance to practice the vocabulary and structures that you learn in each lesson, and, of course, to test yourself on retention. Take the time to write out the entire sentences to get the most out of the practice. Don't limit yourself to just reading and writing. Read the sentences and answer aloud so that you'll also be practicing pronunciation and spoken proficiency. As you gain more confidence, try to adapt the practice sentences by substituting different vocabulary or grammatical constructions, too. Be creative and push the practices as far as you can to get the most out of them.

TIPS ON LEARNING GRAMMAR
Each grammar point is designed to be as small and digestible as possible, while at the same time complete enough to teach you what you need to know. The explanations are intended to be simple and straightforward, but one of the best things you can do is to take notes on each grammar section, putting the explanations into your own words and then copying the example sentences or tables slowly and carefully. This will do two things. It will give you a nice, clear notebook that you can take with you so you can review and practice, and it will also force you to take enough time with each section that it's really driven home. Of course, a lot of grammar is memorization—verb endings, irregular forms, pronouns, and so on. So a lot of the vocabulary learning tips will come in handy for learning grammar, too.

1. AUDIO REPETITION
Listen to the audio several times while you're looking at the words or sentences. For example, for a verb conjugation, listen to all of the forms several times, reading along to activate your visual memory as well.

2. SPOKEN REPETITION

Listen to the audio and repeat several times for practice. For example, to learn the conjugation of an irregular verb, repeat all of the forms of the verb until you're able to produce them without looking at the screen. It's a little bit like memorizing lines for a play—practice until you can make them sound natural. Practice the example sentences that way as well, focusing of course on the grammar section at hand.

3. WRITTEN REPETITION

Write the new forms again and again, saying them slowly and carefully as well. Do this until you're able to produce all of the forms without any help.

4. FLASH CARDS

Copy the grammar point, whether it's a list of pronouns, a conjugation, or a list of irregular forms, on a flash card. Stick the cards in your pocket so that you can practice them when you have time to kill. Glance over the cards, saying the forms to yourself several times, and when you're ready to test yourself, flip the cards over and see if you can produce all of the information.

5. GRAMMAR IN THE WILD

Do you want to see an amazing number of example sentences that use some particular grammatical form? Well, just type that form into a search engine. Pick a few of the examples you find at random, and copy them down into your notebook or language journal. Pick them apart, look up words you don't know, and try to figure out the other grammatical constructions. You may not get everything one hundred percent correct, but you'll definitely learn and practice in the process.

6. COME BACK TO IT

Just like vocabulary, grammar is best learned through repetition and review. Go back over your notes, go back to previous lessons and read over the grammar sections, listen to the audio, or check out the relevant section in the grammar summary. Even after you've completed lessons, it's never a bad idea to go back and keep the "old" grammar fresh.

HOW TO EXPAND YOUR LEARNING EXPERIENCE
Your experience with your new language should not be limited to this course alone. Like anything, learning a language will be more enjoyable if you're able to make it a part of your life in some way. And you'd be surprised to discover how easily you can do that these days!

1. USE THE INTERNET
The internet is an absolutely amazing resource for people learning new languages. You're never more than a few clicks away from on-line newspapers, magazines, reference material, cultural sites, travel and tourism sites, images, sounds, and so much more. Develop your own list of favorite sites that match your needs and interests, whether business, cooking, fashion, film, kayaking, rock climbing, or . . . well, you get the picture. Use search engines creatively to find examples of vocabulary or grammar "in the wild." Find a favorite blog or periodical and take the time to work your way through an article or entry. Think of what you use the internet for in English, and look for similar sites in your target language.

2. CHECK OUT COMMUNITY RESOURCES
Depending on where you live, there may be plenty of practice opportunities in your own community. There may be a cultural organization or social club where people meet. There may be a local college or university with a department that hosts such cultural events as films or discussion groups. There may be a restaurant where you can go for a good meal and a chance to practice a bit of your target language. Of course, you can find a lot of this information online, and there are sites that allow groups of people to organize and meet to pursue their interests.

3. FOREIGN FILMS
Films are a wonderful way to practice hearing and understanding a new language. With English subtitles and the pause and rewind

functions, they're practically really long dialogues with pictures, not to mention the cultural insight and experience they provide! And nowadays, it's simple to rent foreign DVDs online or even access films online. So, if you're starting to learn a new language today, go online and rent yourself some movies that you can watch over the next few weeks or months.

4. Music
Even if you have a horrible singing voice, music is a great way to learn new vocabulary. After hearing a song just a few times, the lyrics somehow manage to plant themselves in the mind. And with the internet, it's often very easy to find the lyrics of a song online, print them out, and have them ready for whenever you feel like singing.

5. Television
If you have access to television programming in the language you're studying, including, of course, anything you can find on the internet, take advantage of that! You'll most likely hear very natural and colloquial language, including idiomatic expressions and rapid speech, all of which will be a healthy challenge for your comprehension skills. But the visual cues, including body language and gestures, will help. Plus, you'll get to see how the language interacts with the culture, which is also a very important part of learning a language.

6. Food
A great way to learn a language is through the cuisine. What could be better than going out and trying new dishes at a restaurant with the intention of practicing your newly acquired language? Go to a restaurant, and if the names of the dishes are printed in the target language, try to decipher them. Then, try to order in the target language, provided, of course, that your server speaks the language! At the very least, you'll learn a few new vocabulary items, not to mention sample some wonderful new food.

ALPHABET

English and French share the same alphabet, but the pronunciation of the letters is a little different.

a	[ah]	n	[ehn]
b	[beh]	o	[o]
c	[seh]	p	[peh]
d	[deh]	q	[kü]
e	[uh]	r	[ehr]
f	[ehf]	s	[ehss]
g	[zheh]	t	[teh]
h	[ahsh]	u	[ü], very sharp
i	[ee]	v	[veh]
j	[zhee]	w	[doobluhveh]
k	[kah]	x	[eeks]
l	[ehl]	y	[eegrehk]
m	[ehm]	z	[zehd]

CONSONANTS

Here is the list of French consonant sounds in comparison with English and accompanied by example words in French.

Letter(s)	Approximate sound	Example
b, d, k, l, m, n, p, s, t, v, z	same as in English	
c before e, i, y	ss	cinéma (*movie theater*)
c before a, o, u	k	cave (*cave*)
ç (always before a, o, u)	s	français (*French*)
ch	sh	chaud (*hot*)
g before e, i, y	s in *measure*	âge (*age*)
g before a, o, u	g in *game*	gâteau (*cake*)
gn	ni in *onion*	agneau (*lamb*)
h	always silent	homme (*man*)
j	s in *measure*	je (*I*)
l, final, after i	y in *yes*	fauteuil (*armchair*)
ll between i and e	y in *yes*	billet (*ticket*)
ll	ll in *ill*	elle (*she*)
qu, final q	k	qui (*who*), cinq (*five*)
r	pronounced in the back of the mouth, like a light gargling sound	Paris (*Paris*)
ss	s	tasse (*cup*)

Letter(s)	Approximate sound	Example
s at beginning of word or before/after another consonant	**s**	**salle** (*hall*), **disque** (*record*)
s between vowels	**z** in *zebra*	**maison** (*house*)
th	**t**	**thé** (*tea*)
x, usually before a vowel	**x** in *exact*	**exact** (*exact*)
x before a consonant or final **e**	**x** in *exterior*	**extérieur** (*exterior*)

VOWELS

Here is the list of French vowel sounds in comparison with English and accompanied by example words in French.

Letter(s)	Approximate sound	Examples
a, à, â	**a** in *father*	**laver** (*to wash*), **à** (*to*), **pâte** (*dough*)
é, er, ez, et	**e** as in *bed*, with tight lips	**été** (*summer*), **aller** (*to go*), **Allez!** (*Go!*)
e before a consonant, **è, ei, ai, aî**	**e** in *bed*, with very relaxed lips	**belle** (*beautiful*), **père** (*father*), **veine** (*vein*), **faire** (*to do*), **connaître** (*to know*)

Letter(s)	Approximate sound	Examples
e at the end of a word or without an accent	**a** in *above*	**le** (*the*), **lever** (*to lift*)
eu, œu	**u** in *fur,* with lips very rounded	**feu** (*fire*), **cœur** (*heart*)
i	**ee** in *beet*	**ici** (*here*)
o, au, eau, ô	**au** in *caught*	**mot** (*word*), **auteur** (*author*), **eau** (*water*), **hôtel** (*hotel*)
ou	**oo** in *tool*	**fou** (*crazy*)
u	keep your lips rounded while pronouncing **ee**	**tu** (*you*)

VOWEL COMBINATIONS

Letter(s)	Approximate sound	Examples
ey, eille	**ey** in *hey*	**seyant** (*becoming*), **bouteille** (*bottle*)
ie	**ye** in *yes*	**hier** (*yesterday*)
œil	**uhy** (no equivalent)	**oeil** (*eye*)
ille	**eey** (no equivalent)	**fille** (*girl, daughter*)
oi	**oi** in the first part of *choir*	**moi** (*me*)

Letter(s)	Approximate sound	Examples
oui	(w)ooee	**Louis** (*Louis*)
oy	wah + y	**foyer** (*home*)
ui	wee	**lui** (*he, to him*)

NASAL VOWELS

Letter(s)	Approximate sound	Examples
an, en/em	a in *balm*, pronounced through both the mouth and the nose	**France** (*France*), **entrer** (*enter*), **emmener** (*to take along*)
in/im, ain/aim, ein/eim, ien, oin	a in *mad*, pronounced through both the mouth and the nose	**vin** (*wine*), **vain** (*vain*), **faim** (*hunger*), **sein** (*bosom*), **rien** (*nothing*), **loin** (*far*)
on/om, ion	o in *song*, pronounced through both the mouth and the nose	**bon** (*good*), **tomber** (*to fall*), **station** (*station, stop*)
un/um	u in *lung*, pronounced through both the mouth and the nose	**un** (*one, a*), **parfum** (*perfume*)

Vowel E, without and with accents

Letter(s)	Approximate sound	Examples
e without an accent, three different pronunciations	**uh;** short **eh,** tight lips, followed by silent **r, z,** or **t;** silent at the end of a word	**lever** (*to lift*), **aller** (*to go*), **allez** (*go*), **et** (*and*); **bonne** (*good*)
é	long **eh**	**été** (*summer*), **déjeuner** (*lunch*)
è, ê, e before a consonant	short **eh,** relaxed lips	**scène** (*scene*), **forêt** (*forest*), **belle** (*beautiful*)

UNIT 1
Greetings and introductions

Bonjour et bienvenue! *Hello and welcome!* We'll begin our first unit with some basic words and useful expressions so that you can start to speak French right away. You will learn how to say your name, introduce yourself to others, say where you are from, and ask other people for basic information about themselves. You will also learn greetings and various other expressions of courtesy that will help you communicate with other people more smoothly.

French is **fantastique!** Enjoy your new adventure! **Allons-y!** *Let's go!*

———————————— Lesson 1 (words) ————————————

WORD LIST 1
LES SALUTATIONS *(Greetings)*

Bonjour!	*Good day!/Hello!*
Salut!	*Hello!/Hi!/Bye!*
Ça va?	*How's everything?*
Ça va.	*Everything is well.*
	(lit., Everything is going well.)
Comment allez-vous?	*How are you? (fml.)*[1]
Comment vas-tu?	*How are you? (infml.)*
Très bien.	*Very well.*
Merci.	*Thank you.*

[1] The following abbreviations will be used in this course: *(m.)* = masculine; *(f.)* = feminine; *(sg.)* = singular; *(pl.)* = plural; *(fml.)* = formal, polite; *(infml.)* = informal, familiar. If a word has two grammatical genders, *(m./f.)* is used.

Enchanté./Enchantée.	*Nice to meet you. (lit., Delighted.)*
oui	*yes*
non	*no*
Bienvenue!	*Welcome!*
Au revoir!	*Good-bye!*
À bientôt!	*See you soon!*
À tout à l'heure!	*See you later!*
Bonsoir!	*Good evening!*
Bonne nuit!	*Good night!*

Notes

The expression **Bonjour!** combines two French words: **bon,** which means *good,* and **jour,** which means *day.* When greeting each other, the French give a firm handshake or a kiss on each cheek. Similarly, **Bonsoir!** *(Good evening!)* contains **bon,** which means *good,* and **soir,** which means *evening.*

Enchanté is an adjective meaning *delighted,* used conversationally to mean *Nice to meet you.* A man uses the form **enchanté,** and the form **enchantée,** with an additional -**e** at the end in writing, should be used by a woman. We'll talk more about the reasons for this distinction later in the lesson.

NUTS & BOLTS 1
Personal pronouns
The following table lists the French personal pronouns.

SINGULAR		PLURAL	
je	*I*	**nous**	*we*
tu *(sg. infml.)*	*you*	**vous** *(pl., sg. fml.)*	*you*
il	*he*	**ils** *(m.)*	*they*
elle	*she*	**elles** *(f.)*	*they*

Notice that in the vocabulary list at the beginning of the lesson, there are two ways of saying *How are you?*

Comment allez-vous?
How are you? (fml.)
Comment vas-tu?
How are you? (infml.)

The first expression uses the word **vous** *(you),* while the other expression ends in **tu** *(you).* **Vous** is a pronoun used to address two or more people (cf., English *y'all* or *you guys);* it is also used when talking to a person you do not know or to whom you need to show respect, such as an older person or a superior. **Tu** is used with family members, friends, and other people with whom you are more familiar, even pets!

Note that there are also two ways to say *they* in French—**ils,** which refers to plural subjects of masculine gender, and **elles,** which refers to plural subjects of feminine gender. When we have a mixed group of subjects—for instance, a boy and two girls—the masculine form **ils** is used.

PRACTICE 1
Tu or **vous**? Which pronoun would you use when speaking to . . . ?

1. *your dog*

2. *a stranger on a bus*

3. *your sister*

4. *your parents*

5. *your two best friends*

6. *your new boss*

7. *a group of your friends*

8. *your girlfriend or boyfriend*

Check your answers at the end of this lesson.

PRACTICE 2
Decide which French pronoun—**je, tu, il, elle, nous, vous, ils,** or **elles**—replaces the following nouns.

1. *Marc and Marie*

2. *the parents*

3. *the teacher*

4. *Sophia*

5. *Sophia and Robert*

6. *Paul and I*

7. *Sylvia and Helen*

8. *the girls*

WORD LIST 2
ENCORE DES SALUTATIONS ET DES MOTS UTILS *(More greetings and useful words)*

Pardon.	*Pardon me.*
Excusez-moi.	*Excuse me.*
Entrez.	*Come in.*
Entendu.	*All right.*
D'accord.	*All right./Okay.*
voilà	*there is, there are*
voici	*here is, here are*
l'homme	*man*
la femme	*woman*
la fille	*girl*
le garçon	*boy*
l'étudiant/l'étudiante	*student (male/female)*

moi	*me*
toi	*you*
aussi	*also*
qui	*who*
maintenant	*now*
devant	*in front (of)*

NUTS & BOLTS 2
Nouns, definite articles, and gender

Like English nouns, French nouns are always preceded by articles. Take a look at the following examples.

la fille
the girl

le garçon
the boy

The words **le** and **la** are definite articles and correspond to the English *the*. The definite articles are given in the following table.

SINGULAR		PLURAL
Masculine	Feminine	Masculine/feminine
le, l'	**la**	**les**

The articles tell us the "gender" of nouns. When a word is masculine, we use **le**. When a word is feminine, we use the article **la**. In French, all nouns are either masculine or feminine, whether they refer to people, things, animals, or abstract concepts.

When a singular noun begins with a vowel or an **h,** we use **l'** before the word. The **a** or **e** from the article is dropped, and the article and the following noun are pronounced together as one word. This rule is referred to as **élision** *(elision)*. Look at the following examples.

l'ami *(m.)*
the friend (male)

l'amie *(f.)*
the friend (female)

l'étudiant *(m.)*
the student (male)

l'étudiante *(f.)*
the student (female)

l'homme *(m.)*
the man

The article **les** is used with both masculine and feminine plural nouns. Note that the final **-s** in the article, which is pronounced *leh,* is silent. Plural nouns also carry this final plural **-s** marker, which is also silent.

les garçons
the boys

les filles
the girls

les amis *(m.)*
the friends (male)

les amies *(f.)*
the friends (female)

les étudiants *(m.)*
the students (male)

les étudiantes *(f.)*
the students (female)

les hommes
the men

It is best to learn each new noun together with its definite article, which indicates the noun's gender, otherwise often unpredictable.

le crayon
the pencil

le papier
the paper

la porte
the door

la classe
the class

There are some general rules that will help you identify the gender of a noun, when, as in most cases, it does not correspond to the sex of a person. For example, we can generally say that if a noun ends with a consonant, it is masculine, and if it ends with a vowel, it is feminine.

le ticket
the ticket

la blouse
the blouse

le train
the train

la lampe
the lamp

Unfortunately, there are many exceptions to this rule.

le livre
the book

la maison
the house

le café
the café

la nation
the nation

Many nouns for professions derive their feminine form by adding the feminine ending **-e** to the masculine form.

l'avocat *(m.)*
the lawyer (male)

l'avocate *(f.)*
the lawyer (female)

l'étudiant *(m.)*
the student (male)

l'étudiante *(f.)*
the student (female)

PRACTICE 3
Fill in the blanks with the correct definite article—**le, la, l',** or **les.**

1. _____ fille

2. _____ amie

3. _____ enfants

4. _____ professeur

5. _____ étudiante

Culture note

French in the world

French, a Romance language related to Spanish and Italian, is spoken as either a first or a second language in more than 30 countries around the world. **Le monde francophone** (*the Francophone world*) consists of approximately 125 million people.

Many English speakers do not realize that a very large number of the English words are actually French in origin. They were borrowed into English in the course of centuries, following the Norman conquest in 1066.

Here are the names for some of the **langues** (*languages*) of the world besides **le français** (*French*).

l'allemand	*German*
l'anglais	*English*
l'espagnol	*Spanish*
le grec	*Greek*
l'italien	*Italian*
le polonais	*Polish*
le portugais	*Portuguese*
le russe	*Russian*

ANSWERS

PRACTICE 1: 1. tu; **2.** vous; **3.** tu; **4.** vous; **5.** vous; **6.** vous; **7.** vous; **8.** tu

PRACTICE 2: 1. elles; **2.** ils; **3.** il; **4.** elle; **5.** ils; **6.** nous; **7.** elles; **8.** elles

PRACTICE 3: 1. la; **2.** l'; **3.** les; **4.** le; **5.** l'

PHRASE LIST 1
ENCORE DES EXPRESSIONS DE POLITESSE *(More polite expressions)*

S'il vous plaît.	*Please.*
Il n'y a pas de quoi.	*You're welcome.*
De rien.	*You're welcome.*
Je vous en prie.	*You're welcome. (lit., I beg of you.)*
Me voici.	*Here I am.*
Je suis ravi/ravie de faire votre connaissance.	*I'm delighted to make your acquaintance.*
Ça va bien.	*Everything is well.*
Ça va très bien.	*Everything is really well.*
Ça va mal.	*It's not going well. (lit., It's going badly.)*
Ça va comme-ci comme-ça.	*Everything is so-so.*
en français	*in French*
en anglais	*in English*
de Paris	*from Paris*
en France	*in France*
C'est . . .	*It is . . .*
des États-Unis	*from the United States*
aux États-Unis	*to the United States*

NUTS & BOLTS 1
THE VERB ÊTRE *(to be)* IN THE PRESENT TENSE

Now let's look at one of the most important verbs, **être** *(to be)*. The subject pronouns that you have previously learned are paired with present tense forms of the verb **être** in the table below. When we change the forms of a verb to match the different subjects, as in the English *I speak* but *she speaks*, we say that we conjugate the verb. So, let's learn how to conjugate the verb **être**.

SINGULAR		PLURAL	
je suis	*I am*	**nous sommes**	*we are*
tu es *(infml.)*	*you are*	**vous êtes** *(pl., sg. fml.)*	*you are*
il est	*he is*	**ils sont** *(m.)*	*they are*
elle est	*she is*	**elles sont** *(f.)*	*they are*

Marie est américaine.
Marie is American.

Marie takes the place of **elle**; therefore, we have **Marie est** *(Marie is)*.

Mes amis sont français.
My friends are French.

Mes amis takes the place of **ils**; therefore, we have **Mes amis sont** *(My friends are)*.

PRACTICE 1
Look at the following sentences. Fill in the blanks with the correct form of the verb **être.** Use the English translation for help.

1. Tu _____ mon ami. *You are my friend.*

2. Marie _____ de Paris. *Marie is from Paris.*

3. Marc _____ anglais. *Marc is English.*

4. Nous _____ français. *We are French.*

5. Jean et Louis, vous _____ français. *Jean and Louis, you are French.*

6. Je _____ professeur. *I am a teacher.*

7. Mon ami Paul _____ de Nice. *My friend Paul is from Nice.*

8. Hélène et Geneviève _____ de Paris. *Hélène and Geneviève are from Paris.*

PHRASE LIST 2
LES PROFESSIONS *(Professions)*

Il est professeur.	*He is a teacher.*
Elle est professeur.	*She is a teacher.*
l'agent de police	*police officer*
l'agent de change	*stockbroker*
l'agent de service	*janitor*
l'avocat/l'avocate	*lawyer (male/female)*
l'artiste	*artist*
l'architecte	*architect*
le baby-sitter/la baby-sitter	*babysitter (male/female)*
le chef d'orchestre	*conductor*
l'assistante sociale	*social worker*
le commissaire aux comptes	*auditor*
le clown	*clown*
le bibliothècaire/la bibliothècaire	*librarian (male/female)*

NOTES
You have learned that, in French, an article is always used before the noun. When indicating a person's profession, however, the article is omitted.

Il est bibliothècaire.
He's a librarian.

Elle est avocate.
She's a lawyer.

Je suis professeur.
I am a teacher.

NUTS & BOLTS 2
ADJECTIVES AND AGREEMENT

An adjective is a word used to describe a noun. The French adjective **intelligent** looks very similar to the English word, but unlike the English equivalent, *intelligent*, it has four different forms—masculine singular, feminine singular, masculine plural, and feminine plural—depending on the gender and number specification of the noun. Consider the four forms of the adjective **intelligent** in French.

intelligent *(m. sg.)*
intelligente *(f. sg.)*
intelligents *(f. pl.)*
intelligentes *(m. pl.)*

Notice how the different forms are used in sentences.

Luc est intelligent.
Luc is intelligent.

Luc is a masculine noun, and **intelligent** is a masculine adjective. Note that most final consonants in French are not pronounced, so intelligent in French is pronounced without the final **t,** as *ehn-teh-lee-zhen.*

Contrast that with the following.

Martine est intelligente.
Martine is intelligent.

Martine is a feminine singular noun, and **intelligente** is an adjective in the feminine singular form. Typically, feminine adjectives are marked by the feminine ending **-e**. This final **-e** is silent, but due to its presence, the preceding consonant **t** is pronounced: *ehn-teh-lee-zhent.* When an adjective modifies a plural subject, we also add the plural marker, **-s,** to either the masculine or the feminine form of the adjective.

Luc et Joseph sont intelligents.
Luc and Joseph are intelligent.

Recall that this final plural **-s** is not pronounced, so there is no audible distinction between the singular and plural forms of adjectives. However, the distinction is present and important to maintain in writing. Here's an example involving a feminine plural subject.

Martine et Julie sont intelligentes.
Martine and Julie are intelligent.

Here are more examples of regular adjectives, which simply require adding an **-e** to form the feminine and **-s** to form the plural.

MASCULINE SINGULAR	FEMININE SINGULAR	MASCULINE PLURAL	FEMININE PLURAL	
important	**importante**	**importants**	**importantes**	*important*
grand	**grande**	**grands**	**grandes**	*big, tall*
petit	**petite**	**petits**	**petites**	*small*
bleu	**bleue**	**bleus**	**bleues**	*blue*
gris	**grise**	**gris**	**grises**	*gray*
noir	**noire**	**noirs**	**noires**	*black*
vert	**verte**	**verts**	**vertes**	*green*
brun	**brune**	**bruns**	**brunes**	*brown*

If the masculine form of an adjective already ends in a silent **-e**, the feminine is the same as the masculine form. One such adjective is **sincère** *(sincere)*, which has only two different forms.

sincère *(m./f. sg.)*
sincères *(m./f. pl.)*

Roger est sincère.
Roger is sincere.

Brigitte est sincère.
Brigitte is sincere.

Roger et Brigitte sont sincères.
Roger and Brigitte are sincere.

Here are other adjectives like **sincère**.

MASCULINE/ FEMININE SINGULAR	MASCULINE/ FEMININE PLURAL	
agréable	**agréables**	*pleasant*
aimable	**aimables**	*kind*
autre	**autres**	*other*
brave	**braves**	*brave, fine*
difficile	**difficiles**	*difficult*
drôle	**drôles**	*funny*
énorme	**énormes**	*enormous*
étrange	**étranges**	*strange*
facile	**faciles**	*easy*

MASCULINE/ FEMININE SINGULAR	MASCULINE/ FEMININE PLURAL	
large	larges	*wide*
magnifique	magnifiques	*magnificent*
mince	minces	*thin*
rapide	rapides	*quick*
sympathique	sympathiques	*friendly*
rouge	rouges	*red*
jaune	jaunes	*yellow*
rose	roses	*pink*

The feminine of irregular adjectives is formed by changing the masculine endings from -x to -se, -f to -ve, -er to -ère, and -et to either -ète or -ette. In the latter case, the spelling of the feminine form needs to be memorized; there is no distinction in pronunciation. Look at the following examples.

MASCULINE SINGULAR	FEMININE SINGULAR	MASCULINE PLURAL	FEMININE PLURAL	
sérieux	sérieuse	sérieux	sérieuses	*serious*
actif	active	actifs	actives	*active*
fier	fière	fiers	fières	*proud*
inquiet	inquiète	inquiets	inquiètes	*worried*
violet	violette	violets	violettes	*violet*

If the masculine singular ends in **-s** or **-x,** the masculine plural is the same as the singular.

Il est français.
He is French.

Ils sont français.
They are French.

Il est paresseux.
He is lazy.

Ils sont paresseux.
They are lazy.

Most masculine adjectives ending in **-al** in the singular change that ending to **-aux** in the plural form.

MASCULINE SINGULAR	FEMININE SINGULAR	MASCULINE PLURAL	FEMININE PLURAL	
égal	**égale**	**égaux**	**égales**	*equal*
général	**générale**	**généraux**	**générales**	*general*
principal	**principale**	**principaux**	**principales**	*principal*
national	**nationale**	**nationaux**	**nationales**	*national*

PRACTICE 2
Choose the correct form of the adjective.

1. Sophie est (américain, américaine).

2. Le professeur est (intelligente, intelligent).

3. Le garçon et la fille sont (sincères, sincère).

4. La femme est (intelligente, intelligent).

5. L'avocate est (américain, américaine).

6. Elles sont (actifs, actives).

7. Françoise et Carol sont (fière, fières).

8. Ils sont (paresseux, paresseuses).

Some adjectives double the final consonant before adding an **-e** to form the feminine.

MASCULINE SINGULAR	FEMININE SINGULAR	MASCULINE PLURAL	FEMININE PLURAL	
ancien	**ancienne**	**anciens**	**anciennes**	*old*
bon	**bonne**	**bons**	**bonnes**	*good*
gentil	**gentille**	**gentils**	**gentilles**	*nice, kind*
parisien	**parisienne**	**parisiens**	**parisiennes**	*Parisian*
violet	**violette**	**violets**	**violettes**	*violet*

Some adjectives are completely irregular, and their forms need to be memorized. They also have an additional form when placed in front of a masculine singular word starting with a vowel.

MASCULINE SINGULAR	FEMININE SINGULAR	MASCULINE PLURAL	FEMININE PLURAL	BEFORE A VOWEL	
beau	**belle**	**beaux**	**belles**	**bel**	*beautiful*
vieux	**vieille**	**vieux**	**vieilles**	**vieil**	*old*
nouveau	**nouvelle**	**nouveaux**	**nouvelles**	**nouvel**	*new*

Il a un nouvel imperméable.
He has a new raincoat.

Tip!

There is no magic to learning vocabulary, but there are some simple tricks that you may want to consider. First, write down all of your new words, taking the time to really focus on the spelling. Accents count, too! A good way to approach the study of vocabulary is to read and concentrate on the new words several times a day instead of spending a large amount of time in one sitting. For example, spend a few minutes reviewing vocabulary in the morning, when your mind is refreshed from sleep, and then again before bedtime. Flash cards also work well, as does labeling things in French around the house using stick-on notes.

ANSWERS

PRACTICE 1: 1. es; **2.** est; **3.** est; **4.** sommes; **5.** êtes; **6.** suis; **7.** est; **8.** sont

PRACTICE 2: 1. américaine; **2.** intelligent; **3.** sincères; **4.** intelligente; **5.** américaine; **6.** actives; **7.** fières; **8.** paresseux

---
Lesson 3 (sentences)

SENTENCE GROUP 1

Here are some general terms you will find helpful when having a conversation with someone.

Comment vous appelez-vous? *(fml.)*	*What is your name?*
Comment t'appelles-tu? *(infml.)*	*What is your name?*
Je m'appelle Pierre Dupont.	*My name is Pierre Dupont.*
Je m'appelle Michèle Soubrié.	*My name is Michèle Soubrié.*
Enchanté/Enchantée de faire votre connaissance.	*Pleased to meet you.*
Bonjour, Monsieur Dupont.	*Good day, Mr. Dupont.*

Bonjour, Madame La Salle.	*Good day, Ms. La Salle.*
Bonjour, Mademoiselle La Salle.	*Good day, Miss La Salle.*
Salut, tout le monde!	*Hi, everyone!*
Quel plaisir de te voir!	*Nice to see you!*
Quelle joie d'être ici!	*It's a joy to be here!*
À plus tard!	*See you later!*
Où habitez-vous? *(fml.)*	*Where do you live?*
Où habites-tu? *(infml.)*	*Where do you live?*
J'habite aux États-Unis.	*I live in the United States.*
Je suis des États-Unis.	*I'm from the United States.*

NOTES

Note the titles in French: **Monsieur** *(Sir)*, **Madame** *(Madam)*, and **Mademoiselle** *(Miss)*. Their abbreviations are **M.** *(Mr.)*, **Mme** *(Mrs., Ms.)*, and **Mlle** *(Miss)*. Use **Messieurs** for *gentlemen* and **Mesdames** for *ladies*. So *ladies and gentlemen* is **Mesdames et Messieurs**.

PRACTICE 1
Select the best response to each question.

1. Comment vous appelez-vous?

   a. Je suis de Paris.

   b. Je suis américain.

   c. Je m'appelle Pierre.

2. Où habitez-vous?

   a. Je suis français.

   b. J'habite à Montréal.

   c. Où habites-tu?

3. Comment allez-vous?

   a. Je m'appelle Jean.

b. Très bien, merci, et vous?

c. J'habite à Paris.

4. Où habites-tu?

a. Je suis de Paris.

b. Ça va.

c. Je suis français.

5. Tu es professeur?

a. Non. Je suis artiste.

b. Oui. Je m'appelle Philippe.

c. Non. J'habite à Nice.

SENTENCE GROUP 2

Now look at some useful terms and sentences you can use to inquire about and describe people.

Qui est-ce?	*Who is this?/Who is it?*
Voici mon mari.	*Here is my husband.*
Voici ma femme.	*Here is my wife.*
Il est charmant.	*He is charming.*
Elle est charmante.	*She is charming.*
L'homme est français.	*The man is French.*
La femme est française.	*The woman is French.*
L'homme et la femme sont français.	*The man and the woman are French.*
Tu es marié/mariée?	*Are you married?*
Non, je suis célibataire. *(m./f.)*	*No, I am single.*
De quelle nationalité êtes-vous? *(fml.)*	*What's your nationality?*
De quelle nationalité es-tu? *(infml.)*	*What's your nationality?*
Je suis italien/ canadien/irlandais.	*I am Italian/Canadian/Irish.*

Here are more adjectives of nationality.

français/française	*French*
anglais/anglaise	*English*
irlandais/irlandaise	*Irish*
américain/américaine	*American*
mexicain/mexicaine	*Mexican*
italien/italienne	*Italian*
canadien/canadienne	*Canadian*
espagnol/espagnole	*Spanish*

NUTS & BOLTS 1
PLACEMENT OF ADJECTIVES

Notice that nationality adjectives follow the noun **l'origine** *(the origin)* or **la nationalité** *(the nationality)*.

Je suis d'origine américaine.

I am of American origin.

Pierre est d'origine irlandaise.

Pierre is of Irish origin.

Jean-Luc est d'origine canadienne.

Jean-Luc is of Canadian origin.

The adjectives of nationality also follow the noun in these examples.

Voici un homme français.

Here is a French man.

Voici un homme américain.

Here is an American man.

Voici une femme française.

Here is a French woman.

Voici une femme américaine.
Here is an American woman.

In fact, most adjectives in French follow the noun they modify.

Voici un homme intelligent.
Here is an intelligent man.

Voici une femme charmante.
Here is a charming woman.

PRACTICE 2
Choose the appropriate words from the list below to fill in the blanks.

intelligente, appelle, Etats-Unis, es, intelligents, ça, célibataire, êtes

1. Bonjour, je m'_____ Henri de la Salle. Ça va?

2. Oui, _____ va bien, merci.

3. Où habitez-vous? Je suis des _____.

4. Ah! Vous _____ américaine!

5. Tu _____ marié?

6. Non, je suis _____.

7. Le garçon est intelligent et la fille est _____.

8. L'étudiant et le professeur sont _____.

Language link
If you would like to forge ahead on your own to explore and expand your French vocabulary, a fun place to start could be www.languageguide.org/francais. The website's mission is to provide resources for language learning and cultural enrichment.

ANSWERS

PRACTICE 1: 1. c; 2. b; 3. b; 4. a; 5. a

PRACTICE 2: 1. appelle; 2. ça; 3. États-Unis; 4. êtes; 5. es;
6. célibataire; 7. intelligente; 8. intelligents

——————— Lesson 4 (conversations) ———————

CONVERSATION 1

Sophie and Olivier meet at a friend's party.

Olivier: Bonjour! Je m'appelle Olivier.
Sophie: Je suis enchantée, Olivier. Je m'appelle Sophie.
Comment allez-vous?
Olivier: Ça va bien, merci. Vous êtes de Paris?
Sophie: Oui, je suis de Paris. Et vous, vous êtes
français?
Olivier: Non! Je suis américain.
Sophie: C'est super! Je suis professeur d'anglais au
collège.
Olivier: Et moi, je suis étudiant à l'université. La France
est magnifique.
Sophie: Bienvenue, Olivier!
Olivier: Merci beaucoup!

Olivier: *Hello! My name is Olivier.*
Sophie: *I am pleased to meet you, Olivier. My name is Sophie.*
How are you?
Olivier: *Very well, thank you. You are from Paris?*
Sophie: *Yes, I am from Paris. And you, are you French?*
Olivier: *No! I am American.*
Sophie: *That's great. I am an English teacher in high school.*
Olivier: *And I am a student at the university. France is*
wonderful.
Sophie: *Welcome, Olivier!*
Olivier: *Thank you very much.*

NOTES

Remember that there is no article before nouns denoting professions, as in Olivier's and Sophie's statements above.

Je suis étudiant.
I am a student. (male)

Je suis professeur.
I am a professeur. (female)

Also note that word **le collège** is not the equivalent of the English word *college*; it means *secondary school* or *high school*. Other French words for *high school* are **le lycée** and **l'école secondaire**. Finally, the French word for *college* is **l'université**.

NUTS & BOLTS 1
COGNATES

There are many words in French that look very similar to their English translations. They are called *cognates*. They may be pronounced differently in the two languages, but they are usually spelled similarly and have the same meanings. You probably do not even realize how many French words you already know! Here are some examples.

blond	la blouse
certain	la boutique
cruel	la nation
différent	la photo
élégant	la phrase
excellent	la question
horrible	la table
le boulevard	l'accident
le bureau	l'âge
le chef	l'animal
le client	l'automobile

le fruit	l'avenue
le guide	l'éléphant
le menu	l'hôtel
le zoo	l'océan
orange	la télévision

Keep in mind that there are also "false cognates," which, like **le collège,** are words that may sound or be spelled the same or nearly the same as in English but have a different meaning. Another example of a false cognate is the French word **sale** *(dirty),* which has nothing at all to do with shopping. The word **blessé** may look similar to the word *blessed,* but its actual meaning is *wounded.*

PRACTICE 1
Look at the following definitions in English and fill in the blanks in French using the cognates you have just learned.

1. *A broad avenue often lined with trees is called* le _____.

2. *A woman's article of clothing often worn with a skirt is called* la _____.

3. *While seated in a restaurant, a person wishing to order a meal consults* le _____.

4. *The colors often associated with Halloween are black and* _____.

5. *This word can refer to a main office or a piece of furniture in a bedroom*: le _____.

CONVERSATION 2
Fabienne and her cousin Martine are in a café. Luc, Fabienne's friend, arrives just as Martine excuses herself from the table.

> Luc: Salut, Fabienne! Comment vas-tu, chère amie?
> Fabienne: Ah! Bonjour, Luc. Ça va très bien, et toi?
> Luc: Pas mal, merci. La fille blonde, c'est une amie?

Fabienne:	C'est ma cousine Martine.
Luc:	Elle est française?
Fabienne:	Non, elle est américaine.
Luc:	Elle est marieé?
Fabinne:	Non, Martine est célibataire.
Luc:	C'est bien. Elle habite ici?
Fabienne:	Non, elle est des États-Unis.
Luc:	Eh bien! Pas de chance!

Luc:	*Hi, Fabienne! How are you, my dear friend?*
Fabienne:	*Ah! Hello, Luc. Everything's fine, my friend, and how about·you?*
Luc:	*Not bad, thanks. The blonde-haired girl, is she a friend?*
Fabienne:	*It's my cousin Martine.*
Luc:	*Is she French?*
Fabienne:	*No, she's American.*
Luc:	*Is she married?*
Fabienne:	*No, Martine is single.*
Luc:	*That's good. Does she live here?*
Fabienne:	*No, she's from the United States.*
Luc:	*Oh well! No luck!*

NUTS & BOLTS 2
Asking questions

Some of the most commonly used question words are **comment** *(how)*, **qui** *(who)*, **où** *(where)*, **(de) quel/de quelle** *(what [+ noun])*, **pourquoi** *(why)*, **quand** *(when)*, and **à quelle heure** *(at what time)*. Let's look at the examples from the conversations in this lesson.

Comment vas-tu? *(infml.)*

How are you?

Comment allez-vous? *(fml.)*

How are you?

Comment t'appelles-tu? *(infml.)*

What is your name?

Comment vous appelez-vous? *(fml.)*
What is your name?

De quelle nationalité es-tu?
What's your nationality?

De quelle origine es-tu?
What's your origin?

Où est Paul?
Where is Paul?

Où habites-tu?
Where do you live?

Quel is used before a masculine noun.

Quel homme est français?
Which man is French?

Quelle is used before a feminine noun.

Quelle femme est canadienne?
Which woman is Canadian?

The question **Comment?** can also be used informally to mean *What?* or *How's that again?*

PRACTICE 2
Write a question that could lead to each of the following answers.

1. Voici Martine. *(Ask where she is.)*

2. J'habite à Boston.

3. Je m'appelle Monsieur Le Brun.

4. Voici le médecin. *(Ask where he is.)*

5. Marc est d'origine française.

France, the country

Although metropolitan France is smaller than the state of Texas, it has the population of more than sixty million people, almost three times that of Texas. It is made up of twenty-two **provinces** (*provinces*). Here are their names in French: **Alsace, Aquitaine, Auvergne, Basse-Normandie, Bourgogne, Bretagne, Centre, Champagne-Ardenne, Corse, Franche-Comte, Haute-Normandie, Ile-de-France, Languedoc-Roussillon, Limousin, Lorraine, Midi-Pyrenees, Nord-Pas-de-Calais, Pays de la Loire, Picardie, Poitou-Charentes, Provence-Alpes-Côte d'Azur,** and **Rhone-Alpes.** The scenery, weather, and way of life vary greatly from region to region. In the east, the mountains of the Alps are covered with snow all year and are a popular skiing location. Normandy, in the north, has a flat coastline with long sandy beaches. Brittany, located in the northwest, has a rocky coastline with many inlets.

France also has **départements d'outre-mer** (*overseas departments*): **Guyane** (*French Guiana*) in Northern South America, **Guadeloupe** in the Caribbean, **Martinique** in the Caribbean, and **Réunion** in the Indian Ocean.

ANSWERS

PRACTICE 1: 1. boulevard; **2.** blouse; **3.** menu; **4.** orange; **5.** bureau

PRACTICE 2: 1. Où est Martine? **2.** Où habites-tu?/Où habitez-vous? **3.** Comment vous appelez-vous? **4.** Où est le médecin? **5.** De quelle origine est Marc?

UNIT 1 ESSENTIALS

Here are some of the most important phrases and expressions you've learned in this unit.

Bonjour!	*Good day!*
Bonsoir!	*Good evening!*
Comment allez-vous?	*How are you?*
Ça va?	*Is everything okay?/How's it going?*
Ça va bien.	*Everything is well./It's going well.*
Comment vous appelez-vous? *(fml.)*	*What is your name?*
Je m'appelle . . .	*My name is . . .*
De quelle origine/nationalité êtes-vous? *(fml.)*	*What's your origin/nationality?*
Salut!	*Hello!/Hi!/Bye!*
Au revoir!	*Good-bye!*
À bientôt!	*See you soon!*
Où est . . . ?	*Where is . . . ?*
Merci!	*Thank you!*
Il n'y a pas de quoi!	*You're welcome!*
S'il vous plaît.	*Please.*
À demain!	*See you tomorrow!*

Unit 2
Talking about family

Continuons! *Let's continue!* You are now familiar with some of the most basic vocabulary in French that you can use to greet people, to ask questions, and to talk about yourself.

In this unit, you will continue building your French skills by learning how to tell others about your family and friends. You will also learn some numbers in French. In Unit 1, you learned the verb **être** *(to be)*. It is useful in describing people and things. In this unit, another important verb will be presented, the verb **avoir** *(to have)*. This new verb is used to talk about family and possessions, as well as in expressions for conditions, such as hunger, thirst, cold, or heat. Now let's take a look at the new vocabulary.

——————————— Lesson 5 (words) ———————————

WORD LIST 1
LA FAMILLE *(The family)*

la famille	*family*
la mère	*mother*
le père	*father*
la sœur	*sister*
le frère	*brother*
la fille	*daughter*
le fils	*son*
la grand-mère	*grandmother*
le grand-père	*grandfather*

la tante	aunt
l'oncle	uncle
le cousin/la cousine	cousin (male/female)
le neveu	nephew
la nièce	niece
l'enfant	child
la femme	wife
le mari	husband

NOTES

Note that the word **la fille** *(girl)*, which you learned in Unit 1, can also mean *daughter*. If you want to talk about your parents, you would refer to them as **mes parents**. When you want to refer to your relatives, use **des parents** instead.

Mes parents sont à Paris.

My parents are in Paris.

J'ai des parents à Paris.

I have relatives in Paris.

NUTS & BOLTS 1
POSSESSIVE ADJECTIVES

In the practice sentences above, you might have noticed some new words used along with the family vocabulary presented: **mon, ma,** and **mes**. These adjectives express possession and agree with the noun they modify in number and gender, just like other adjectives.

MASCULINE SINGULAR	FEMININE SINGULAR	MASCULINE AND FEMININE PLURAL	
mon	**ma**	**mes**	*my*
ton *(infml.)*	**ta**	**tes**	*your*

Let's look at the examples.

mon père
my father

The possessive adjective **mon** is used because the word **père** is masculine.

ma mère
my mother

The possessive adjective **ma** is used because the word **mère** is feminine.

mes parents
my parents

The possessive adjective **mes** is used because the word **parents** is plural.

The possessive adjective agrees in gender and number with the noun it modifies, rather than with the person who is speaking or with the possessor. For example, either a boy or a girl will say **mon père** to refer to his or her father.

Here are a few more examples of nouns with possessive adjectives.

ma famille
my family

mon oncle
my uncle

mes oncles
my uncles

PRACTICE 1

Fill in the blanks with the best answer.

1. La mère de mon père est ma _____.

2. La sœur de ma mère est ma _____.

3. Le frère de mon père est mon _____.

4. Le fils de mon oncle est mon _____.

5. La fille de ma mère est ma _____.

6. Le fils de mon grand-père est mon _____.

7. La fille de ma sœur est ma _____.

8. Le fils de mon frère est mon _____.

Here are the rest of the possessive adjectives.

MASCULINE SINGULAR	FEMININE SINGULAR	MASCULINE AND FEMININE SINGULAR	
son	**sa**	**ses**	*his, her, its*
notre	**notre**	**nos**	*our*
votre	**vòtre**	**vos** *(pl., sg. fml.)*	*your*
leur	**leur**	**leurs**	*their*

Voici Marie et son père.
Here are Marie and her father.

Voici Luc et son père.
Here are Luc and his father.

Voilà notre mère.
There is our mother.

Nos parents sont d'origine italienne.

Our parents are of Italian descent.

Votre famille est italienne.

Your family is Italian.

Jacques et Paul, voici la photo de vos parents.

Jacques and Paul, here is the photo of your parents.

Voilà leur sœur.

There is their sister.

PRACTICE 2

Supply the correct possessive adjective for each sentence.

1. Voici Sylvie et _____ sœur. *Here are Sylvia and her sister.*

2. Jean est avec _____ parents. *John is with his parents.*

3. Voilà _____ amis. *There are our friends.*

5. _____ mari est ici, Madame Dupont. *Your husband is here, Ms. Dupont.*

5. Henri est _____ père. *Henry is their father.*

6. _____ sœur est sincère. *Your (fml.) sister is sincere.*

7. _____ père est grand. *Our father is tall.*

8. _____ cousins sont à la maison. *Our cousins are at home.*

WORD LIST 2
LES NOMBRES CARDINAUX *(Cardinal numbers)*

zéro	*zero*
un/une *(m./f.)*	*one*
deux	*two*
trois	*three*
quatre	*four*

cinq	*five*
six	*six*
sept	*seven*
huit	*eight*
neuf	*nine*
dix	*ten*

NOTES

Here's a quick note to help you pronounce the numbers. A *liaison*, a binding or joining of words, is used between a number ending in an **s** and the following word starting with a vowel. Compare the following two pronunciations.

trois filles [trwah feey]

three girls

trois enfants [trwah z-ah^n-fah^n]

three children

In the latter example, the **s** in the word **trois** is pronounced like a **z** and "joined" to the word **enfants.**

The same happens with the numbers **deux, six,** and **dix.** The letter **x** is pronouced like a **z** when it is followed by a word beginning with a vowel.

deux Italiens [duh z-ih-tah-lyeh^n]

two Italians

In the number *nine,* **neuf,** the **f** sound changes to a **v** sound in front of a word beginning with a vowel, especially before words such as **ans** *(years),* **heures** *(o'clock),* and **hommes** *(men).*

neuf heures [nuhv uhr]

nine o'clock

Finally, when the numbers **cinq, six, huit,** and **dix** are followed by a word beginning with a consonant, the final consonant of each word is silent. This rule is sometimes not followed with **cinq.**

cinq minutes
five minutes

six filles
six girls

dix garçons
ten boys

Here are the rest of the numbers up to twenty.

onze	*eleven*
douze	*twelve*
treize	*thirteen*
quatorze	*fourteen*
quinze	*fifteen*
seize	*sixteen*
dix-sept	*seventeen*
dix-huit	*eighteen*
dix-neuf	*nineteen*
vingt	*twenty*

Dix-neuf et un font vingt.
Nineteen and one make twenty.

Il y a onze statues dans le parc.
There are eleven statues in the park.

Note that **dix-neuf** is pronounced *diz nuhf.*

LES NOMBRES ORDINAUX *(Ordinal numbers)*

premier/première *(m./f.)*	*first*
deuxième	*second*
second/seconde *(m./f.)*	*second*
troisième	*third*
quatrième	*fourth*
cinquième	*fifth*
sixième	*sixth*
septième	*seventh*
huitième	*eighth*
neuvième	*ninth*
dixième	*tenth*
onzième	*eleventh*
quinzième	*fifteenth*
vingtième	*twentieth*

NOTES

Ordinal numbers are adjectives and must agree with the nouns they modify. With the exception of the words **premier** and **second,** ordinal numbers are formed by adding -**ième** to the corresponding cardinal numbers.

Note also that the silent **e** in the number **quatre** is dropped before -**ième** is added to form **quatrième.**

Also notice that the letter **u** is added in **cinquième** and the letter **f** in **neuf** is replaced with the letter **v** in **neuvième.**

le huit septembre
the eighth of September

les premiers jours
the first days

Premier is the only ordinal number used in numerical titles of rulers; otherwise, cardinal numbers are used.

François Premier
Francis the First

Louis Seize
Louis XVI

NUTS & BOLTS 2
INDEFINITE ARTICLES

In Unit 1, you learned about definite articles—**le, la, l'**, and **les.** In addition to definite articles, French also uses indefinite articles.

SINGULAR		PLURAL
Masculine	Feminine	Masculine and feminine
un	**une**	**des**

J'ai un cousin à Boston et une cousine à Paris.
I have a (male) cousin in Boston and a (female) cousin in Paris.

The plural form of **un** and **une** is **des,** which has no English equivalent and can also mean *some,* as in **des amis** *(friends, some friends).*

J'ai des cousins en Angleterre.
I have cousins in England.

PRACTICE 3

Replace the definite articles with the appropriate indefinite articles.

1. Jonathan est le neveu de Carol.
2. L'oncle de Sophie est américain.

3. Le professeur est présent.

4. La grand-mère de Paul habite à Paris.

5. La sœur de Roger habite en France.

6. La tante de mon amie est canadienne.

7. Marie est la fille de ma tante.

8. Voici le médecin.

Culture note

Family time

French families are close-knit and spend a lot of quality time together. For example, **les vacances** (*vacations*), **les repas** (*mealtimes*), and **les fêtes** (*holidays*) are occasions that the French like to spend together with parents, grandparents, and other close relatives. The average worker in France has five to six weeks of vacation time. Most people spend the larger part of their vacation in the summer, often by the sea; summer vacation is referred to as **les grandes vacances** (*lit., the big vacation*). Another week or two are spent at another time, often skiing, referred to as **le ski en montagne** (*skiing in the mountains*). The time off from school in the winter is called **les vacances de neige** (*lit., snow vacation*).

ANSWERS

PRACTICE 1: 1. grand-mère; 2. tante; 3. oncle; 4. cousin; 5. sœur; 6. père; 7. nièce; 8. neveu

PRACTICE 2: 1. sa; 2. ses; 3. nos; 4. votre; 5. leur; 6. ta; 7. notre; 8. nos

PRACTICE 3: 1. un; 2. un; 3. un; 4. une; 5. une; 6. une; 7. une; 8. un

PHRASE LIST 1
LES EXPRESSIONS AVEC LES GENS *(Expressions for people)*

Voilà des gens.	*There are some people.*
quelqu'un	*someone*
la personne	*person*
tout le monde	*everyone, everybody*
l'adulte	*adult, grown-up*
le bébé	*baby*
le nouveau-né	*newborn*
le cadet/la cadette	*youngest child (male/female)*
l'aîné/l'aînée	*oldest child (male/female)*
l'être humain	*human being*
l'individu	*individual*
Moi aussi.	*Me, too.*
une personne âgée	*elderly person*
bien sûr	*of course*
J'aime bien . . .	*I like . . .*
C'est une foule.	*It's a crowd.*

NUTS & BOLTS 1
THE VERB AVOIR *(to have)* IN THE PRESENT TENSE—SINGULAR FORMS

The first verb you learned in Unit 1 was the verb **être** *(to be)*. Now it's time to learn the second important verb—the verb **avoir** *(to have)*. Here are the singular forms of the verb **avoir**.

SINGULAR	
j'ai	*I have*
tu as	*you have (infml.)*
il a	*he has*
elle a	*she has*

Notice the apostrophe in **j'ai** *(I have)*. Remember from Unit 1 that the definite articles **le** and **la** become **l'** when used in front of a noun beginning with a vowel. The same thing happens with the pronoun **je** *(I)* before a verb beginning with a vowel, so **je ai** becomes **j'ai**. Let's see some examples of the verb **avoir** in the singular form.

J'ai deux frères.
I have two brothers.

Il a une grande famille.
He has a big family.

Tu as une sœur?
Do you have a sister?

Elle a une question.
She has a question.

Marie a un problème.
Marie has a problem.

J'ai un frère et une sœur.
I have a brother and a sister.

PRACTICE 1
Use the appropriate form of the verb **avoir** *(to have)*.

1. Pierre _____ des parents en France.

2. Tu _____ une sœur et un frère, n'est-ce pas?

3. Non, j'_____ deux sœurs.

4. Il _____ beaucoup de cousins.

5. Elle _____ trois enfants.

PHRASE LIST 2
ENCORE DES EXPRESSIONS AVEC LES GENS *(More expressions for people)*

J'ai un frère.	*I have one brother./I have a brother.*
mon père	*my father*
ma mère	*my mother*
mon frère	*my brother*
ma sœur	*my sister*
mes amis	*my friends*
N'est-ce pas?	*Right?/Don't you think so?/Isn't that so?*
ton père	*your father (infml.)*
ta mère	*your mother (infml.)*
tes parents	*your parents (infml.)*
Il y a . . .	*There is . . . /There are . . .*
Mon Dieu!	*My God!/My goodness!*

NUTS & BOLTS 2
THE VERB AVOIR *(to have)* IN THE PRESENT TENSE—PLURAL FORMS
Let's learn the plural forms of the verb **avoir**.

PLURAL	
nous avons	*we have*
vous avez *(fml.)*	*you have*
ils ont *(m.)*	*they have*
elles ont *(f.)*	*they have*

Note that the final **s** in the pronouns **nous, vous, ils,** and **elles,** normally silent, is pronounced as **z** in front of the forms of the verb **avoir**—e.g., **nous avons** is *noo z-ah-voh^n.*

Also keep in mind that **ils** is used to refer to subjects that are masculine as well as combinations of masculine and feminine.

Philippe et Geneviève ont quatre enfants.
Philippe and Geneviève have four children.

Vous avez une sœur.
You have one sister.

Nous avons un album de photos.
We have a photo album.

Ils ont trois nièces.
They have three nieces.

Here is one more look at the verb **avoir** with both the singular and plural forms in one place.

SINGULAR		PLURAL	
j'ai	*I have*	**nous avons**	*we have*
tu as *(infml.)*	*you have*	**vous avez** *(pl., sg. fml.)*	*you have*
il a	*he has*	**ils ont** *(m./f.)*	*they have*
elle a	*she has*	**elles ont** *(f.)*	*they have*

PRACTICE 2
Choose the correct form of the verb **avoir** *(to have)* to complete the sentences.

1. Marcel et Jean _____ (a, ont, avons) deux enfants.

2. Madame Dupont _____ (avez, ont, a) une question.

3. Nous _____ (avons, a, ont) une fête.

4. Elles _____ (a, ont, avons) un problème.

5. Vous _____ (avez, ai, avons) trois sœurs.

PRACTICE 3

Fill in the blanks with the correct form of the verb **avoir** *(to have)*.

1. Ils _____ trois enfants.

2. Suzanne et Chantal _____ un album de photos.

3. L'enfant _____ deux parents.

4. Vous _____ des cousins en France.

5. Nous _____ une sœur et un frère.

6. J'_____ quatre enfants.

7. Monsieur Dupont _____ une femme.

8. Tu _____ un fils.

Tip!

Learning verbs can be challenging! In Unit 1, you learned about making flash cards for new vocabulary. The same advice holds true for verbs. On one side, write the French forms, and on the other side, write the English equivalents. You can practice by yourself whenever you have a spare moment. The more exposure you have to the verb forms, the better! You can have a friend shuffle the cards and hold them up to prompt you to give the correct answer.

There are also different language games that make studying with a partner more fun. Here is one idea: Find a ball that can be easily tossed back and forth between two people. One person starts the game by tossing the ball to the other person and calling out a subject and verb in English—for example, *I am*. The person catching the ball must quickly give the translation in French—**je suis**—and toss the ball back while calling out another subject and verb in English for the other player. Points are scored when a player successfully gives an answer in French.

ANSWERS

PRACTICE 1: 1. a; 2. as; 3. ai; 4. a; 5. a

PRACTICE 2: 1. ont; 2. a; 3. avons; 4. ont; 5. avez

PRACTICE 3: 1. ont; 2. ont; 3. a; 4. avez; 5. avons; 6. ai; 7. a;
8. as

——————— Lesson 7 (sentences) ———————

SENTENCE GROUP 1
PARLONS DE LA FAMILLE *(Let's talk about the family)*

Il y a combien de personnes dans ta famille?	*How many people are there in your family?*
Il y a quatre personnes dans ma famille.	*There are four people in my family.*
Combien de frères as-tu?	*How many brothers do you have?*
J'ai deux frères.	*I have two brothers.*
Quel garçon a sept sœurs?	*Which boy has seven sisters?*
Jean-Luc a sept sœurs.	*Jean-Luc has seven sisters.*
Quel enfant est le cadet?	*Which child is the youngest?*
Quel enfant est l'aîné?	*Which child is the oldest?*
Il y a combien d'enfants dans ta famille?	*How many children are there in your family?*
Il y a trois enfants dans ma famille.	*There are three children in my family.*
Qu'est-ce que c'est?	*What is this?*
Qu'est-ce que tu fais?	*What are you doing?*

NOTES

Take note of the expression **il y a** *(there is, there are)*. This expression is used very often, so learn it and keep it handy.

Note also the expression **qu'est-ce que,** which simply means *what.*

NUTS & BOLTS 1
THE INTERROGATIVE ADJECTIVES
Note the following question words:

combien (de) *(how much, how many)*
quel/quelle *(what, which [m./f.])*

These question adjectives appear in front of nouns, unlike most other French adjectives. **Quel** and **quelle** sound the same, but **quel** is used with masculine nouns and **quelle** with feminine nouns.

PRACTICE 1
Supply the missing word in French.

1. Il y a _____ *(how many)* de personnes dans ta famille?

2. _____ *(There are)* trois personnes dans ma famille.

3. _____ *(Which)* homme est ton père?

4. _____ *(Which)* fille est ta sœur?

5. Tu as _____ *(how many)* d'enfants?

SENTENCE GROUP 2
LES DESCRIPTIONS DE FAMILLE *(Family descriptions)*

Mon père a les yeux bleus.	*My father has blue eyes.*
Ma mère a les cheveux blonds.	*My mother has blonde hair.*
Ma mère est blonde.	*My mother is blonde.*
Mon frère a vingt ans.	*My brother is twenty years old (lit., has twenty years).*
J'ai faim.	*I'm hungry (lit., have hunger).*
Elle a soif.	*She's thirsty (lit., has thirst).*

Tes cousins ont froid.	*Your cousins are cold (lit., have cold).*
Mon oncle et ma tante ont beaucoup d'enfants.	*My uncle and my aunt have many children.*
Tu as raison.	*You are right (lit., have reason).*
Nous avons raison.	*We are right (lit., have reason).*
Mon père a chaud.	*My father is warm (lit., has warmth).*
Le bébé a peur.	*The baby is afraid (lit., has fear).*

NUTS & BOLTS 2
USES OF ÊTRE *(to be)* AND AVOIR *(to have)*

Let's focus on the differences in use between the verbs **être** and **avoir**. The verb **être** is used with adjectives to describe people, places, and things.

Tu es blond.
You're blond.

Paris est magnifique.
Paris is wonderful.

Mes parents sont intelligents.
My parents are intelligent.

Now let's look again at the verb **avoir** *(to have)*. It's used to say that someone is in possession of something, whether it's an object or a quality.

Marc a un album.
Marc has an album.

Ma sœur a les yeux bleus.
My sister has blue eyes.

J'ai les cheveux bruns.
I have brown hair.

Mon ami Paul a les cheveux roux.
My friend Paul has red hair.

The verb **avoir** (and not **être**) is also used to talk about age.

J'ai vingt ans.
I'm twenty years old (lit., have twenty years).

Finally, it's used in many different fixed expressions where English usually uses *to be*.

avoir les yeux bleus/bruns/verts	*to have blue/brown/green eyes*
avoir les cheveux bruns/blonds/roux/noirs	*to have brown/blond/red/black hair*
avoir faim	*to be hungry (lit., to have hunger)*
avoir soif	*to be thirsty (lit., to have thirst)*
avoir froid	*to be cold (lit., to have cold)*
avoir chaud	*to be hot, to be warm (lit., to have warmth)*
avoir peur	*to be afraid (lit., to have fear)*
avoir raison	*to be right (lit., to have reason)*
avoir sommeil	*to be sleepy (lit., to have sleep)*

PRACTICE 2
Translate the following sentences into French. Be sure to use the verb **avoir,** and write the numbers in French.

1. *Marie is twelve years old.*

2. *The child has a mother.*

3. *We are right.*

4. *They have blue eyes.*

5. *My sister is six years old.*

6. *You have an album. (sg. fml.)*

You may want to explore the following useful website in order to practice conjugating verbs some more: www.verbix.com/languages/french.shtml.

Language link

You may want to explore the following useful website in order to practice conjugating verbs some more: www.verbix.com/languages/french.shtml.

ANSWERS

PRACTICE 1: 1. combien; 2. Il y a; 3. Quel; 4. Quelle; 5. combien

PRACTICE 2: 1. Marie a douze ans. 2. L'enfant a une mère. 3. Nous avons raison. 4. Ils ont les yeux bleus. 5. Ma sœur a six ans. 6. Vous avez un album.

—————— Lesson 8 (conversations) ——————

CONVERSATION 1
Patrick and Jeanne are looking at family photographs.

Patrick: Tu as ton album de photos aujourd'hui?

Jeanne: Voici mon album de photos.

Patrick: Et voilà mon album. Il y a combien de personnes dans ta famille?

Jeanne: Dans ma famille, il y a cinq personnes, mon père, ma mère, mon frère, ma sœur, et moi! Et dans ta famille?

Patrick: J'ai une grande famille! Il y a neuf personnes dans ma famille, mon père et ma mère, bien sûr, et sept enfants.

Jeanne: Mon Dieu! Sept enfants! Oh là là!

Patrick: Oui. Nous avons sept enfants dans notre famille. J'ai deux sœurs et quatre frères.

Jeanne: J'aime bien les grandes familles!

Patrick: Moi aussi! C'est amusant.

Jeanne: Oui, tu as raison, Patrick. Surtout pour les fêtes!

Patrick: C'est vrai. J'aime bien quand tout le monde est là!

> Patrick: Do you have your photo album today?
>
> Jeanne: Here is my photo album.
>
> Patrick: And here's my album. How many people are there in your family?
>
> Jeanne: In my family, there are five people: my father, my mother, my brother, my sister, and me. And in your family?
>
> Patrick: I have a big family. There are nine people in my family: my father and my mother, of course, and seven children.
>
> Jeanne: My goodness! Seven children! Wow!
>
> Patrick: Yes, we have seven children in our family. I have two sisters and four brothers.
>
> Jeanne: I like big families.
>
> Patrick: Me, too. It's fun.
>
> Jeanne: You're right, Patrick. Especially for holidays!
>
> Patrick: It's true. I like it when everyone is there!

NOTES

Tout le monde, meaning *everybody* or *everyone,* literally means *all the world.* This expression comes up often in conversation.

Bonjour, tout le monde!

Hi, everyone!

Tout le monde est ici.

Everybody is here.

NUTS & BOLTS 1
C'EST *(it is)* + ADJECTIVE

The phrase **c'est** *(it is)* is often used with various adjectives to express opinions.

C'est bon!

It's good!

C'est vrai.

It's true.

C'est amusant!
It's amusing!

When the food is good, you can use the following expression.

C'est bon!
It's good!

You can also say the following.

C'est délicieux!
It's delicious!

When you are having fun, you can say:

C'est amusant!
It's amusing!

C'est intéressant!
It's interesting!

C'est cool!
It's cool!

C'est super!
It's super!

C'est extra!
It's great!

Or, you can simply say:

Oh là là!
Wow!

PRACTICE 1
Match the French sentences with their English translations.

1. C'est intéressant!	a. *Wow!*
2. Oh là là!	b. *It's amusing!*
3. C'est extra!	c. *It's great!*
4. C'est bon!	d. *It's interesting!*
5. C'est amusant!	e. *It's good!*

CONVERSATION 2
Julia and her friend Jean are discussing their families and the Christmas holiday.

Julia: Eh bien, qu'est-ce que tu fais pour la fête de Noël?

Jean: Tout le monde est à la maison pour la fête.

Julia: C'est extra! Tes enfants sont mariés, n'est-ce pas? Ils sont là?

Jean: Oui. Mes enfants sont là avec leurs femmes et leurs maris et nous avons des parents de Paris. C'est bon d'avoir la famille ensemble.

Julia: Bien sûr, et vous avez une grande famille.

Jean: Et toi, qu'est-ce que tu fais pour la fête?

Julia: Le dîner a lieu à la maison. Mon fils, Robert, qui est étudiant à l'université, est à la maison aussi avec mon mari et moi, et ses grands-parents.

Jean: Tu as une photo de Robert?

Julia: Oui, voilà une photo de Robert avec ses cousins et ses cousines.

Jean: Il a les cheveux blonds comme toi, Julia.

Julia: Et il a les yeux bleus comme son père.

Julia: Well, what are you doing for the Christmas holiday?

Jean: Everyone is at home for the holiday.

Julia: That's great. Your children are married, right? They are there?

Jean:	Yes. My children will be there with their wives and their husbands, and we have relatives from Paris. It's good to have the family together.
Julia:	Of course. And you have a big family.
Jean:	What are you doing for the holiday?
Julia:	The dinner is being held at home. My son, Robert, who is a student at the university, is also at home with my husband and me, and his grandparents.
Jean:	Do you have a picture of Robert?
Julia:	Yes, here's a photo of Robert with his male and female cousins.
Jean:	He has blond hair, like you, Julia.
Julia:	And he has blue eyes, like his father.

NUTS & BOLTS 2

MORE FIXED EXPRESSIONS WITH THE VERB AVOIR *(to have)*

Take a look at several more common expressions with **avoir** *(to have)*.

avoir tort	*to be wrong (lit., to have wrong)*
avoir lieu	*to take place, to be held*
avoir honte	*to be ashamed (lit., to have shame)*
avoir envie de	*to feel like (lit., to have the desire for)*
avoir besoin de	*to need (lit., to have need of)*

PRACTICE 2

Fill in the blanks with the correct **avoir** expression. Choose from the words below.

avoir besoin de, avoir tort, avoir lieu, avoir honte, avoir envie de

1. Sophie _____.

Sophie is ashamed (lit., has shame).

2. Mon frère _____.

My brother is wrong.

3. Mes grands-parents _____ de danser.

My grandparents feel like dancing.

4. Tu _____.

You are wrong.

5. Le concert _____ à New York.

The concert takes place in New York.

6. Le ballet _____ à Paris.

The ballet is held in Paris.

7. J' _____ de mes amis.

I need my friends.

Discovery activity

It's your turn to create your own family album, complete with pictures and dialogues in French! Search for a few family pictures of yourself growing up along with other family members. Arrange them in your scrapbook with captions in French. Feel free to use some of the sentences from the dialogues to help you form your own sentences describing the members of your family. Then, you might want to entitle your booklet **La famille Smith** *(The Smith Family)*, for example. Note that if you just wanted to say *The Smiths*, you would use the plural article **les** with your family name, so you would have **Les Smith**.

ANSWERS
PRACTICE 1: 1. d; **2.** a; **3.** c; **4.** e; **5.** b

PRACTICE 2: 1. a honte; **2.** a tort; **3.** ont envie; **4.** as tort; **5.** a lieu; **6.** a lieu; **7.** ai besoin

Bonjour, tout le monde!	*Hello, everybody!*
Voilà mon père.	*There is my father.*
Voici ma mère.	*Here is my mother.*
J'ai une grande famille.	*I have a big family.*
Il y a combien d'enfants dans ta famille?	*How many children are there in your family?*
Il y a trois enfants dans ma famille.	*There are three children in my family.*
Quel âge as-tu?	*How old are you?*
J'ai dix-sept ans.	*I'm seventeen years old.*
C'est amusant, n'est-ce pas?	*That's amusing, don't you agree?*
J'ai faim.	*I'm hungry.*
J'ai soif.	*I'm thirsty.*
Mon frère a les yeux bleus.	*My brother has blue eyes.*
Ma tante a les cheveux bruns.	*My aunt has brown hair.*
C'est vrai!	*That's true!/It's true!*
C'est bon!	*It's good!/That's good!*

UNIT 3
Everyday life

In this unit, you will learn more vocabulary, expressions, and verbs for everyday conversations concerning the things you like and dislike. To begin, let's start with some necessary vocabulary, the days of the week.

———————— Lesson 9 (words) ————————

WORD LIST 1
LES JOURS DE LA SEMAINE *(Days of the week)*

les jours de la semaine	*the days of the week*
lundi	*Monday*
mardi	*Tuesday*
mercredi	*Wednesday*
jeudi	*Thursday*
vendredi	*Friday*
samedi	*Saturday*
dimanche	*Sunday*

Here are a few more vocabulary words associated with the days of the week.

le week-end	*weekend*
hier	*yesterday*
aujourd'hui	*today*
demain	*tomorrow*
le soir	*evening*
l'après-midi	*afternoon*

NOTES

You will notice that the days of the week are not capitalized in French as they are in English. Also note that, in French, the week starts with **lundi** *(Monday)* and not **dimanche** *(Sunday)*, as in English. Finally, notice that in French all of the days end in **-di** except for **dimanche** *(Sunday)*, which begins with **di-**.

NUTS & BOLTS 1
DAYS OF THE WEEK: WHEN AND WHEN NOT TO USE AN ARTICLE

You have learned that an article is almost always used before a noun in French. The days of the week, however, are not normally preceded by an article.

Samedi, il y a un concert.
On Saturday, there is a concert.

J'ai un rendez-vous mardi.
I have an appointment on Tuesday.

However, to indicate something that takes place repeatedly or habitually, the definite article is used with the days of the week, too. The definite article is always in the masculine singular form, **le**, and it corresponds to the English *every* + *the day of the week* or *on* + *the day of the week in the plural*.

Le lundi, j'ai ma classe de français.
On Mondays (Every Monday), I have my French class.

Le dimanche je suis à la maison.
On Sundays (Every Sunday), I am at home.

PRACTICE 1

Decide whether a definite article is needed in the following sentences. If the article is not needed in the sentence, leave the space blank.

1. Marie a une classe de science _____ lundi et _____ jeudi.

   Marie has a science class on Mondays and Thursdays.

2. _____ samedi, nous avons une fête.

   On Saturday, we have a party.

3. Julie est libre _____ dimanche.

   Julie is free on Sundays.

4. Mes parents ont un dîner _____ mardi.

   My parents have a dinner (to go to) on Tuesday.

5. _____ mercredi je visite le Louvre.

   On Wednesday, I am visiting the Louvre.

PRACTICE 2

Match the French words with the correct English equivalent.

1. mercredi   a. *week*

2. hier   b. *Sunday*

3. jeudi   c. *Friday*

4. lundi   d. *Wednesday*

5. demain   e. *yesterday*

6. semaine   f. *Tuesday*

7. dimanche   g. *evening*

8. soir   h. *Thursday*

9. mardi   i. *tomorrow*

10. vendredi   j. *Monday*

WORD LIST 2
LES MOIS DE L'ANNÉE *(The months of the year)*

le mois de l'année	*the month of the year*
janvier	*January*
février	*February*
mars	*March*
avril	*April*
mai	*May*
juin	*June*
juillet	*July*
août	*August*
septembre	*September*
octobre	*October*
novembre	*November*
décembre	*December*

NOTES

The months of the year are not capitalized in French. When giving a date in French, always place the definite article **le** first, before the date, and then give the month.

La date de la fête nationale française est le 14 juillet.
The date of the French national holiday is the fourteenth of July.

Le jour de la Saint-Valentin est le 14 février.
Valentine's Day is on the fourteenth of February.

La fête de Noël est le 25 décembre.
Christmas is on the twenty-fifth of December.

Mon anniversaire est le 21 mai.
My birthday is on the twenty-first of May.

The following are some useful weather expressions including the months of the year.

Il fait beau en mai.
It's beautiful in May.

Il fait frais en mars.
It's cool in March.

Il fait chaud en juillet.
It's hot in July.

Il fait froid en janvier.
It's cold in January.

Il fait du vent en mars.
It's windy in March.

Il fait du soleil en juin.
It's sunny in June.

Il pleut en avril.
It rains in April.

Il neige en décembre.
It snows in December.

Il y a une tempête de neige en janvier.
There is a snow storm in January.

Il gèle en février.
It freezes in February.

You will notice that all but three of the weather expressions—**il neige** *(it snows)*, **il pleut** *(it rains)*, and **il gèle** *(it freezes)*—include **il fait** *(lit., it makes)*. Note as well the use of the preposition **en** *(in)* before the name of the month.

NUTS & BOLTS 2
Verbs ending in -er in the present tense

Verbs are the class of words that express existence, action, or occurrence. French regular verbs are divided into three groups depending on their ending in the infinitive form, the form in which they appear in the dictionary. These are the three groups of verbs.

Group 1: Verbs ending in **-er**

Group 2: Verbs ending in **-ir**

Group 3: Verbs ending in **-re**

In this lesson, we will look at the Group 1 verbs. Here are some common examples.

-er verbs	
parler	*to speak*
danser	*to dance*
jouer	*to play*
aimer	*to like, to love*
préparer	*to prepare*
regarder	*to watch, to look at*
écouter	*to listen (to)*

To create the present tense forms of an **-er** verb, take the ending **-er** off of the infinitive and add the following endings that correspond to the subject pronouns.

-er verb endings			
je	-e	nous	-ons
tu	-es	vous	-ez
il	-e	ils	-ent
elle	-e	elles	-ent

Now let's look at the present tense forms of the verb **parler** *(to speak)*.

je parle	*I speak, I am speaking, I do speak*	nous parlons	*we speak, we are speaking, we do speak*
tu parles *(infml.)*	*you speak, you are speaking, you do speak*	vous parlez *(pl., sg. fml.)*	*you speak, you are speaking, you do speak*
il parle	*he speaks, he is speaking, he does speak*	ils parlent	*they speak, they are speaking, they do speak*
elle parle	*she speaks, she is speaking, she does speak*	elles parlent	*they speak, they are speaking, they do speak*

Note that each form of **parler** corresponds to three forms in English. For example, **je parle** can be translated as *I speak, I'm speaking,* or *I do speak,* according to the context.

Joelle parle italien avec moi.
Joelle speaks Italian with me.

Le professeur parle devant la classe.

The teacher is speaking in front of the class.

Oui, je parle français.

Yes, I speak French.

Here are more useful **-er** verbs.

-er verbs	
accompagner	*to accompany*
aider	*to help*
chanter	*to sing*
décider	*to decide*
dîner	*to dine*
donner	*to give*
laver	*to wash*
marcher	*to walk*
quitter	*to leave*
skier	*to ski*
travailler	*to work*
visiter	*to visit*

PRACTICE 3

Fill in the blanks with the correct present tense form of the verbs in parentheses.

1. Jean _____ un film. (regarder)

   Jean is watching a movie.

2. Nous _____ la musique. (écouter)

We are listening to the music.

3. Ils _____ ensemble. (danser)

They are dancing together.

4. Mes parents _____ le jazz. (aimer)

My parents like jazz.

5. Je _____ le dîner pour ma famille. (préparer)

I'm preparing dinner for my family.

6. Tu _____ au tennis? (jouer)

Do you play tennis?

7. Vous _____ au football. (jouer)

You play soccer.

8. Les filles et les garçons _____. (danser)

The girls and the boys are dancing.

9. Elle _____ la télévision. (regarder)

She is watching television.

10. Tu _____ la musique? (aimer)

Do you like music?

Language link

A good way to practice **-er** verbs and other verbs as we continue in the course is to go to www.laits.utexas.edu/fi/vp/. This is an excellent interactive page that lets you work on verb conjugations at your own pace and then check your progress.

ANSWERS
PRACTICE 1: 1. le, le; 2. -; 3. le; 4. -; 5. -;

PRACTICE 2: 1. d; 2. e; 3. h; 4. j; 5. i; 6. a; 7. b; 8. g; 9. f; 10. c

PRACTICE 3: 1. regarde; 2. écoutons; 3. dansent; 4. aiment; 5. prépare; 6. joues; 7. jouez; 8. dansent; 9. regarde; 10. aimes

--------- Lesson 10 (phrases) ---------

PHRASE LIST 1
LES PIÈCES *(Rooms of the house and objects in the house)*

à la maison	*at the house, at home*
la pièce	*room*
la cuisine	*kitchen*
dans la salle à manger	*in the dining room*
la chambre à coucher	*bedroom*
la salle de bains	*bathroom*
le salon	*parlor, living room*
les toilettes	*restroom*
le jardin	*garden*
sous le lit	*under the bed*
la chaise	*chair*
sur la table	*on the table*
derrière le canapé	*behind the sofa*
la lampe	*lamp*
le meuble	*furniture*

NOTES
You may have noticed three words in the list above for bathroom. This is because in France, **la salle de bains** *(the bathroom)* is a room set aside for the sole purpose of bathing and washing up. In a French bathroom, you will generally find the following items.

le lavabo	*sink*
la baignoire	*bathtub*
la douche	*shower*
le bidet	*bidet*

The toilet is in a separate room called **le W.C.** *(lit., the water closet).*

Now take note of some basic prepositions and prepositional phrases used in the vocabulary above.

à	*to, at, in*
dans	*in*
sur	*on*
sous	*under*
derrière	*behind*
à côté de	*next to*
en face de	*facing, across from*

Here are some examples of the prepositions used in sentences.

La lampe est derrière le sofa.
The lamp is behind the sofa.

Le journal est sur la table.
The newspaper is on the table.

Le chat est sous la chaise.
The cat is under the chair.

Je suis dans la baignoire.
I'm in the bathtub.

La télévision est en face du sofa.
The television is facing the sofa.

La chaise est à côté de la table.
The chair is next to the table.

NUTS & BOLTS 1

The placement and agreement of adjectives

In Unit 1, you learned basic rules about adjectives. In French, an adjective must agree with the noun it modifies in gender (masculine or feminine) as well as number (singular or plural). Generally, in French, most adjectives follow the noun.

un homme intelligent
an intelligent man

une femme intelligente
an intelligent woman

un garçon charmant
a charming boy

une fille charmante
a charming girl

des parents charmants
(some) charming parents

Now, in contrast to the phrases above, look at the examples below. Notice the placement of the adjectives.

une jeune fille
a young girl

un beau garçon
a handsome boy

les petits enfants
the little children

If you noticed that the adjective comes before the noun in the second set, you are correct. There are special adjectives that always precede nouns. We will call them BAGS (Beauty-Age-Goodness-Size) adjectives.

B for beauty

beau/belle/bel *(m./f./m. + vowel)*	*beautiful, handsome*
joli/jolie *(m./f.)*	*pretty*

A for age

jeune	*young*
vieux/vieille/vieil *(m./f./m. + vowel)*	*old*
nouveau/nouvelle/nouvel *(m./f./m. + vowel)*	*new*
ancien/ancienne *(m./f.)*	*old, former*

G for goodness

bon/bonne *(m./f.)*	*good*
mauvais/mauvaise *(m./f.)*	*bad*

S for size

petit/petite *(m./f.)*	*small, little*
grand/grande *(m./f.)*	*big, tall*
long/longue *(m./f.)*	*long*
mince *(m. and f.)*	*thin*

Notice also that some of the BAGS adjectives have irregular forms.

Marc est un beau garçon.
Marc is a handsome boy.

Christine est une belle fille.
Christine is a beautiful girl.

Nous avons un long voyage.
We have a long trip.

C'est une longue histoire.
It's a long story.

Here are examples with nouns modified by two adjectives.

un nouveau garçon intelligent
a new, intelligent boy

une vieille dame charmante
a charming old lady

une jeune fille sincère
a sincere young girl

une bonne classe intéressante
a good, interesting class

les bons amis sincères
the sincere good friends

PRACTICE 1
Choose the forms of the adjectives that best fit the sentences.

1. C'est un (petit/petite) jardin.

   It's a small garden.

2. Tu as une (beau/belle) maison.

   You have a beautiful house.

3. J'ai deux (grand/grands) frères.

   I have two big brothers.

4. Ils ont une (nouveau/nouvelle) cuisine.

   They have a new kitchen.

5. C'est un (long/longue) voyage.

   It's a long trip.

PHRASE LIST 2
Les couleurs *(Colors)*

bleu/bleue	*blue*
noir/noire	*black*
vert/verte	*green*
brun/brune	*brown*
orange	*orange*
rouge	*red*
beige	*beige, tan*
jaune	*yellow*
rose	*pink*
blanc/blanche	*white*
violet/violette	*violet*

Notes
Notice that several English words and expressions related to colors come from French—for example, the colors *beige* and *violet* and the expressions *carte blanche, bête noire,* and *jaundice.*

NUTS & BOLTS 2
Placement of color adjectives
Like other adjectives, color adjectives must agree with the noun they modify in gender (masculine or feminine) and in number (singular or plural). All color adjectives are placed after the noun. Look at the following examples and notice the changes in the forms of the color adjectives.

le tapis brun
the brown rug

la chaise brune
the brown chair

les tapis bruns
the brown rugs

les chaises brunes
the brown chairs

Here are some more examples.

le canapé vert
the green sofa

la maison verte
the green house

les canapés verts
the green sofas

les maisons vertes
the green houses

Some color adjectives are exactly the same in the masculine and feminine forms.

un mur beige
a beige wall

une cuisine beige
a beige kitchen

des murs beiges
(some) beige walls

des cuisines beiges
(some) beige kitchens

Here are some more examples.

un salon rouge
a red parlor

une pièce rouge
a red room

des salons rouges
(some) red parlors

des pièces rouges
(some) red rooms

Some color adjectives do not simply add an **-e** to the masculine form to construct the feminine form; they have irregular forms in the feminine.

le mur blanc
the white wall

la maison blanche
the white house

le tapis violet
the violet rug

la table violette
the violet table

PRACTICE 2
Choose the sentences containing correctly placed adjectives.

1. a. C'est une longue chaise bleue.

   b. C'est une bleue chaise longue.

2. a. Voici le blanc mur grand.

   b. Voici le grand mur blanc.

3. a. C'est un nouveau meuble brun.

   b. C'est un brun meuble nouveau.

4. a. Vous avez un joli canapé vert.

   b. Vous avez un vert canapé joli.

5. a. C'est un intéressant jardin beau.

   b. C'est un beau jardin intéressant.

PRACTICE 3

Choose the correct translation of each English sentence by checking the placement and agreement of the adjectives. Hint: Look at the articles to figure out the gender of the nouns.

1. *This is an intelligent old lady.*

   a. C'est une vieille dame intelligente.

   b. C'est une vieux dame intelligent.

   c. C'est une vieille dame intelligent.

2. *There's a pretty green garden.*

   a. Voilà un jolie jardin vert.

   b. Voilà un vert jardin joli.

   c. Voilà un joli jardin vert.

3. *You have a beautiful white house.*

   a. Tu as une beau maison blanc.

   b. Tu as une belle maison blanche.

   c. Tu as une blanche maison belle.

4. *It's a good, amusing day.*

    a. C'est un bonne jour amusant.

    b. C'est un amusant jour bon.

    c. C'est un bon jour amusant.

5. *He is watching a new French film.*

    a. Il regarde un nouveau film français.

    b. Il regarde un français film nouveau.

    c. Il regarde un nouvelle film français.

Culture note

The floors in France

It is important to note that the numbering of floors of buildings in France differs from the numbering of floors in the United States. The floor on which a building is entered, sometimes called *the first floor* in the United States, is considered *the ground floor* in France and is referred to as **le rez-de-chaussée.** The floor above **le rez-de-chaussée** is called **le premier étage** *(the first floor* in France, but *the second floor* in the U.S.); the floor above that is **le deuxième étage** *(the second floor* in France, but *the third floor* in the U.S.); the next floor is **le troisième étage** *(the third floor* in France, but *the fourth floor* in the U.S.), and so on.

ANSWERS

PRACTICE 1: 1. petit; **2.** belle; **3.** grands; **4.** nouvelle; **5.** long

PRACTICE 2: 1. a; **2.** b; **3.** a; **4.** a; **5.** b

PRACTICE 3: 1. a; **2.** c; **3.** b; **4.** c; **5.** a

SENTENCE GROUP 1
LES PLAISIRS DU JOUR *(Everyday likes and dislikes)*

Look at these simple sentences that express likes and dislikes. They will be useful in everyday conversations.

J'aime ça.	*I like that./I love that.*
Ça me plaît.	*I like that. (Lit., That pleases me.)*
Ça m'intéresse.	*That interests me.*
C'est parfait.	*It's perfect.*
C'est super.	*It's great./It's super.*
Il est très gentil.	*He is very nice.*
Elle est très gentille.	*She is very nice.*
Il/Elle est sympa.	*He/She is nice.*
Vous êtes très aimable.	*You are very kind.*
Je n'aime pas ça.	*I don't like that.*
Ça ne m'intéresse pas.	*That doesn't interest me.*
Ça me dérange.	*That bothers me.*
C'est mauvais.	*That's bad.*
C'est bizarre.	*It's strange.*
C'est ennuyeux.	*It's boring.*

NUTS & BOLTS 1
NEGATIVES

Negative sentences are formed using **ne** and **pas.** To form the negative, put **ne** before the verb and **pas** after the verb. Look at the following examples using **-er** verbs.

Je marche.	*I walk.*
Je ne marche pas.	*I do not walk.*
Tu regardes.	*You watch.*
Tu ne regardes pas.	*You do not watch.*
Il prépare.	*He prepares.*

Il ne prépare pas.	*He does not prepare.*
Elle chante.	*She sings.*
Elle ne chante pas.	*She does not sing.*
Nous jouons.	*We play.*
Nous ne jouons pas.	*We do not play.*
Vous parlez.	*You speak.*
Vous ne parlez pas.	*You do not speak.*
Ils donnent . . .	*They give . . .*
Ils ne donnent pas . . .	*They do not give . . .*
J'aime . . .	*I like . . .*
Je n'aime pas . . .	*I do not like . . .*
Tu aimes . . .	*You like . . .*
Tu n'aimes pas . . .	*You do not like . . .*
Jean écoute.	*Jean listens.*
Jean n'écoute pas.	*Jean does not listen.*
Nous aidons.	*We help.*
Nous n'aidons pas.	*We do not help.*
Elles aiment . . .	*They like . . .*
Elles n'aiment pas . . .	*They do not like . . .*

When a verb begins with a vowel, the **ne** becomes **n'**.

Je n'accompagne pas mon ami.
I do not accompany my friend.

Je n'écoute pas la radio.
I'm not listening to the radio.

Ils n'aiment pas le chocolat.
They do not like chocolate.

Nous n'aimons pas la pizza.
We do not like pizza.

Tu n'invites pas ton ami.
You do not invite your friend.

PRACTICE 1

Change the following sentences from the affirmative form to the negative form.

1. Sophie accompagne son amie mardi.

2. Mes parents dînent avec moi le soir.

3. Luc et Martine regardent la maison.

4. Tu prépares le dîner à la maison.

5. Aujourd'hui les enfants jouent dans le jardin.

6. Le vendredi, mon mari travaille à New York.

7. J'aime ma chambre à coucher.

8. En décembre mes amis chantent.

9. Ma femme marche dans le jardin quand il fait beau.

10. Vous quittez la maison.

NUTS & BOLTS 2

FORMING QUESTIONS

There are three ways to form *yes/no* questions in French. The first way is simply to raise the intonation in speech or place a question mark at the end of the sentence in writing. The second way is to place the question marker **est-ce que** at the beginning of an affirmative or negative sentence meant as a question.

Je chante bien.
I sing well.

Est-ce que je chante bien?
Do I sing well?

Tu ne joues pas.
You are not playing.

Est-ce que tu ne joues pas?
Aren't you playing?

Notice that the phrase **est-ce que** becomes **est-ce qu'** before a word that begins with a vowel.

Est-ce qu'il chante bien?

Does he sing well?

Est-ce qu'elle chante bien?

Does she sing well?

The third way to form a question is by placing the verb in front of the subject in the sentence. Perhaps the most classic example of this type of question is the following.

Parlez-vous français?

Do you speak French?

Note that the verb **parlez** precedes the pronoun **vous** and a hyphen separates them. Here are some more examples.

Parles-tu anglais?

Do you speak English?

Avons-nous une fête?

Are we having a party?

Chantent-ils bien?

Do they sing well?

Où habites-tu?

Where do you live?

It is important to notice that the verb can precede the subject only if the subject is a pronoun, so if the statement doesn't have a subject pronoun, it needs to be added in the corresponding question.

Ta chambre à coucher est bleue.

Your bedroom is blue.

Ta chambre à coucher est-elle bleue?

Is your bedroom blue?

Here are two more examples.

Leur salon est-il grand?
Is their parlor big?

Luc est-il français?
Is Luc French?

The letter **t** is inserted between the subject pronoun and the verb when the verb ends with an **e**.

Marie parle-t-elle anglais?
Does Marie speak English?

Invite-t-il ses amis?
Is he inviting his friends?

Look at the table summarizing the three ways to form *yes/no* questions in French.

YES/NO QUESTIONS			
Tu aimes Paris?	**Est-ce que tu aimes Paris?**	**Aimes-tu Paris?**	*Do you like Paris?*
Luc aime Marie?	**Est-ce que Luc aime Marie?**	**Luc aime-t-il Marie?**	*Does Luc like Marie?*
Nous jouons?	**Est-ce que nous jouons?**	**Jouons-nous?**	*Are we playing?*
Vous travaillez?	**Est-ce que vous travaillez?**	**Travaillez-vous?**	*Do you work?*
Ils aident?	**Est-ce qu'ils aident?**	**Aident-ils?**	*Are they helping?*

Elles dansent?	Est-ce qu'elles dansent?	Dansent-elles?	*Are they dancing?*
Il donne le livre à son ami?	Est-ce qu'il donne le livre à son ami?	Donne-t-il le livre à son ami?	*Is he giving the book to his friend?*
Elle décide?	Est-ce qu'elle décide?	Décide-t-elle?	*Is she deciding?*

Finally, here is how questions asking for specific information are formed. In Lesson 4, you learned a few question words: **comment** *(how)*, **qui** *(who)*, **où** *(where)*, **(de) quel/quelle** *(what [+ noun])*, **pourquoi** *(why)*, **quand** *(when)*, and **à quelle heure** *(at what time)*. Here are some examples combining question words with different question forms.

À quelle heure arrive-t-elle?
At what time is she arriving?

Pourquoi aimez-vous le français?
Why do you like French?

Comment danse-t-elle?
How does she dance?

Qui est-ce qu'elle écoute?
To whom does she listen?

PRACTICE 2
Change the following sentences into questions using **est-ce que.**

1. Ghislaine danse avec Georges.
2. Nous regardons un nouveau livre.
3. Tu aimes la maison blanche.
4. Elle aime la couleur de la chambre à coucher.
5. Tes parents dînent à la maison le soir.
6. Ils invitent tout le monde.
7. Vous parlez français.
8. Elles aiment les enfants.

PRACTICE 3
Now change the same sentences above into questions by placing the verb in front of the subject.

Tip!

Memorization is the key to learning to speak a foreign language. For some, it is easy, and for others, it may be difficult. The more you say a certain expression out loud, the better it will be retained in your memory. If you have access to a tape recorder, you may want to record yourself saying some of the phrases and expressions that you find most useful. You can do that after having listened to the audio component of the book for regular pronunciation and memorization practice. Then, listen to your recordings, comparing them to the recordings by the native speakers on the audio component. Gradually, your pronunciation will get better through regular practice!

ANSWERS

PRACTICE 1: 1. Sophie n'accompagne pas son amie mardi.
2. Mes parents ne dînent pas avec moi le soir. **3.** Luc et Martine ne regardent pas la maison. **4.** Tu ne prépares pas le dîner à la maison. **5.** Aujourd'hui, les enfants ne jouent pas dans le jardin.
6. Le vendredi, mon mari ne travaille pas à New York. **7.** Je n'aime pas ma chambre à coucher. **8.** En décembre mes amis ne chantent pas. **9.** Ma femme ne marche pas dans le jardin quand il fait beau. **10.** Vous ne quittez pas la maison.

PRACTICE 2: 1. Est-ce que Ghislaine danse avec Georges?
2. Est-ce que nous regardons un nouveau livre? **3.** Est-ce que tu aimes la maison blanche? **4.** Est-ce qu'elle aime la couleur de la chambre à coucher? **5.** Est-ce que tes parents dînent à la maison le soir? **6.** Est-ce qu'ils invitent tout le monde? **7.** Est-ce que vous parlez français? **8.** Est-ce qu'elles aiment les enfants?

PRACTICE 3: 1. Ghislaine, danse-t-elle avec Georges?
2. Regardons-nous un nouveau livre? **3.** Aimes-tu la maison blanche? **4.** Aime-t-elle la couleur de la chambre à coucher?
5. Tes parents, dînent-ils à la maison le soir? **6.** Invitent-ils tout le monde? **7.** Parlez-vous français? **8.** Aiment-elles les enfants?

Lesson 12 (conversations)

CONVERSATION 1

Martine has invited her friend Claudine to her new home for lunch. Claudine has just arrived at the door.

Martine:	Bonjour, Claudine. Bienvenue!
Claudine:	Tu es très aimable. Quelle jolie maison!
Martine:	Merci. Entre. Voici le salon et maintenant nous allons dans la cuisine.
Claudine:	Ah, c'est une grande cuisine. Ça m'intéresse parce que j'aime cuisiner.
Martine:	Mon mari aime la cuisine. En général, il prépare le dîner le soir.

Claudine:	Voilà le jardin. C'est super! Est-ce que tu travailles dans le jardin?
Martine:	Oui, j'aime travailler avec mes plantes.
Claudine:	C'est parfait ici. Je ne vais pas dans mon jardin. C'est trop petit.
Martine:	Eh bien, est-ce que tu as faim? Le déjeuner est prêt.
Claudine:	Oui, j'ai vraiment faim.

Martine:	*Hello, Claudine. Welcome!*
Claudine:	*This is very nice of you. (lit., You are very kind.) What a pretty house!*
Martine:	*Thank you. Come in. Here's the living room, and now we're going to the kitchen.*
Claudine:	*Oh, it's a big kitchen. That interests me because I like to cook.*
Martine:	*My husband loves the kitchen. He usually prepares dinner at night.*
Claudine:	*There's the garden. It's great! Do you work in the garden?*
Martine:	*Yes, I like doing work on my plants.*
Claudine:	*It's perfect here. I don't go into my garden. It's too small.*
Martine:	*So, are you hungry? Lunch is ready.*
Claudine:	*Yes, I'm really hungry.*

NUTS & BOLTS 1
THE VERB ALLER *(to go)* IN THE PRESENT TENSE

Here are the present tense forms of the verb **aller** *(to go)*, another important irregular verb.

je vais	*I go*	nous allons	*we go*
tu vas *(infml.)*	*you go*	vous allez *(pl., sg. fml.)*	*you go*
il va	*he goes*	ils vont	*they go*
elle va	*she goes*	elles vont	*they go*

Remember that a single French present tense verb form–for example, **je vais**–can be translated into English in three different ways–e.g., *I go, I am going,* or *I do go*–depending on the context.

PRACTICE 1
Complete the sentences below with the verb **aller** *(to go)* in the appropriate form.

1. Il _____ aux États-Unis.

2. Vous _____ à New York.

3. Pierre _____ à la maison.

4. Luc et Jean _____ dans le jardin.

5. Nous _____ dans la salle à manger.

6. Je _____ dans ma chambre à coucher.

7. Est-ce que tu _____ à Paris.

8. Elle ne _____ pas à la maison.

CONVERSATION 2
Marcel wants to ask his friend Chantal to go out with him. They just can't seem to agree on an activity for the day.

Marcel: **Tiens, Chantal! Tu es libre samedi soir?**
Chantal: **Oui, je suis à la maison samedi soir. Pourquoi?**
Marcel: **Je t'invite à Paris. Tu viens[1] avec moi?**
Chantal: **Où vas-tu?**
Marcel: **Eh bien, il y a une nouvelle discothèque à Paris. Est-ce que tu danses?**
Chantal: **Je ne danse pas très bien. Ça ne me plaît pas.**
Marcel: **Est-ce que tu aimes regarder les films?**
Chantal: **Ah oui! J'adore les westerns. Ça m'intéresse.**

---

1 **Tu viens** is a present tense form of the verb **venir** *(to come)*. See Lesson 24 for other present tense forms.

Marcel: C'est bien! Moi, aussi j'aime bien les westerns. Alors, rendez-vous samedi soir?

Chantal: D'accord, Marcel. C'est super!

Marcel: *Say, Chantal! Are you free Saturday night?*

Chantal: *Yes, I am at home Saturday night. Why?*

Marcel: *I'm inviting you to go to Paris. Are you coming with me?*

Chantal: *Where are you going?*

Marcel: *Well, there's a new club in Paris. Do you dance?*

Chantal: *I don't dance very well. I don't like it. (lit., That doesn't please me.)*

Marcel: *Do you like to watch movies?*

Chantal: *Oh yes. I love westerns. I find them interesting. (lit., That interests me.)*

Marcel: *That's good! I really like westerns, too. So, it's a date Saturday night?*

Chantal: *Okay, Marcel. That sounds great!*

NOTES

When Americans hear the expression **rendez-vous,** they often think of a secret getaway or dinner date. In French, however, the term **rendez-vous** can refer to any kind of appointment, such as a doctor's appointment, a business meeting, or a lunch date with a friend.

NUTS & BOLTS 2
ALLER *(to go)* IN IDIOMATIC EXPRESSIONS

Like **avoir** *(to have)*, the verb **aller** *(to go)* is used in many fixed and idiomatic expressions, some of which you have already learned in the previous lessons.

Comment vas-tu?

How are you? (lit., How are you going?)

Ça va?

How is it going?/How are things? (lit., Is is going?)

Comment-allez-vous?

How are you? (lit., How are you going?)

Je vais bien.

I am well. (lit., I am going well.)

Richard va très bien.

Richard is very well. (lit., Richard is going well.)

Françoise va bien aussi.

Françoise is well, also. (lit., Françoise is going well, also.)

PRACTICE 2

Match the French sentences with their English translations.

1. Je vais très bien.   a. *He's going home.*
2. Nous allons dans le salon. b. *You're well.*
3. Vous allez bien.   c. *She's not doing well.*
4. Il va à la maison.   d. *You're doing well.*
5. Elle ne va pas bien.   e. *I'm very well.*
6. Tu vas à la maison.   f. *We're going into the parlor.*
7. Elle va dans la cuisine. g. *You're going home.*
8. Tu vas bien.   h. *She is going into the kitchen.*
9. Ils vont à la maison.   i. *Is everything fine?*
10. Ça va bien?   j. *They are going home.*

ANSWERS

PRACTICE 1: 1. va; 2. allez; 3. va; 4. vont; 5. allons; 6. vais; 7. vas; 8. va

PRACTICE 2: 1. e; 2. f; 3. b or d; 4. a; 5. c; 6. g; 7. h; 8. b or d; 9. j; 10. i

les jours de la semaine	*the days of the week*
les mois de l'année	*the months of the year*
Il fait beau.	*It's beautiful out.*
Il fait chaud.	*It's hot.*
Il fait froid.	*It's cold.*
Il fait soleil./Il fait du soleil.	*It's sunny out.*
Il fait du vent.	*It's windy.*
Il pleut.	*It's raining.*
Il neige.	*It's snowing.*
Ça me plaît.	*I like that. (lit., That pleases me.)*
Est-ce que tu aimes . . . ?	*Do you like . . . ?*
Tu aimes . . . ?	*Do you like . . . ?*
Aimes-tu . . . ?	*Do you like . . . ?*
Je ne danse pas bien.	*I don't dance well.*
C'est un vieux monsieur.	*It's an old man.*
C'est une nouvelle lampe rouge.	*It's a new red lamp.*
Je vais à la maison.	*I'm going home.*
Nous allons regarder la télé.	*We're going to watch TV.*

UNIT 4
At a restaurant

—————— Lesson 13 (words) ——————

In this unit, you will learn many new words and expressions in French that pertain to food, mealtimes, and restaurants. You will see that English has borrowed many expressions from French in this area. In France, good food and food preparation are very serious matters. You can be a **gourmet** *(lover of fine food)* or a **gourmand** *(glutton)*. **La gastronomie** *(gastronomy)* is something that just about everyone loves to discuss!

WORD LIST 1
LA NOURRITURE *(Foods)*

le repas	*meal (m.)*
le petit déjeuner	*breakfast*
le déjeuner	*lunch*
le dîner	*dinner*
le fruit	*fruit*
la cerise	*cherry*
la tomate	*tomato*
le citron	*lemon*
le citron vert	*lime*
le raisin	*grape*
le légume	*vegetable*
la pomme de terre	*potato*
la carotte	*carrot*
la laitue	*lettuce*
le maïs	*corn*
le concombre	*cucumber*

le céleri	celery
les petits pois *(m.)*	peas
les épinards *(m.)*	spinach
les haricots verts *(m.)*	green beans

NOTES

Note the similarity between **la pomme** *(apple)* and **la pomme de terre** *(potato)*, which literally means *the apple of the earth.*

NUTS & BOLTS 1
THE VERB MANGER *(to eat)*

We have studied the present tense forms of **-er** verbs. Let's now look at the verb **manger** *(to eat)*, also an **-er** verb but with a spelling change in the **nous** form.

je mange	*I eat*	**nous mangeons**	*we eat*
tu manges *(infml.)*	*you eat*	**vous mangez** *(pl., sg. fml.)*	*you eat*
il mange	*he eats*	**ils mangent**	*they eat*
elle mange	*she eats*	**elles mangent**	*they eat*

An **e** is added to the **nous** form of the verb in order to ensure the "soft" pronunciation of the letter **g** as **zh,** the sound in the English word *measure,* because in French, a **g** followed by an **o, a** or **u** corresponds to a "hard" **g** sound, as in the English word *goose.* In fact, all verbs ending in **-ger** follow this rule. Here are some other verbs of this type: **nager** *(to swim),* **ranger** *(to put away),* **voyager** *(to travel),* **déménager** *(to move out),* **changer** *(to change),* and **éponger** *(to mop, to soak up).*

A similar spelling change is required in the **nous** form of verbs that end in **-cer,** such as **commencer** *(to begin)*: **nous commençons** *(we begin).* The letter **c** is pronounced like the **c** in *cat* when it is followed by **a, o,** or **u;** to keep its pronunciation "soft" (as in *cent*), a cedilla is added to the letter **c.** Here are a few other verbs ending in **-cer: avancer** *(to advance),* **annoncer** *(to announce),* and **menacer** *(to threaten).*

PRACTICE 1
Fill in the blanks with the correct present tense forms of the verbs in parentheses. Remember, these are **-er** verbs with a spelling change in the **nous** form.

1. Je _____ un sandwich. (manger)

2. Nous _____ un croissant. (manger)

3. Vous _____ le dîner. (manger)

4. Tu _____ en France. (voyager)

5. Nous _____ aux Etats-Unis. (voyager)

6. Ils _____ dans l'océan. (nager)

7. Nous _____ dans l'océan. (nager)

8. Nous _____ le plan. (changer)

WORD LIST 2
LES HORS-D'ŒUVRE *(Appetizers)*
The French will often begin their meal with **un hors-d'œuvre** *(an appetizer).* Here are some common French appetizers.

la soupe	*soup*
le potage	*soup*
les crudités	*raw vegetables (f. pl.)*
le pâté (de foie gras)	*goose liver pâté*
le melon	*cantaloupe*

Here are some words that will be useful in describing **le plat principal** *(the main course).*

la viande	meat
le steak	steak
le bœuf	beef
le jambon	ham
le porc	pork
le poulet	chicken
le canard	duck
le veau	veal
le poisson	fish
le homard	lobster

Here are the words for the utensils used with the above main course foods.

la fourchette	fork (placed to the left of the plate)
l'assiette	plate
le couteau	knife (placed to the right of the plate)
la cuiller, la cuillère	spoon (placed above the plate)
le couvert	table setting
la nappe	tablecloth (used at every meal)
la serviette	napkin (most families use cloth napkins)
le verre	glass
la tasse	cup

NUTS & BOLTS 2
PARTITIVE ARTICLES

We have already learned that articles, both definite and indefinite, always precede nouns in French. A third kind of article is called *partitive;* the partitive articles are **de, de la, de l', du,** and **des.**

The partitive articles in French indicate unspecified amounts or quantities of the items referred to by nouns. They correspond to the English *some* or *any*. The partitive *some* is optional in English, but the partitive article is obligatory in French.

Partitive articles are made up of the preposition **de** *(of)* and a definite article. There are two contractions, **du** and **des**.

de + la = de la
de + l' = de l'
de + le = du
de + les = des

Here are some examples of sentences containing these articles.

Je mange de la glace.
I eat (some) ice cream.

Je bois de l'eau.
I drink (some) water.

Je bois du vin.
I drink (some) wine.

Je mange des fraises.
I eat (some) strawberries.

Elle a des bananes.
She has (some) bananas.

Il mange de la salade.
He eats (some) salad.

J'ai de la chance.
I am lucky. (lit., I have some luck.)

Notice that we do not use the partitive article in French—and we use no article at all in English—when we speak in general about things that we like or dislike.

J'aime la glace au chocolat.
I like chocolate ice cream.

Elle adore la salade.
She loves salad.

Mon mari aime le vin.
My husband likes wine.

Philippe aime l'eau.
Philippe likes water.

Nous aimons les escargots comme hors-d'œuvre.
We like snails/escargot as an hors d'oeuvre.

The negative form of the partitive article is **pas de/pas d'** + noun. In other words, the definite article, which is part of the partitive article, is dropped in a negative sentence.

Je ne bois pas de vin.
I don't drink wine.

Il ne mange pas de salade.
He doesn't eat salad.

Elle ne mange pas d'escargots.
She doesn't eat snails.

Ils n'ont pas de chance.
They have no luck.

PRACTICE 2
Fill in the blanks with the correct partitive article: **de, de la, de l', du,** or **des.**

1. J'ai _____ eau.

   I have (some) water.

2. Mes amis mangent _____ cerises.

   My friends are eating (some) cherries.

3. Il mange _____ viande.

   He's eating (some) meat.

4. Nous avons _____ chance.

   We are lucky./We have some luck.

5. Elle mange _____ poulet.

   She's eating chicken.

6. Ils ont _____ pommes.

   They have (some) apples.

7. Le bébé désire _____ lait.

   The baby wants (some) milk.

8. Je mange _____ salade.

   I'm eating (some) salad.

PRACTICE 3

Fill in the blanks with the appropriate type of article—either a definite article (**le, la, l', or les**) or a partitive article (**de, de la, de l', du, or des**). (Remember the rule for general likes and dislikes as well as the rule for negative forms.)

1. Je ne mange pas _____ soupe.

   I don't eat soup.

2. Je n'aime pas _____ soupe.

   I don't like (the) soup.

3. Le bébé mange _____ petits pois.

   The baby eats (some) peas.

4. J'aime _____cerises.

I like cherries.

5. Est-ce que vous désirez _____ café?

Do you want some coffee?

6. Elle n'aime pas _____ artichauts.

She doesn't like artichokes.

7. Je mange _____ salade.

I eat (some) salad.

8. Ils ont _____ bananes.

They have (some) bananas.

9. Les enfants désirent _____ eau.

The children want (some) water.

10. J'aime _____ fraises.

I like strawberries.

Culture note

French food

When one thinks of France, besides art, fashion, and perfumes, immediately the words "cuisine" and "cooking" come to mind, as the French are well known for their food. Consider some of the famous French dishes that have made their way onto American menus, such as **quiche, soufflé, parfait,** and **fondue,** just to name a few!

Mealtimes are very important to the French, as they are social occasions as well. The French eat more slowly than Americans do. Let's start with the first meal of the day, which is breakfast.

Le petit déjeuner *(breakfast)* is light and often consists of **le café noir** *(black coffee)*, **le café crème** *(coffee with cream)*, or **le café au lait** *(coffee with milk)*, consumed from a large cup or bowl. Children often drink **le chocolat chaud** *(hot chocolate)*. A flaky **croissant** *(crescent roll)*, a **brioche** *(muffin)*, or a **tartine** *(French bread with butter and jelly)* accompanies the coffee.

Le déjeuner *(lunch)* used to be the most important meal of the day, where families would gather at home for an hour and a half to two hours sharing a meal. However, it is losing its place as the main meal, especially in large cities where people are too busy. A quick meal at a fast-food restaurant or a sandwich on a **baguette** at a nearby **café** or **brasserie** has become a common substitute. In smaller towns and especially the provinces, **le déjeuner** is still considered the most important meal of the day.

Le dîner *(dinner)* has become the most important meal instead, and families who do not share a leisurely meal at lunch will make sure that everyone is together in the evening. **Le dîner** is served around seven, eight, or even nine in the evening. When the French are going out in the evening—for example, to a concert or a play—a late meal is eaten afterward, around eleven or midnight. This is called **le souper** *(supper)* because very often soup is on the menu.

ANSWERS

PRACTICE 1: 1. mange; 2. mangeons; 3. mangez; 4. voyages; 5. voyageons; 6. nagent; 7. nageons; 8. changeons

PRACTICE 2: 1. de l'; 2. des; 3. de la; 4. de la; 5. du; 6. des; 7. du; 8. de la

PRACTICE 3: 1. de; 2. la; 3. des; 4. les; 5. du; 6. les; 7. de la; 8. des; 9. de l'; 10. les

PHRASE LIST 1
LES ALIMENTS *(Food)*
Here are more vocabulary items for foods.

un œuf poché	*a poached egg*
un œuf au plat, un oeuf sur le plat	*a fried egg*
un œuf à la coque	*a soft-boiled egg*
un croque-monsieur	*a grilled ham and cheese sandwich*
les radis au beurre	*rosette-cut radishes served with butter on top*
les coquilles Saint-Jacques	*scallops*
des saucisses	*sausages*
la purée de pommes de terre	*mashed potatoes*
les pommes de terre en robe des champs	*boiled potatoes in their skins*
les frites	*french fries*
la moutarde de Dijon	*Dijon mustard*
une tarte aux pommes	*apple pie*
une tarte à la citrouille	*pumpkin pie*
un gâteau au chocolat	*chocolate cake*
une mousse au chocolat	*chocolat mousse*
la crème chantilly	*whipped cream*
la glace à la vanille	*vanilla ice cream*
la glace à la fraise	*strawberry ice cream*
la glace au chocolat	*chocolate ice cream*
la tisane	*herbal tea*

NOTES

You will find that the French use the crusty baguette to make sandwiches, which are then buttered, and usually not served with mustard or mayonnaise. Most French people prefer to use unsalted butter when they cook. A naturally salted butter comes from the province of Normandy in the northwest of France, where cows graze on the grasses watered with the sea salt of the English Channel.

NUTS & BOLTS 1
THE VERB PRENDRE *(to take)* IN THE PRESENT TENSE

We are going to learn another irregular verb, **prendre** *(to take)*.

Je prends la fourchette.
I take the fork.

Ils prennent les livres.
They take the books.

Prendre is also often used when ordering in a restaurant or café to say *I will have . . .* or *What will you have?*

Here is the verb **prendre** *(to take)* in the present tense.

je prends	*I'm taking*	nous prenons	*we take*
tu prends (infml.)	*you take*	vous prenez (pl., sg. fml.)	*you take*
il prend	*he takes*	ils prennent	*they take*
elle prend	*she takes*	elles prennent	*they take*

Because this is an irregular verb, you must memorize the verb form for each person. Note that all of the persons have only one **n** except for the **ils/elles** forms, which have a double **n**. Other common irregular verbs that follow the same pattern as **prendre** are below.

comprendre *(to understand)*
apprendre *(to learn)*
surprendre *(to surprise)*

En général, qu'est-ce que vous prenez pour le petit déjeuner?
In general, what do you have for breakfast?

Ils prennent des œufs.
They have eggs.

Je comprends le français.
I understand French.

Les enfants apprennent à lire.
The children are learning to read.

Nous apprenons l'anglais.
We're learning English.

PRACTICE 1

Complete the sentences with an appropriate form of **prendre, apprendre, comprendre,** or **surprendre.**

1. Il _____ un sandwich au restaurant. (prendre)

2. Est-ce que tu _____ des frites? (prendre)

3. Nous _____ du thé. (prendre)

4. Mes amis _____ de la glace. (prendre)

5. Je _____ du vin. (prendre)

6. Elle _____ la recette pour la sauce. (comprendre)

7. Vous _____ le menu en français? (comprendre)

8. Oui, je _____ le menu. (comprendre)

9. Tu _____ à cuisiner. (apprendre)

10. Ils _____ la recette pour le potage. (apprendre)

PHRASE LIST 2
LES EXPRESSIONS DE QUANTITÉ *(Expressions of quantity)*

une boîte de jus d'orange	*a carton of orange juice*
une bouteille de champagne	*a bottle of champagne*
une tasse de thé	*a cup of tea*
un verre de lait	*a glass of milk*
une tranche de fromage	*a slice of cheese*
un panier de prunes	*a basket of plums*
un kilo de	*a kilo of (1 kilogram = 2.2 lbs.)*
une livre de beurre	*a pound of butter*
une carafe de vin	*a pitcher of wine*
une douzaine d'œufs	*a dozen eggs*
trop de sauce	*too much sauce*
un peu d'épinards	*a little spinach*
beaucoup de glace	*a lot of ice cream*
moins de légumes	*less vegetables*
plus de bonbons	*more candy*

All expressions of quantity are followed by the preposition **de**, not the partitive article. For example, note the contrast with the partitive article and the expressions of quantity followed by **de**.

Je prends du vin.
I'm having some wine. (lit., I'm taking some wine.)

Je prends un peu de vin.
I'm having a little wine.

Nous prenons de l'eau.
We're having some water.

Nous prenons un verre d'eau.
We're having a glass of water.

Tu prends de la bière.

You're having some beer.

Tu prends une bouteille de vin.

You're having a bottle of wine.

Il mange des bonbons.

He's eating some candy.

Il mange beaucoup de bonbons.

He's eating a lot of candy.

NUTS & BOLTS 2
THE VERB BOIRE *(to drink)*

Here is another irregular verb that is useful to learn, the verb **boire** *(to drink)*.

je bois	*I drink*	**nous buvons**	*we drink*
tu bois (infml.)	*you drink*	**vous buvez** (pl., sg. fml.)	*you drink*
il boit	*he drinks*	**ils boivent**	*they drink*
elle boit	*she drinks*	**elles boivent**	*they drink*

Qu'est-ce que tu bois avec le dîner ce soir?

What are you drinking with dinner tonight?

Il boit de l'eau.

He's drinking water.

Nous buvons du vin rouge.

We're drinking red wine.

Mes amis boivent du champagne.

My friends are drinking some champagne.

Je bois du thé.

I'm drinking tea.

PRACTICE 2

Fill in the blanks with the correct form of the verb **boire.**

1. Il _____ du vin.

2. Nous _____ du café.

3. Je _____ du café le matin.

4. _____-vous du vin rouge ou du vin blanc?

5. Tu _____ de l'eau minérale.

Discovery activity

English has borrowed many words and expressions pertaining to the world of food from the French language. How many of the following examples have you heard or used? Try covering up the English equivalent on the right to see if you know the definition of the term before looking at the answer. Can you think of more?

à la carte	*a term used in dining when foods are individually ordered from the menu*
apéritif	*wine served before meal to stimulate the appetite*
bistro	*small restaurant*
connoisseur	*a person competent to make a judgment in taste or art*
crêpes	*thin pancakes*
croissant	*flaky crescent roll*
cuisine	*a style of cooking*
demi-tasse	*small cup of black coffee*
étiquette	*polite rules of conduct*

escargots	snails
gourmet	a person who knows fine food
hors-d'œuvre	appetizer
pâté de foie gras	goose liver paste
quiche	a baked dish made primarily with eggs, cheese, and bacon
R.S.V.P.	acronym for **Répondez, s'il vous plaît** (Respond, please) on invitations requiring a response
sauté	to fry quickly in a pan with little or no oil

ANSWERS

PRACTICE 1: 1. prend; 2. prends; 3. prenons; 4. prennent; 5. prends; 6. comprend; 7. comprenez; 8. comprends; 9. apprends; 10. apprennent

PRACTICE 2: 1. boit; 2. buvons; 3. bois; 4. Buvez; 5. bois

—————— Lesson 15 (sentences) ——————

SENTENCE GROUP 1
COMMANDER UN REPAS *(Ordering a meal)*

Garçon, le menu/ la carte s'il vous plaît.	*Waiter, the menu please.*
Quelle est la spécialité de la maison?	*What is the specialty of the house?*
Qu'est-ce que vous recommandez?	*What do you recommend?*
Je prends une soupe à l'oignon.	*I'll have onion soup.*
Il prend un croque-monsieur.	*He's having a grilled ham and cheese sandwich.*

Elle prend une salade niçoise.	*She's having a chef's salad.*
Mon ami prend un poulet frites.	*My friend is having chicken and fries.*
Nous n'avons plus de steak frites.	*We are out of steak and fries.*
Prenez-vous un sandwich au jambon, au fromage ou jambon-fromage?	*Are you having a ham sandwich, a cheese sandwich, or ham and cheese?*
Je prends une omelette aux champignons.	*I'm having a mushroom omelette.*
Est-ce que tu prends un dessert?	*Are you having desert?*
Je bois un kir.	*I'm drinking white wine with cassis.*
un kir royal	*champagne with cassis*
Tu prends une menthe à l'eau.	*You're having mint water.*
À table!	*Dinner's ready!/The food is ready! (lit., To the table!)*
À votre santé!	*To your health! (a toast before a drink)*

NOTES

In contrast to the many cocktails served in the United States, the French usually order simple drinks in a café or restaurant, such as a glass of wine, beer, or often, mineral water, which has its source in many of the natural springs found in France, such as Évian, Vichy, Volvic, and Perrier. Quite often, flavored syrup, such as **menthe** *(mint)*, is mixed into the water.

NUTS & BOLTS 1
THE NEAR FUTURE
In Unit 3, you learned the verb **aller** *(to go)*.

Je vais à Paris.
I'm going to Paris.

Marc va à la maison.
Marc is going home.

Ils vont en France.
They are going to France.

We also saw how it is used in conversational expressions, such as the following.

Ça va?
Is everything fine?

Je vais bien.
I'm doing well.

Elle va mal.
She's doing badly.

Now we'll see that this verb can also be used to express the near future, similar to the English *going to* future. The near future tense is often used in conversation instead of the regular future tense, which you will learn about in Lesson 20.

The near future is put together by combining the present tense form of the verb **aller** and the main verb in the infinitive form. For example, here's the near future of the verb **manger** *(to eat)*.

je vais manger	*I'm going to eat*	nous allons manger	*we're going to eat*
tu vas manger	*you're going to eat*	vous allez manger	*you're going to eat*
il va manger	*he's going to eat*	ils vont manger	*they're going to eat*
elle va manger	*she's going to eat*	elles vont manger	*they're going to eat*

Je vais prendre des crudités comme hors-d'œuvre.
I'm going to have some raw vegetables as an hors d'oeuvre.

Il va boire un coca.
He's going to drink a cola.

Qu'est-ce que tu vas prendre?
What are you going to have?

Elle va commander une bouteille de vin rouge.
She's going to order a bottle of red wine.

Nous allons dîner à la maison.
We're going to dine at home.

Je vais préparer de la soupe à l'oignon.
I'm going to prepare some onion soup.

PRACTICE 1
Translate the English into French using the near future.

1. Tu _____ *(are going to eat)* au restaurant.

2. Est-ce que ma mère _____ *(going to prepare)* le déjeuner?

3. Nous _____ *(are going to eat)* ensemble.

4. Mes parents _____ *(are going to dine)* au bistro.

5. Je _____ *(am going to drink)* du lait.

SENTENCE GROUP 2
DES EXPRESSIONS AU RESTAURANT *(Expressions at a restaurant)*
Here are some expressions that may be useful when you are in a restaurant.

Qu'est-ce qu'il y a à manger?	*What is there to eat?*
Qu'est-ce qu'il y a à boire?	*What is there to drink?*
On va prendre un pot.	*Let's have a drink.*

Qu'est-ce que tu vas boire?	*What are you going to drink?*
Comme boisson, je vais prendre un vin rouge (blanc, rosé).	*As a drink, I'm going to have red (white, rosé) wine.*
Qu'est-ce que tu prends?	*What are you having?*
Comme plat principal je prends du coq au vin.	*For the main course, I'm having chicken cooked in wine.*
Comme dessert, je prends un éclair.	*For dessert, I'm having an éclair.*
Apportez-moi du sel (du poivre) s'il vous plaît.	*Bring me some salt (pepper), please.*
Bon appétit!	*Enjoy your meal!*
C'est délicieux!	*It's delicious.*
L'addition, s'il vous plaît.	*The check, please.*
Il a une faim de loup.	*He's as hungry as a bear. (lit., He's as hungry as a wolf.)*
J'ai faim.	*I'm hungry.*
Je n'ai plus faim.	*I'm not hungry anymore.*

NOTES

Most cafés and restaurants in France display their menu selections outside so that patrons can see the choices and prices before entering. The expression **service compris** means the tip is automatically included in the bill.

Also, do not be surprised to find a dog or cat seated with its owner at the table. The French love their pets and take them just about everywhere, especially their dogs.

NUTS & BOLTS 2
CONTRACTIONS WITH THE PREPOSITION À
Similar to the preposition **de,** the preposition **à** *(to, at, in)* is combined with the definite articles.

à + la = à la
à + l' = à l'
à + le = au
à + les = aux

Here are some examples with **à** followed by the article.

Je suis à la maison.
I am at home.

Étienne va à l'université.
Étienne goes to college.

Nous allons au café.
We're going to the café.

Ils habitent aux Etats-Unis.
They live in the United States.

Note the two contractions, **au** and **aux.** Note also that **à** is used alone with proper names.

Je parle à Jean.
I speak to Jean.

Je vais à Paris.
I'm going to Paris.

The contractions with **à** are also used in food expressions to denote a flavor or main ingredient.

Elle prépare une tarte à la fraise.
She prepares a strawberry pie.

Nous aimons la tarte aux pommes.
We like apple pie.

La tarte à la mode est délicieuse dans ce restaurant.
The apple pie with vanilla ice cream is delicious in this restaurant.

PRACTICE 2
Fill in the blanks with **à, à la, à l', au,** or **aux.**

1. J'aime la tarte _____ citron.

2. Je prends une omelette _____ champignons.

3. Elle prépare un soufflé _____ chocolat.

4. Nous aimons la glace _____ fraise.

5. Ils boivent une menthe _____ eau.

Language link

Why not try to cook or bake something French? There are many wonderful French recipes that can be found in various cookbooks, such as those written by the renowned chefs Julia Child and Jacques Pépin. Some of the recipes may be easier than you think. The website www.foodnetwork.com also has information about French dishes created by the television chefs. For a good authentic source of French recipes, from main courses to desserts, go to www.aftouch-cuisine.com.

ANSWERS
PRACTICE 1: 1. vas manger; **2.** va préparer; **3.** allons manger; **4.** vont dîner; **5.** vais boire

PRACTICE 2: 1. au; **2.** aux; **3.** au; **4.** à la; **5.** à l'

——————— Lesson 16 (conversations) ———————

CONVERSATION 1
Paul and Thomas work at the same bank in Paris. It has been a busy morning, and now that it's lunchtime, they decide to grab a bite to eat at a nearby café.

Paul: J'ai faim. On va au café du quartier?

Thomas: C'est une bonne idée, car moi aussi, j'ai envie de manger quelque chose.

Paul: De toute façon, nous travaillons trop. C'est l'heure de déjeuner.

(They arrive, and after having looked at the menu, they decide what to order.)

Paul: Qu'est-ce que tu prends comme hors-d'œuvre ?

Thomas: Je pense que je vais prendre des crudités et après, un croque-monsieur. Et toi, qu'est-ce que tu prends?

Paul: Je ne sais pas. Peut-être une salade verte et un poulet frites.

Thomas: La soupe à l'oignon gratinée dans ce café est délicieuse.

Paul: Ah bon, alors, je voudrais une soupe à l'oignon gratinée et un poulet frites.

Thomas: Comme boisson, je prends une bière. J'ai soif.

Paul: Je vais commander un Perrier cassis.

Paul: *I'm hungry. Want to go to the café up the block?*

Thomas: *Good idea, because I feel like eating something, too.*

Paul: *At any rate, we've been working too much. It's time for lunch.*

Paul: *What are you having as an appetizer?*

Thomas: *I think I'll have the crudités and a grilled ham and cheese sandwich. What are you having?*

Paul: *I don't know. Maybe a green salad and chicken with fries.*

Thomas: *The baked onion soup at this café is delicious.*

Paul: *Good. I would like the onion soup and the chicken with fries.*

Thomas: *As a drink, I'm having a beer. I'm thirsty.*

Paul: *I'm going to order a Perrier cassis.*

Notes

Cassis is a black currant liquor that is used in many French drinks. Its taste is similar to that of blackberry brandy, but the consistency is much thicker, and the drink adds a strong flavor to mineral water **(Perrier cassis)**, white wine **(kir)**, or champagne **(kir royal)**. Syrup of cassis is also available for those who do not drink alcohol.

NUTS & BOLTS 1
The polite form, je voudrais *(I would like)*

In this unit, you encountered the polite expression **je voudrais** *(I would like)*. This expression is extremely useful in everyday conversation. It is used to ask politely for something. It may be used with a noun, as in the following example.

Je voudrais un bonbon.
I would like a candy.

It may be used with an infinitive.

Je voudrais danser.
I would like to dance.

Je voudrais is the conditional form of the verb **vouloir** *(to wish, to want)*. Look at the following table and learn the conditional forms of **vouloir**.

je voudrais	*I would like*	nous voudrions	*we would like*
tu voudrais	*you would like*	**vous voudriez**	*you would like*
il voudrait	*he would like*	**ils voudraient**	*they would like*
elle voudrait	*she would like*	**elles voudraient**	*they would like*

PRACTICE 1

Complete the sentences by translating the English into French.

1. *(We would like)* _____ des pommes.

2. *(They would like)* _____ prendre un dessert.

3. Jean *(would like)* _____ un croque monsieur.

4. Qu'est-ce que *(would you [infml.] like)* _____ boire?

5. *(I'd like)* _____ un verre de lait.

CONVERSATION 2

Mireille and her husband Étienne are at a **crêperie** *(restaurant that specializes in various kinds of crêpes for dinner or dessert).*

Étienne: Qu'est-ce que tu vas prendre ce soir, chérie?

Mireille: Il y a beaucoup de crêpes au menu. C'est difficile de se décider.

Étienne: Et bien, moi, je voudrais une crêpe au poulet.

Mireille: J'ai envie de prendre un dessert. On prépare de bons desserts ici.

Étienne: Quel parfum prends-tu?

Mireille: Alors, je pense que je prends une crêpe aux marrons.

Étienne: Est-ce que tu voudrais boire du cidre ce soir?

Mireille: Bonne idée! Je voudrais bien du cidre doux. Qu'est-ce que tu en penses?

Étienne: D'accord, nous allons prendre une bouteille de cidre doux.

Étienne: *What are you going to have tonight, dear?*

Mireille: *There are a lot of crêpes on the menu. It's difficult to decide.*

Étienne: *Well, I'm having a crêpe stuffed with chicken.*

Mireille: *I feel like eating dessert. They make good dessert crêpes here.*

Étienne:	What flavor are you having?
Mireille:	Well, I think I'll have the chestnut crêpe.
Étienne:	Do you want to have some cider tonight?
Mireille:	Good idea! I would really like some sweet cider. What do you think?
Étienne:	Okay, we'll get a bottle of sweet cider.

NOTES

Cider is produced in various regions of France, especially in Normandy, which is famous for growing apples. However, cider in France is not the same as that in the United States. It contains alcohol and comes in two varieties, **doux** *(sweet)* and **brut** *(dry)*, and it can be sparkling.

NUTS & BOLTS 2

THE SUBJECT PRONOUN ON *(one, we, you, they)*

The subject pronoun **on** is used for indefinite reference. It is always combined with a singular verb of the **il/elle** form. It often corresponds to the "generic" *one, we, you,* or *they* in English—e.g., *What can you do in Hawaii?* The possible answer to this question might be *You can surf, you can sightsee, and you can enjoy the sunsets.*

Other translations for the pronoun **on** are possible, as you can see in the French examples below.

Dans un café, on mange.
In a café, one eats/we eats/you eat/they eat/people eat.

Pendant l'été, on nage.
During the summer, you can swim/we can swim/one can swim/people can swim.

En hiver, on fait du ski et on patine.
In the winter, we ski and we ice-skate.

Le dimanche, on mange des croissants pour le petit déjeuner à la maison.
On Sundays, we eat croissants for breakfast at home.

PRACTICE 2
Write the correct form of each verb in the sentence.

1. Dans un jardin, on _____. (marcher)

   In a garden, one walks.

2. On _____ dans un restaurant. (dîner)

   People dine at a restaurant./We dine at the restaurant.

3. En général, on _____ du café avec le petit déjeuner en France. (boire)

   In general, they have coffee with breakfast in France.

4. On _____ en ville. (aller)

   They're going to town.

5. Le soir, on _____ le dîner. (préparer)

   At night, they make dinner.

Tip!

A good way remember vocabulary for food items is, again, to create flash cards. This time, instead of writing the vocabulary words in French on one side and the English equivalents on the other, browse through magazines that feature pictures of food. Cut out the various food items and paste them on one side, with the French on the other. Visual association is an excellent way to reinforce vocabulary.

ANSWERS
PRACTICE 1: 1. nous voudrions; **2.** ils voudraient; **3.** voudrait; **4.** tu voudrais; **5.** je voudrais

PRACTICE 2: 1. marche; **2.** dîne; **3.** boit; **4.** va; **5.** prépare

UNIT 4 ESSENTIALS

le repas	*meal*
Nous prenons le petit déjeuner.	*We're having breakfast.*
Je prends une quiche pour le déjeuner.	*I'm having quiche for lunch.*
Qu'est-ce que tu prends pour le dîner?	*What are you having for dinner?*
Je voudrais commander.	*I would like to order.*
Garçon, apportez-moi, s'il vous plaît, le menu (la carte).	*Waiter, please bring me the menu.*
La liste des vins, s'il vous plaît.	*The wine list, please.*
L'addition, s'il vous plaît!	*The check, please!*
Bon appétit!	*Enjoy your meal!*
Je recommande la soupe du jour.	*I recommend the soup of the day.*
J'aime la glace à la fraise.	*I like strawberry ice cream.*
Service compris.	*The tip is included.*
À votre santé!	*To your health!*
Je bois un verre de vin blanc.	*I'm drinking a glass of white wine.*
Je prends un croque-monsieur.	*I'm having a grilled ham and cheese sandwich.*

UNIT 5
Using the telephone and making appointments

In this unit, you will learn how to tell time, as well as various expressions associated with time. You will also learn several useful expressions for making telephone calls and making appointments in French.

―――――――――――― Lesson 17 (words) ――――――――――――

WORD LIST 1
COMMENT DIRE L'HEURE *(How to tell time)*

Quelle heure est-il?	*What time is it?* *(Lit., What hour is it?)*
Il est une heure.	*It is one o'clock.*
Il est deux heures.	*It is two o'clock.*
Il est deux heures cinq.	*It is five minutes after two.*
Il est deux heures dix.	*It is ten minutes after two.*
Il est deux heures et quart.	*It is a quarter after two.*
Il est deux heures vingt.	*It is twenty minutes after two.*
Il est deux heures vingt-cinq.	*It is twenty-five minutes after two.*
Il est deux heures et demie.	*It is half past two.*
Il est trois heures moins vingt-cinq.	*It is twenty-five minutes to three (lit., the hour of three minus twenty-five).*
Il est trois heures moins vingt.	*It is twenty minutes to three (lit., the hour of three minus twenty).*
Il est trois heures moins le quart.	*It is a quarter to three (lit., the hour of three minus the quarter).*
Il est trois heures moins dix.	*It is ten minutes to three.*
Il est trois heures moins cinq.	*It is five minutes to three.*

| Il est midi. | *It is noon.* |
| Il est minuit. | *It is midnight.* |

NOTES

To express time up to thirty minutes after the hour, the number of minutes is added. We use the word **et** *(and)* only with **quart** *(quarter)* and **demi/e** *(half)*.

To express time from thirty minutes before a certain hour, use the word **moins** *(minus, less)*. The word **heure** *(hour)* is feminine; therefore, we say **Il est une heure** *(It is one o'clock)*, using the feminine indefinite article.

Note that the words **midi** *(noon)* and **minuit** *(midnight)* are both masculine. After a masculine noun, the form **demi** is used.

Il est minuit et demi.
It is twelve thirty a.m.

After a feminine noun it becomes **demie**.

Il est six heures et demie.
It is six thirty.

PRACTICE 1

Say and write down the following times in French. There may be more than one way of saying a certain time.

1. 1:10
2. 2:25 a.m.
3. 12 a.m.
4. 12 p.m.
5. 5:30
6. 7:45
7. 9:50
8. 10:15

GROUP 2 VERBS: VERBS ENDING IN -IR

You have already learned the present tense forms of **-er** verbs. In the table below you will find some common **-ir** verbs.

-ir VERBS	
bâtir	*to build*
choisir	*to choose*
finir	*to finish*
obéir	*to obey*
punir	*to punish*
rougir	*to blush*

The **-ir** verbs will follow the same basic pattern as the **-er** verbs, with some changes in the endings. To conjugate an **-ir** verb, we cut off the ending **-ir** from the infinitive and add the following endings to the stem.

-ir VERB ENDINGS	
je: -is	**nous: -issons**
tu: -is	**vous: -issez**
il: -it	**ils: -issent**
elle: -it	**elles: -issent**

Let's look at the conjugated verb **finir** *(to finish)*.

je finis	*I finish*	nous finissons	*we finish*
tu finis (infml.)	*you finish*	vous finissez (pl., sg. fml.)	*you finish*
il finit	*he finishes*	ils finissent	*they finish*
elle finit	*she finishes*	elles finissent	*they finish*

Each form of **finir** corresponds to several forms in English. For example, **je finis** can be translated as *I finish* or *I'm finishing* or *I do finish*, depending on the context.

Le bébé finit son petit déjeuner.
The baby finishes his breakfast.

Je finis mon croissant.
I'm finishing my croissant.

En général, les enfants finissent leurs devoirs.
Generally, the children finish their homework.

Here are more **-ir** verbs.

-ir VERBS	
agir	*to act*
désobéir	*to disobey*
nourrir	*to feed*
réfléchir	*to think, to reflect*
réussir	*to succeed, to do well*
remplir	*to fill (in)*

maigrir	to lose weight
grossir	to gain weight
grandir	to grow

PRACTICE 2

Choose the correct verb form in each of the following sentences.

1. Nous (finissez, finissons, finissent) à dix heures.

   We're finishing at ten o'clock.

2. L'étudiant (choisis, choisissez, choisit) le train de deux heures.

   The student chooses the two o'clock train.

3. La fille (rougit, rougis, rougir) devant ses amis.

   The girl blushes in front of her friends.

4. L'architecte (bâtis, bâtissent, bâtit) la maison.

   The architect builds the house.

5. Est-ce que vous (obéissez, obéis, obéit) à vos parents?

   Do you obey your parents?

PRACTICE 3

Fill in the blanks with the correct form of the verb in parentheses.

1. Tu _____ à tout. (réussir)

   You do succeed in everything.

2. Le professeur _____ le mauvais élève. (punir)

   The teacher punishes the bad student.

3. Le garçon _____ le sandwich. (finir)

   The boy is finishing the sandwich.

4. Ils _____ à leurs parents. (obéir)

   They obey their parents.

5. Vous _____ une maison. (bâtir)

   You're building a house.

6. Je _____ un dessert. (choisir)

   I choose a dessert.

7. _____-nous avec le projet? (réussir)

   Are we succeeding with the project?

8. Les étudiants _____ à l'examen. (réussir)

   The students do well on the exam.

9. L'enfant _____ à son père. (désobéir)

   The child disobeys his father.

10. Quand elle a tort, elle _____. (rougir)

    When she's wrong, she blushes.

PRACTICE 4
Complete each sentence by giving the correct form of the verb. Follow the model.

Ex. Je finis mon travail.
    Tu finis ton travail.

1. Tu nourris le bébé. Nicole _____ les enfants.

2. Elles obéissent à leurs parents. Il _____ à ses parents.

3. Finissez-vous le déjeuner? Non, je ne _____ pas le déjeuner.

4. Elle rougit devant la classe. Quand _____-tu?

5. Réfléchis-tu? Oui, je _____ toujours.

WORD LIST 2
LES ADVERBES DE TEMPS *(Adverbs of time)*

toujours	*always, still*
encore	*still, more*
jamais	*ever, never*
souvent	*often*
maintenant	*now*
rarement	*rarely*
longtemps	*long, for a long time*
tôt	*early*
tard	*late*
bientôt	*soon*
autrefois	*formerly, in the past*
avant-hier	*the day before yesterday*
après-demain	*the day after tomorrow*

NOTES

You have learned that to form the negative, two words are used: **ne,** placed before the verb, and **pas,** directly after the verb. We can form more negatives by substituting different negative words for **pas.**

ne . . . jamais *(never)*
Il ne finit jamais son dîner.
He never finishes his dinner.

ne . . . plus *(no longer, no more, anymore)*
Nous ne parlons plus.
We don't speak anymore./We no longer speak.

ne . . . pas encore *(not yet)*

Tu ne réussis pas encore.

You're not yet succeeding.

NUTS & BOLTS 2
GROUP 3 VERBS: VERBS ENDING IN -RE

Now you are going to learn the present tense forms of verbs ending in **-re**. Here are some common **-re** verbs.

-re VERBS	
attendre	*to wait (for), to expect*
défendre	*to defend*
descendre	*to go down, to come down*
entendre	*to hear*
interrompre	*to interrupt*
perdre	*to lose*
rendre	*to give back, to return*
répondre	*to answer, to respond*
rompre	*to break*
vendre	*to sell*

To conjugate an **-re** verb, we cut off the ending **-re** from the infinitive and add the following endings to the stem in the appropriate persons.

-re VERB ENDINGS

je: -s	nous: -ons
tu: -s	vous: -ez
il: -	ils: -ent
elle: -	elles: -ent

Let's look at the conjugated verb **vendre** *(to sell)*.

je vends	*I sell*	nous vendons	*we sell*
tu vends (infml.)	*you sell*	vous vendez (pl., sg. fml.)	*you sell*
il vend	*he sells*	ils vendent	*they sell*
elle vend	*she sells*	elles vendent	*they sell*

Note the similarities in verb endings that are shared by all three groups of regular verbs that you have studied. The **nous** form always has **-ons** in the ending; **vous** has **-ez** in the ending, and the plural forms **ils** and **elles** have **-ent**.

However, the third person singular of **rompre** *(to break)* and **interrompre** *(to interrupt)* ends in **-t**.

elle rompt
she breaks

il interrompt
he interrupts

Remember that the verbs **prendre, apprendre,** and **comprendre** are irregular.

The **-ir** and **-re** verbs form their negative and interrogative in the same manner as **-er** verbs. Here are some examples of the negative forms for **-ir** verbs.

Je ne finis pas.
I don't finish.

Ils ne choisissent pas.
They do not choose.

Elle ne rougit pas.
She doesn't blush.

Here are some examples of **-re** verbs in the negative form.

Elles ne vendent pas de pommes.
They don't sell apples.

Je n'attends pas l'autobus.
I'm not waiting for the bus.

Marc n'entend pas la musique.
Marc doesn't hear the music.

Now let's look at some examples of the interrogative forms of **-ir** verbs.

Est-ce que nous choisissons un dessert?
Are we choosing a dessert?

Choisissons-nous un dessert?
Are we choosing a dessert?

Est-ce que vous réussissez vos études?
Are you doing well in your studies?

Réussissez-vous vos études?
Are you doing well in your studies?

Here are examples of **-re** verbs in the interrogative form.

Est-ce que vous répondez à la question?
Are you answering the question?

Répondez-vous à la question?
Are you answering the question?

Est-ce que Jean descend?
Is Jean coming down?

Jean descend-il?
Is Jean coming down?

PRACTICE 5
Fill in the blanks with the correct form of the verb in parentheses.

1. Je _____ à la question. (répondre)

   I'm answering the question.

2. Qu'est-ce que vous _____? (attendre)

   What are you waiting for?

3. Est-ce qu'elle _____ la musique? (entendre)

   Does she hear the music?

4. Il _____ son auto. (vendre)

   He's selling his car.

5. Mes amis _____ l'autobus. (attendre)

   My friends are waiting for the bus.

6. Nous ne _____ pas. (répondre)

   We don't answer.

7. Vous _____ cinq dollars. (perdre)

   You lose five dollars.

8. Tu _____ ta place. (perdre)

   You lose your place.

9. Je n'_____ pas. (entendre)

   I do not hear.

10. Elles _____ les livres. (rendre)

   They give back the books.

Tip!

Now that you have learned about the three groups of regular verbs, it is important to practice what you have learned. Creating a flip chart for verb conjugations is an excellent way to review verbs. Using a piece of oak tag or cardboard, approximately 12 x 14 inches, write the singular subject pronouns on the left and the plural subject pronouns in a middle column. For each verb included in your flip chart, you will need two separate strips of paper (or cardboard), equal to the 12 inches—one for the singular forms of the verb and one for the plural forms. Write the various verb forms on the two strips, and secure them at the top of your chart with loose-leaf rings. Each time you "flip the verb," you will have the appropriate forms with the corresponding pronouns. Try to conjugate your verb correctly before flipping to your answers. You can add more verbs as your studies progress.

ANSWERS

PRACTICE 1: 1. une heure dix; **2.** deux heures vingt-cinq; **3.** minuit; **4.** midi; **5.** cinq heures et demie; **6.** sept heures quarante-cinq *or* huit heures moins le quart; **7.** neuf heures cinquante *or* dix heures moins dix; **8.** dix heures et quart

PRACTICE 2: 1. finissons; **2.** choisit; **3.** rougit; **4.** bâtit; **5.** obéissez

PRACTICE 3: 1. réussis; **2.** punit; **3.** finit; **4.** obéissent; **5.** bâtissez; **6.** choisis; **7.** réussissons; **8.** réussissent; **9.** désobéit; **10.** rougit

PRACTICE 4: 1. nourrit; **2.** obéit; **3.** finis; **4.** rougis; **5.** réfléchis

PRACTICE 5: 1. réponds; **2.** attendez; **3.** entend; **4.** vend; **5.** attendent; **6.** répondons; **7.** perdez; **8.** perds; **9.** entends; **10.** rendent

———————— Lesson 18 (phrases) ————————

PHRASE LIST 1
LES EXPRESSIONS DE TEMPS *(Expressions of time)*

À quelle heure?	*at what time?*
à midi précis	*exactly at noon*
à une heure précise	*at one o'clock sharp*
à dix heures précises	*at ten o'clock sharp*
trois heures du matin	*three o'clock in the morning*
trois heures de l'après-midi	*three o'clock in the afternoon*
huit heures du soir	*eight o'clock in the evening*
vers neuf heures	*around nine o'clock*
dans un quart d'heure	*in a quarter of an hour*
une demi-heure	*a half hour*
en retard	*late*
à l'heure	*on time*
en avance	*early*
la semaine prochaine	*next week*
l'année dernière	*last year*
dans un mois	*in one month*

NOTES
Notice that the French equivalent of *a.m.* is **du matin** *(in the morning)*, and *p.m.* is translated as **de l'après-midi** *(in the afternoon)* or

du soir, which can also mean *in the evening*. The word **demi** is invariable when used before the word **heure** but changes to **demie** when it appears after it, as in **une heure et demie** *(an hour and a half)*. The adjective **précis/précise/précises** must agree with the noun that it modifies.

NUTS & BOLTS 1
THE PAST TENSE (LE PASSÉ COMPOSÉ)

Remember that the most important verb, **avoir** *(to have),* is used in many expressions. Now we are going to see it used to create the past tense in French.

To form the past tense, or in French, **le passé composé,** we combine the present tense of the verb **avoir** with the past participle of the verb. The participle is a special form of the verb used in compound tenses.

To form the past participle of an **-er** verb, we cut off the ending **-er** from the infinitive and add **-é,** e.g., **dansé.**

Let's look at an example of the past tense of the verb **danser** *(to dance).*

j'ai dansé	*I danced*	nous avons dansé	*we danced*
tu as dansé	*you danced*	vous avez dansé	*you danced*
il a dansé	*he danced*	ils ont dansé	*they have danced*
elle a dansé	*she danced*	elles ont dansé	*they danced*

There are three ways to translate the French past tense into English: **j'ai dansé** can mean *I danced, I have danced,* or *I did dance.*

PRACTICE 1
Fill in the blanks with the correct past tense form of the verbs in parentheses.

1. Tu _____ au professeur. (parler)

2. Elle _____. (chanter)

3. À midi, nous _____ au café. (manger)

4. Ils _____ de manger à sept heures. (décider)

5. Est-ce que vous _____ le livre? (donner)

6. Ils _____ un match de tennis. (jouer)

7. Marc _____ avec Marie. (danser)

8. Ma mère _____ bon dîner. (préparer)

9. Vous _____. (marcher)

10. J' _____ à six heures et quart. (terminer)

To form the negative of a verb in the past tense, place the negative words **ne** and **pas** around the forms of the verb **avoir**.

Je n'ai pas regardé la télévision.
I didn't watch TV.

Tu n'as pas mangé à neuf heures.
You didn't eat at nine o'clock.

Il n'a pas donné le livre à Jean.
He did not give the book to Jean.

Nous n'avons pas chanté.
We didn't sing.

Vous n'avez pas parlé.

You have not spoken.

Ils n'ont pas joué au basket.

They didn't play basketball.

Note the varied translations of the negative sentences above.

The interrogative form of the past tense verbs is not difficult. You may use one of the three ways of asking questions you learned about earlier—the intonational question, the **est-ce que** question, or the subject-verb inversion question.

Vous avez parlé?/Est-ce que vous avez parlé?/Avez-vous parlé?

Did you speak?/Have you spoken?/You spoke?

Now, here are the endings for the past participles of **-ir** verbs and **-re** verbs.

For **-ir** verbs, cut off the **-ir** from the infinitive and add **-i** to form the past participle; for **-re** verbs, cut off the **-re** from the infinitive and add **u**.

finir—fini

to finish—finished

vendre—vendu

to sell—sold

PRACTICE 2
Put the sentences in the past tense.

1. Nous _____ le dessert. (finir)

   We finished dessert.

2. J'_____ la musique. (entendre)

   I heard the music.

3. Ma famille _____ la maison. (vendre)

My family sold the house.

4. Elle _____. (répondre)

She responded.

5. Tu _____ un sujet. (choisir)

She did choose.

PRACTICE 3
Negate the following sentences.

1. La fille a chanté une belle chanson.

2. Nous avons mangé bien.

3. Il a parlé anglais.

4. Ils ont dîné à sept heures et demie.

5. J'ai joué au tennis.

PRACTICE 4
Change the following questions from the **est-ce que** form to the subject-verb inversion form.

1. Est-ce qu'elle a mangé à six heures dix?

2. Est-ce que nous avons fini?

3. Est-ce que vous avez regardé la télé?

4. Est-ce que tu as préparé le dîner?

5. Est-ce qu'ils ont répondu à la lettre?

Now let's look at the table below to review all three groups of regular verbs at a glance, in the past tense.

parler *(to speak)*	finir *(to finish)*	répondre *(to answer)*
j'ai parlé	j'ai fini	j'ai répondu
tu as parlé	tu as fini	tu as répondu
il a parlé	il a fini	il a répondu
elle a parlé	elle a fini	elle a répondu
nous avons parlé	nous avons fini	nous avons répondu
vous avez parlé	vous avez fini	vous avez répondu
ils ont parlé	ils ont fini	ils ont répondu
elles ont parlé	elles ont fini	elles ont répondu

PRACTICE 5
Put the verbs in parentheses in the correct past tense form.

1. Il _____ à son ami. (répondre)

2. Mes amis _____ le taxi. (attendre)

3. J'_____ la lettre. (finir)

4. Nous _____ la nouvelle chanson. (entendre)

5. Tu _____ au tennis. (jouer)

6. _____-vous _____ le menu hier soir? (regarder)

7. Elle n'_____ pas _____ son auto. (vendre)

8. Vous n'_____ pas _____ une boisson. (choisir)

9. Je n'_____ pas _____. (rougir)

10. Est-ce que les enfants _____? (obéir)

PHRASE LIST 2
EXPRESSIONS POUR PARLER AU TÉLÉPHONE *(Expressions for speaking on the phone)*

Allô?	*Hello?*
le téléphone	*telephone*
le numéro de téléphone	*phone number*
téléphoner	*to make a phone call*
donner un coup de fil	*to make a phone call*
consulter l'annuaire *(m.)*	*to consult a phone book*
le poste 224	*extension 224*
Qui est-ce?	*Who is it?*
Attendez, s'il vous plaît.	*Wait, please.*
Ne quittez pas, s'il vous plaît.	*Hold on, please.*
Vous m'entendez?	*Can you hear me?*
Je ne vous entends pas.	*I can't hear you.*
Raccrochez, s'il vous plaît.	*Hang up, please.*

NOTES
The French use the expression **allô** *(hello)* only when they answer the phone and not for greeting people in conversation.

NUTS & BOLTS 2
THE PAST TENSE OF IRREGULAR VERBS
The past tense of some irregular verbs is formed the same way as for the regular verbs. However, for the irregular verbs, you must memorize the past participles because they have unpredictable, irregular forms.

IRREGULAR PAST PARTICIPLES	
avoir *(to have)*	**eu** *(had)*
boire *(to drink)*	**bu** *(drunk)*

être *(to be)*	été *(been)*
comprendre *(to understand)*	compris *(understood)*
prendre *(to take)*	pris *(taken)*
apprendre *(to learn)*	appris *(learned)*

Here is the irregular verb **prendre** *(to take)* in the past tense.

j'ai pris	*I took*	nous avons pris	*we took*
tu as pris	*you took*	vous avez pris	*you took*
il a pris	*he took*	ils ont pris	*they took*
elle a pris	*she took*	elles ont pris	*they took*

PRACTICE 6
Fill in the blanks with the correct past tense form of the verb in parentheses.

1. Paul _____ un verre de vin rouge. (boire)

2. Mes amis _____ en France. (être)

3. J'_____ le livre. (comprendre)

4. Nous _____ un problème. (avoir)

5. Vous _____ aux États-Unis. (être)

6. Elle _____ mes clés. (prendre)

> *Discovery activity*
>
> To practice the past tense of verbs, try keeping a journal in French of the day's activities. Keep it simple, but try to write down some of the activities or things you accomplished during the course of the day.

ANSWERS

PRACTICE 1: 1. as parlé; **2.** a chanté; **3.** avons mangé; **4.** ont décidé; **5.** avez donné; **6.** ont joué; **7.** a dansé; **8.** a préparé; **9.** avez marché; **10.** ai terminé

PRACTICE 2: 1. avons fini; **2.** ai entendu; **3.** a vendu; **4.** a répondu; **5.** as choisi

PRACTICE 3: 1. La fille n'a pas chanté. **2.** Nous n'avons pas mangé bien. **3.** Il n'a pas parlé anglais. **4.** Ils n'ont pas dîné à sept heures et demie. **5.** Je n'ai pas joué au tennis.

PRACTICE 4: 1. A-t-elle dîné à six heures dix? **2.** Avons-nous fini? **3.** Avez-vous regardé la télévision? **4.** As-tu préparé le dîner? **5.** Ont-ils répondu à la lettre?

PRACTICE 5: 1. a répondu; **2.** ont attendu; **3.** ai fini; **4.** avons entendu; **5.** as joué; **6.** Avez-(vous) regardé; **7.** n'a pas vendu; **8.** n'avez pas choisi; **9.** n'ai pas rougi; **10.** ont obéi

PRACTICE 6: 1. a bu; **2.** ont été; **3.** ai compris; **4.** avons eu; **5.** avez été; **6.** a pris

—————————— Lesson 19 (sentences) ——————————

SENTENCE GROUP 1
AU TÉLÉPHONE *(On the phone)*

Je voudrais téléphoner.	*I would like to make a phone call.*
Je voudrais parler à . . .	*I would like to speak to . . .*
C'est de la part de qui, s'il vous plaît?	*Who is calling, please?*
Je suis désolé/désolée.	*I am sorry.*
Il/Elle n'est pas là.	*He/She isn't here.*
Voulez-vous laisser un message?	*Do you want to leave a message?*
Je voudrais laisser un message.	*I would like to leave a message.*

Pouvez-vous lui dire que j'ai appelé?	*Can you tell him/her that I called?*
Parlez plus lentement, s'il vous plaît.	*Speak slower, please.*
Quel est votre numéro de téléphone?	*What is your telephone number?*
Je vous le/la passe.	*I am getting him/her for you.*
La ligne est occupée.	*The line is busy.*
Je vais rappeler.	*I'm going to call back.*

NOTES

Remember the verb **appeler** in the following expressions.

Comment t'appelles-tu?
What's your name?

Je m'appelle . . .
My name is . . . (lit., I call myself . . .)

The **m'** before the verb in this case, stands for **me**.

The verb **appeler** *(to call)* and its cousin, **rappeler** *(to call back)*, are also used when telephoning someone.

J'appelle le médecin.
I call the doctor.

Vous rappelez votre ami.
You call your friend back.

However, note that with these **-er** verbs, there is a slight spelling change. The infinitive form of the verb **appeler** (and **rappeler**) has one **l**. The verb changes its spelling by doubling the **l** in all forms except the **nous** and **vous** forms.

Let's take a look at the conjugated forms of the verb **appeler** *(to call)*.

j'appelle	*I call*	nous appelons	*we call*
tu appelles	*you call*	vous appelez	*you call*
il appelle	*he calls*	ils appellent	*they call*
elle appelle	*she calls*	elles appellent	*they call*

NUTS & BOLTS 1
THE VERB DEVOIR *(to have to, must, to owe)*

You have already learned various irregular verbs in French, such as **avoir** *(to have)*, **être** *(to be)*, **aller** *(to go)*, **prendre** *(to take)*, and **boire** *(to drink)*. Here is another irregular verb that you can add to your list, the verb **devoir** *(to have to, must, to owe)*.

The verb **devoir** has several meanings that are useful; **devoir** followed by an infinitive verb means *to have to* or *must,* and **devoir** followed by a noun means *to owe.* Here are its present tense forms.

je dois	*I have to*	nous devons	*we have to*
tu dois	*you have to*	vous devez	*you have to*
il doit	*he has to*	ils doivent	*they have to*
elle doit	*she has to*	elles doivent	*they have to*

Let's now see how the verb is used.

Mon père doit travailler de six heures du matin jusqu'à six heures du soir.
My father has to work from six in the morning until six at night.

Nous devons être au théâtre à huit heures pour la pièce.
We have to be at the theater by eight o'clock for the play.

Je dois appeler le restaurant pour faire des réservations.
I have to call the restaurant to make reservations.

Devoir can be used to express things that are supposed to or should take place.

Tu dois être prêt à cinq heures.
You must be ready by five o'clock./You're supposed to be ready by five o'clock.

Leur avion doit arriver à midi.
Their plane is supposed to arrive at noon.

Cela doit être amusant!
This must be fun!/This should be fun!

We can use **devoir** to show a debt that is owed.

Il doit dix dollars.
He owes ten dollars.

Combien est-ce que je dois?
How much (money) do I owe?

When learning irregular verbs in the present tense, you will find that most **nous** and **vous** forms of the verbs take their cue from the infinitive spelling. That is, they will look similar to the infinitive form of the verb.

avoir: nous avons, vous avez
devoir: nous devons, vous devez
aller: nous allons, vous allez

You will see more of these similarities as you continue to learn other irregular verbs.

PRACTICE 1

Fill in the blanks with the appropriate form of the verb **devoir**.

1. Ils _____ finir leur projet.

   They must finish their project.

2. Tu ne _____ pas travailler.

   You don't have to work.

3. Est-ce que nous _____ aller à New York?

   Are we supposed to go to New York?

4. Vous _____ être au café à l'heure.

   You have to be at the café on time.

5. Je _____ retourner à la maison ce soir.

   I have to go home tonight.

6. Elle _____ beaucoup à ses parents.

   She owes a lot to her parents.

7. Le train _____ arriver à sept heures et demie.

   The train is supposed to arrive at seven thirty.

8. À quelle heure est-ce que tu _____ partir?

   At what time do you have to leave?

SENTENCE GROUP 2
PRENDRE RENDEZ-VOUS *(Making an appointment)*

Je voudrais prendre un rendez-vous.	*I would like to make an appointment.*
Est-ce que tu es libre à neuf heures?	*Are you free at nine o'clock?*
Êtes-vous libre à sept heures et quart?	*Are you free at a quarter past seven?*

Avez-vous le temps d'y aller avec moi?	*Do you have time to go there with me?*
As-tu le temps d'y aller avec moi?	*Do you have time to go there with me?*
J'ai le temps d'y aller.	*I have time to go (there).*
Le temps, c'est de l'argent.	*Time is money.*
Je n'ai pas le temps.	*I don't have time.*
Il perd son temps.	*He's wasting his time.*
Il est temps de te reposer.	*It's about time for you to relax.*

NOTES

Remember that when expressing time of day, the word **heure** *(hour)* is always used.

Quelle heure-est-il?
What time is it?

The term **le temps** *(time)* is used when expressing time in general, as in the sentences in the table above.

NUTS & BOLTS 2
THE VERB FAIRE *(to do, to make)*
You already became acquainted with the verb **faire** in Unit 3 when weather expressions were introduced.

Il fait beau.
It's nice out.

Il fait froid.
It's cold.

Now let's look at all of the present tense forms of the verb **faire.**

je fais	*I do, I make*	**nous faisons**	*we do, we make*
tu fais	*you do, you make*	**vous faites**	*you do, you make*
il fait	*he does, he makes*	**ils font**	*they do, they make*
elle fait	*she does, she makes*	**elles font**	*they do, they make*

The verb **faire** is used to form many expressions besides those pertaining to weather. Here are some examples.

Je fais du sport.	*I play sports. (lit., I do some sports.)*
Je fais du ski.	*I ski. (lit., I do some skiing.)*
Je fais du ski nautique.	*I water-ski.*
Je fais du baby-sitting.	*I'm babysitting.*
Je fais la cuisine.	*I'm cooking. (lit., I'm doing the cooking.)*
Je fais des courses.	*I'm shopping.*
Je fais du shopping.	*I'm shopping.*
Je fais des achats.	*I'm running errands.*
Je fais une promenade.	*I'm taking a walk.*

Note that the past participle of the verb **faire** is **fait** *(did, made).*

J'ai fait une erreur.
I made a mistake.

J'ai fait des achats.
I ran some errands.

PRACTICE 2
Use the correct present tense form of the verb **faire.**

1. Je _____ une omelette.

   I'm making an omelet.

2. Qu'est-ce que tu _____?

   What are you doing?/What are you making?

3. Nous _____ un grand dîner.

   We're making a big dinner.

4. Les garçons _____ du ski.

   The boys are skiing.

5. _____-vous du shopping?

   Are you shopping?

Language link

If you are visiting France for the first time and want to make a call either to France or from France, here is a website to consult before doing so: www.ehow.com/how 8495 call-france-united.html.

The French phone system was changed about ten years ago, and the old eight-digit numbers were turned into ten-digit numbers by adding prefixes. The prefix 01 represents Paris, 02 stands for northwest, 03 for northeast, 04 for southeast, and 05 for southwest.

ANSWERS
PRACTICE 1: 1. doivent; **2.** dois; **3.** devons; **4.** devez; **5.** dois; **6.** doit; **7.** doit; **8.** dois

PRACTICE 2: 1. fais; **2.** fais; **3.** faisons; **4.** font; **5.** Faites

CONVERSATION 1

In this dialogue, Jean-Claude is trying to reach his friend Marc at home.

Madame Soubrié:	Allô?
Jean-Claude:	Bonjour, Madame Soubrié. Je voudrais parler à Marc, s'il vous plaît.
Madame Soubrié:	Qui est à l'appareil?
Jean-Claude:	C'est Jean-Claude DuLac. Je suis un ami de Marc.
Madame Soubrié:	Ne quittez pas, s'il vous plaît, je vais le chercher.

(She returns to the line after a few moments.)

Madame Soubrié:	Je regrette, mais Marc n'est plus ici. Il a quitté la maison il y a deux minutes.
Jean-Claude:	Je vais laisser un message pour lui.
Madame Soubrié:	Bien sûr. Il va revenir à cinq heures et quart.
Jean-Claude:	D'accord. Je vais téléphoner ce soir vers sept heures, Madame.
Madame Soubrié:	Bon. Je vais donner le message à Marc.

Madame Soubrié:	*Hello?*
Jean-Claude:	*Hello, Madame Soubrié. I would like to speak with Marc, please.*
Madame Soubrié:	*Who's calling?*
Jean-Claude:	*It's Jean-Claude DuLac. I'm a friend of Marc's.*
Madame Soubrié:	*Hold on, I'll get him for you.*

(She returns to the line after a few moments.)

Madame Soubrié:	*I'm sorry, but Marc is no longer here. He left the house two minutes ago.*
Jean-Claude:	*I am going to leave a message for him.*

> *Madame Soubrié:* Of course. He's going to be back at 5:15.
> *Jean-Claude:* Okay. I'm going to call tonight around 7:00.
> *Madame Soubrié:* Good. I am going to give Marc the message.

NOTES

The expression **il y a,** which means *there is* or *there are* in English, can also mean *ago* when combined with an expression of time.

il y a trois heures *(three hours ago)*
il y a deux minutes *(two minutes ago)*
il y a longtemps *(a long time ago)*

NUTS & BOLTS 1
THE FUTURE TENSE

You have already learned the near future, which uses the verb **aller** + infinitive. Now you will learn the formal future tense.

The future tense is formed by adding the future endings to the infinitive for **-er** verbs and **-ir** verbs. For **-re** verbs, the final **e** is dropped before adding the endings. The endings for the future tense are in the table below.

FUTURE TENSE ENDINGS	
je: -ai	**nous: -ons**
tu: -as	**vous: -ez**
il: -a	**ils: -ont**
elle: -a	**elles: -ont**

Here are examples of the three groups of regular verbs in the future tense.

danser *(to dance)*	finir *(to finish)*	vendre *(to sell)*
je danserai	je finirai	je vendrai
tu danseras	tu finiras	tu vendras
il dansera	il finira	il vendra
elle dansera	elle finira	elle vendra
nous danserons	nous finirons	nous vendrons
vous danserez	vous finirez	vous vendrez
ils danseront	ils finiront	ils vendront
elles danseront	elles finiront	elles vendront

Je marcherai au parc avec toi.
I will walk in the park with you.

Le médecin guérira le bébé.
The doctor will cure the baby.

Qui vendra le bateau?
Who will sell the boat?

Ils inviteront tout le monde.
They will invite everyone.

PRACTICE 1
Fill in the blanks with the correct future tense form of the verbs in parentheses.

1. Les enfants _____ à leurs parents. (obéir)

2. Elles _____ en ville. (dîner)

3. Est-ce que tu _____ à la lettre? (répondre)

4. J' _____ mes mais au restaurant. (accompagner)

5. Vous ne _____ pas la télévision. (regarder)

6. Il _____ au baseball. (jouer)

CONVERSATION 2

Carol calls the restaurant to make reservations for dinner for Saturday evening.

Le maître d'hôtel:	**Allô, bonsoir. Puis-je vous aider?**
Carol:	**Je voudrais faire des réservations pour dîner samedi soir.**
Le maître d'hôtel:	**Vous serez combien de personnes, Madame?**
Carol:	**Nous serons quatre personnes.**
Le maître d'hôtel:	**À quelle heure est-ce que vous désirez réserver une table?**
Carol:	**Nous arriverons vers sept heures et demie, Monsieur.**
Le maître d'hôtel:	**Très bien, Madame. La réservation sera sous quel nom?**
Carol:	**C'est pour la famille Rigaud.**
Le maître d'hôtel:	**Entendu. Quatre personnes pour le dîner samedi soir à sept heures et demie.**

Maître d':	*Hello, good evening. May I help you?*
Carol:	*I would like to make reservations for dinner for Saturday evening.*
Maître d':	*How many people will you be, Madame?*
Carol:	*We will be four people.*
Maître d':	*For what time would you like to make reservations?*
Carol:	*We will be arriving around seven thirty, Monsieur.*
Maître d':	*Very well, Madame. The reservation will be under what name?*
Carol:	*It's for the Rigaud family.*

> *Maître d':* *All right. Four people for dinner on Saturday evening at seven thirty.*

NUTS & BOLTS 2
THE FUTURE TENSE OF IRREGULAR VERBS

Some irregular verbs have an irregular stem in the future tense. You will have to memorize the stem and add the future endings.

aller: ir-
avoir: aur-
être: ser-
faire: fer-
devoir: devr-

J'irai à Paris.
I will go to Paris.

Il devra dix dollars.
He will owe ten dollars.

Nous serons en retard.
We will be late.

J'aurai les tickets ce soir.
I will have the tickets tonight.

Je ferai la cuisine demain soir.
I will do the cooking tomorrow night.

Il fera du soleil demain.
It will be sunny tomorrow.

PRACTICE 2
Put the verbs in parentheses in the future tense.

1. Vous _____ combien de personnes? (être)
2. Nous _____ au restaurant à midi. (être)

3. Ils _____ la fête ce soir. (avoir)

4. Est-ce que vous _____ en France? (aller)

5. Je _____ finir. (devoir)

6. Jeudi, il _____ beau. (faire)

PRACTICE 3

Change the verbs from the near future to the formal future tense. Follow the model.

Ex. Je vais travailler. *I'm going to work.*
    Je travaillerai. *I shall work.*

1. Mes amis vont être à la maison à dix heures.

2. Tu vas aller à New York avec nous.

3. Vous allez être combien de personnes?

4. Je vais attendre.

5. Nous allons dîner en ville.

Culture note

Communications in France

The postal and telephone services in France used to be provided in the same place and were called **les PTT (Postes, Télégraphe et Téléphones).** More recently, this service has been split into two services: **La Poste,** where you go to mail letters and packages, and **France Télécom,** the company that provides telephone services.

Some coin-operated phone booths may still be found in the cities in France, but most of them have been replaced with phones requiring a magnetic phone card called **la télécarte.** When traveling to France, it is wise to purchase **la télécarte** rather than use a hotel phone, as the card is more economical. These cards can be found at magazine kiosks, at the post office, or in tobacco shops.

French phone numbers consist of ten digits. If you would like to make an international call from France, it is necessary to dial 00, the country code (1 for the United States), the area code, and then the number.

ANSWERS

PRACTICE 1: 1. obéiront; **2.** dîneront; **3.** répondras; **4.** accompagnerai; **5.** regarderez; **6.** jouera

PRACTICE 2: 1. serez; **2.** serons; **3.** auront; **4.** irez; **5.** devrai; **6.** fera

PRACTICE 3: 1. Mes amis seront à la maison à dix heures. **2.** Tu iras à New York avec nous. **3.** Vous serez combien de personnes? **4.** J'attendrai. **5.** Nous dînerons en ville.

UNIT 5 ESSENTIALS

There were many new things that you learned in this unit. Some of the most important items are listed below.

Quelle heure est-il?	*What time is it? (lit., What hour is it?)*
Il est une heure.	*It is one o'clock.*
Il est deux heures cinq.	*It is five minutes after two.*
Il est deux heures et quart.	*It is a quarter after two.*
Il est deux heures et demie.	*It is half past three.*
Il est trois heures moins le quart.	*It is a quarter to three.*
Il est midi.	*It is noon.*
Il est minuit.	*It is midnight.*
À quelle heure?	*At what time?*
Je voudrais parler à . . .	*I would like to speak to . . .*
Je finis.	*I finish.*
Je réponds.	*I answer.*
J'ai répondu.	*I answered./I have responded.*
Je parlerai.	*I shall speak.*
Je dois.	*I have to./I must./I've got to./I should.*

UNIT 6
Asking for directions

In this unit, you will learn how to get around **la ville** (*city, town*). You will learn the names of various stores and shops found along **la rue** (*street*), **l'avenue** (*avenue*), **le parc** (*the park*), or in **la place** (*the square*). You will also learn vocabulary for **les transports** (*various means of transportation*).

———————— Lesson 21 (words) ————————

WORD LIST 1
LES BÂTIMENTS *(m. pl.) (Buildings)*
Let's get started with the names of buildings.

l'immeuble	*apartment building*
le musée	*museum*
le magasin	*store*
l'hôtel de ville *(m.)*	*municipal building*
l'école *(f.)*	*school*
le lycée	*high school*
l'église	*church*
la cathédrale	*cathedral*
le temple	*temple*
la mosquée	*mosque*
la banque	*bank*
le cinéma	*movie theater*
le théâtre	*theater*
le supermarché	*supermarket*
la gare	*train station*
l'aéroport *(m.)*	*airport*

Now we'll continue with more important words to know for getting around town.

la bibliothèque	*library*
les boutiques	*shops, stores*
la librairie	*bookstore*
la boulangerie	*bakery*
la pâtisserie	*pastry shop*
la confiserie	*candy store*
la boucherie	*butcher shop*
la charcuterie	*delicatessen*
l'épicerie	*grocery store*
la quincaillerie	*hardware store*
l'institut de beauté	*beauty parlor*

NOTES
You can buy bread in **la boulangerie,** but also in **la pâtisserie.** Sometimes you will find a combination shop called **la pâtisserie-confiserie** that sells candies, cakes, and assorted breads.

Note the false cognates in our vocabulary list above. **La librairie** means *the bookstore* and not *the library.* **La bibliothèque** is *the library.* Many visitors have gone to Paris looking to book a room at **l'hôtel de ville,** which is actually *the town hall,* housing the offices of the mayor. You can book a room at **un hôtel** *(a hotel)* or **une auberge** *(an inn).*

Le magasin means *the store,* while **un grand magasin** refers to *a department store.* You will also find **le centre commercial** *(the mall)* in many cities. In France, despite the modernization of many towns and cities, you will still find smaller *shops,* **les boutiques,** specializing in various items. For example, **la boucherie** is a *butcher shop* for various cuts of *meat,* **la viande,** and *poultry,* **la volaille,** whereas **la charcuterie** *(the delicatessen)* sells mostly smoked pork, because the French eat all parts of **le cochon** *(the pig).*

NUTS & BOLTS 1
THE VERB CONDUIRE *(to drive)* IN THE PRESENT TENSE

Because this unit is devoted to places in town and means of transportation, let's look at a good verb to know, the verb **conduire** *(to drive)*. It is an irregular verb, but it is not difficult to learn.

je conduis	*I drive, I am driving*	nous conduisons	*we drive, we are driving*
tu conduis	*you drive, you are driving*	vous conduisez	*you drive, you are driving*
il conduit	*he drives, he is driving*	ils conduisent	*they drive, they are driving*
elle conduit	*she drives, she is driving*	elles conduisent	*they drive, they are driving*

Other verbs conjugated like **conduire** are **construire** *(to construct)* and **produire** *(to produce)*.

Let's look at some examples of the verb **conduire** and at the same time review the contractions with the preposition **à** that you learned in Unit 4. You learned how to use them in food expressions and when speaking to someone or giving something to someone. Now lets's see how they can be used to talk about places to which we are going.

à + la = à la
à + l' = à l'
à + le = au
à + les = aux

Here are some examples of the verb **conduire** with the preposition **à** preceding the location phrase that usually accompanies it.

Elle conduit les enfants à la bibliothèque.
She's driving the children to the library.

Nous conduisons ma fille à l'école.
We're driving my daughter to school.

Je conduis les touristes au musée.
I'm driving the tourists to the museum.

The past participle of the verb **conduire** is **conduit** *(drove)*, and **avoir** is the helping verb used with it to form past tense.

J'ai conduit aux magasins.
I drove to the stores.

Ils ont conduit pendant quatre heures.
They drove for four hours.

PRACTICE 1

This exercise requires you to think about three things to make the sentences below complete: the verb **conduire** *(to drive)*, the correct form of the preposition **à** with the definite article, and the correct building or store. Follow the model.

Ex. Pour regarder des sculptures, on _____ les touristes _____.
In order for them to look at sculptures, we _____ the tourists _____.

Pour regarder des sculptures, on conduit les touristes au musée.
In order for them to look at sculptures, we drive the tourists to the museum.

1. Pour regarder un film, on _____ les enfants _____.

2. Je voudrais acheter *(to buy)* un steak, donc, je _____.

3. Pour regarder un livre sans acheter *(without buying)* le livre, il
   _____.

4. Pour prendre le train, je _____.

5. Pour prendre l'avion, nous _____ toute la famille _____.

6. Pour acheter un livre, tu _____.

7. Pour visiter le bureau du maire *(the office of the mayor)*, ils _____
   Sophie _____.

8. Je voudrais du porc, donc je _____.

WORD LIST 2
LES TRANSPORTS *(Transportation)*

l'automobile, l'auto *(f.)*	*car*
la voiture	*car*
la bicyclette	*bicycle*
la motocyclette, la moto	*motorcycle*
le vélo	*bike*
le camion	*truck*
le bateau	*boat, ship*
le paquebot	*steamship, liner*
le train	*train*
le métro	*subway*
le solex, le vélomoteur	*moped*
l'avion	*airplane*

NOTES
Besides these various means of transportation, one can always go
à pied *(on foot)*! Many French people walk to various destinations
or travel by bicycle instead of driving. Cars in France and
throughout most of Europe are smaller than American cars and
are easier to maneuver on the tiny streets. **Le solex** *(the moped)*, or,
as it is more often called, **le vélomoteur,** is an economical means
of transportation for getting around town.

NUTS & BOLTS 2

VERBS OF CHANGE OF PLACE AND STATE OF BEING

You have already become familiar with the three groups of regular verbs and some irregular verbs. Now let's take a look at another group of verbs in the table below. Some of these verbs may look familiar to you because you have seen them before in the present tense. (Others are new, but don't worry about them for now.)

These verbs express a change of place or state of being. Notice that many of the verbs are opposites of each other.

aller	*to go*	venir	*to come*
monter	*to go up*	descendre	*to go down*
arriver	*to arrive*	partir	*to leave*
sortir	*to go out*	entrer	*to enter*
naître	*to be born*	mourir	*to die*
rester	*to stay*	retourner	*to return*
revenir	*to come back*	rentrer	*to come home*
devenir	*to become*	tomber	*to fall*

What distinguishes this group of verbs from the others mentioned previously is that they take the verb **être** *(to be)* as the helping verb in the past tense. Like adjectives, past participles conjugated with **être** agree in gender and number with the subject of the sentence. Notice the past participle agreement patterns.

je suis allé(e)	*I went*	**nous sommes allé(e)s**	*we went*
tu es allé(e)	*you went*	**vous êtes allé(e)(s)**	*you went*
il est allé	*he went*	**ils sont allés**	*they went*
elle est allée	*she went*	**elles sont allées**	*they went*

Because the pronouns **je, tu, nous,** and **vous** may be masculine or feminine, and **vous** may be singular or plural, the past participles used with them vary in ending.

Quand êtes-vous arrivée *(f.)*, **Marie?**
When did you arrive, Marie?

Quand êtes-vous arrivés *(m. pl.)*, **messieurs?**
When did you arrive, gentlemen?

Here are more examples.

Je suis allé(e) *(m./f. sg.)* **au cinéma.**
I went to the movies.

Ils sont arrivés *(m. pl.)* **à l'hôtel.**
They arrived at the hotel.

Le petit garçon est tombé *(m. sg.)*.
The little boy fell.

In order to tell which verbs require **être** as the helping verb in the past tense, you will need to memorize the verbs that you use the most.

PRACTICE 2

Complete the sentences in the past tense using the auxiliary verb **être.** Remember to make the past participle agree with the subject.

1. Ils _____ en vacances. (partir)

2. Caroline _____ à l'heure. (arriver)

3. Nous _____ au cinéma. (aller)

4. Vous _____ à l'hôtel, Madame. (rester)

5. Elle _____ au restaurant. (retourner)

PRACTICE 3

Complete the sentences in the past tense below using the appropriate helping verb, **avoir** or **être.** Remember to make the past participle agree with the subject as necessary. Follow the model.

Ex. Elle _____ à huit heures. (dîner) *She dined at eight o'clock.*
Elle a dîné à huit heures.

Elle _____ dans la rue. (tomber) *She fell down in the street.*
Elle est tombée dans la rue.

1. Nous _____ une heure au musée. (rester)

2. Tu _____ les sculptures. (regarder)

3. Mes parents _____ en Suisse. (aller)

4. Marie et Christine _____ au théâtre. (arriver)

5. Je _____ dans le magasin. (attendre)

6. Vous _____ un long voyage. (faire)

7. Ils _____ dans un grand hôtel. (descendre)

8. Est-ce qu'elle _____ avec vous? (aller)

9. Je ne _____ pas _____ à la boulangerie. (aller)

10. Nous _____ la bonne route. (prendre)

ANSWERS

PRACTICE 1: 1. conduit, au cinéma; **2.** conduis, à la boucherie; **3.** conduit, à la bibliothèque; **4.** conduis, à la gare; **5.** conduisons, à l'aéroport; **6.** conduis, à la librairie; **7.** conduisent, à l'hôtel de ville; **8.** conduis, à la charcuterie

PRACTICE 2: 1. sont partis; **2.** est arrivée; **3.** sommes allés; **4.** êtes restée; **5.** est retournée

PRACTICE 3: 1. sommes resté(e)s; **2.** as regardé; **3.** sont allés; **4.** sont arrivées; **5.** j'ai attendu; **6.** avez fait; **7.** sont descendus; **8.** est allée; **9.** ne suis pas allé(e); **10.** avons pris

——————————— Lesson 22 (phrases) ———————————

PHRASE LIST 1
DES PRÉPOSITIONS IDIOMATIQUES DE LOCATION *(Locative prepositions and expressions)*

autour de	*around*
chez (+ person's name)	*at (person's name)'s house*
de l'autre côté de	*on the other side of*
en haut	*upstairs*
en bas	*downstairs*
par ici	*this way*
par là	*that way*
au bout de	*at the end of*
à gauche	*on (to, at) the left*

à droite	on (to, at) the right
au pied de	at the foot of
à travers	through, across
au bord de	at the edge of
au milieu de	in (at) the middle of
y	there

NOTES

Y is a pronoun that can translate as *there, to it, in it, on it, to them, in them,* or *on them* in English. It usually replaces **à** + noun, but it may also replace other prepositions, such as **dans** *(in)*, **sur** *(on)*, or **chez** *(at)*, + noun. It can be used to replace a previously referenced location expression. **Y** is always placed before the verb.

Elle va à Paris au printemps.

She's going to Paris in the springtime.

Elle y va.

She's going there.

Je vais chez mon ami.

I'm going to my friend's house.

J'y vais.

I'm going there.

Je vais à l'épicerie.

I'm going to the grocery store.

J'y vais.

I'm going there.

Qui va au parc?

Who's going to the park?

Charles y va.

Charles is going there.

Répondons aux lettres.

Let's answer the letters.

Répondons-y.
Let's answer them (lit., to them).

Sont-ils sur la chaise?
Are they on the chair?

Non, ils n'y sont pas.
No, they are not there (lit., on it).

NUTS & BOLTS 1
THE IMPERATIVE

The imperative is used to give a command or a directive and to make requests. The imperative forms of regular verbs are the same as the corresponding forms of the present tense, except for the omission of the subject pronouns **tu, nous,** and **vous.** Let's look at three regular verbs in the imperative.

	danser *(to dance)*	**finir** *(to finish)*	**répondre** *(to answer)*
(tu)	**danse** *(infml.) (dance)*	**finis** *(infml.) (finish)*	**réponds** *(infml.) (answer)*
(nous)	**dansons** *(let's dance)*	**finissons** *(let's finish)*	**répondons** *(let's answer)*
(vous)	**dansez** *(pl., sg. fml.) (dance)*	**finissez** *(pl., fml. sg.) (finish)*	**répondez** *(pl., fml. sg.) (answer)*

Note that the **tu** imperative forms of **-er** verbs drop the final **s.**

Danse!
Dance!

Écoute!
Listen!

Mange!
Eat!

The negative forms of the imperative are formed in the same way as the present tense forms—by placing **ne** before the verb and **pas** after.

Ne danse pas!/Ne dansez pas!
Don't dance!

Ne répondons pas!
Don't answer!

The irregular verbs generally follow the same pattern as regular verbs.

	aller *(to go)*	**faire** *(to do, to make)*	**prendre** *(to take)*
(tu)	**va** *(go)*	**fais** *(do, make)*	**prends** *(take)*
(nous)	**allons** *(let's go)*	**faisons** *(let's do, let's make)*	**prenons** *(let's take)*
(vous)	**allez** *(go)*	**faites** *(do, make)*	**prenez** *(take)*

Remember that **-er** verbs drop the final **s** in the **tu** imperative form.

Va au lit!
Go to bed!

But if a pronoun follows, the **s** is there.

Vas-y!
Go there!

PRACTICE 1
Write the three forms of the imperative for each verb.

1. étudier
2. bâtir
3. vendre
4. prendre
5. parler

The irregular verbs **avoir** and **être** have also irregular imperatives.

	avoir *(to have)*	**être** *(to be)*
(tu)	**aie** *(have)*	**sois** *(be)*
(nous)	**ayons** *(let's have)*	**soyons** *(let's be)*
(vous)	**ayez** *(have)*	**soyez** *(be)*

Here are examples of imperatives with **avoir** and **être.**

Soyez patient(s)!
Be patient!

Sois sage!
Be good!

Ayons patience!
Let's have patience!

Note that the adverb **donc** *(then, thus)* may often be used with the imperative for special emphasis.

Pensez donc!
Just think!

Entrez donc!
Come on in!

PRACTICE 2
Give the equivalent in French.

1. *Let's look!*

2. *Let's drink!*

3. *Let us succeed!*

4. *Let's finish!*

5. *Let's dance!*

PRACTICE 3
Complete the English sentences.

1. Donnez le livre à Charles! _____ *the book to Charles!*

2. Soyez donc plus actifs! _____ *more active!*

3. Ne rougissez pas, mes enfants! _____ *my children!*

4. Remplis cette bouteille! _____ *this bottle!*

5. Travaillons vite! _____ *quickly!*

6. Parlons français! _____ *French!*

7. Regardons un film! _____ *a movie!*

8. Allons en ville! _____ *to town!*

PHRASE LIST 2
LES ADVERBES DE PLACE *(Adverbs of place)*

ici	*here*
là	*there*
à côté	*at the side*
entre	*between*
derrière	*behind*
devant	*in front of, before*
dessus	*on top*
dessous	*underneath*
dehors	*outside*
partout	*everywhere*
nulle part	*nowhere*
loin	*far*
près	*near*
ailleurs	*elsewhere*
là-bas	*over there*

NUTS & BOLTS 2
IL FAUT + INFINITIF *(it is necessary to, one has to, one needs)*
The expression **il faut** *(it is necessary to, one has to, one needs)* comes from the verb **falloir** *(to be necessary)*. It is used with an infinitive or a noun.

Il faut traverser la rue.

It's necessary to cross the street./You have to cross the street.

Il faut aller tout droit.

It's necessary to go straight ahead./You have to go straight ahead.

Il faut tourner à gauche.

It's necessary to turn left./You have to turn left.

Il faut boire de l'eau.

It's necessary to drink water./You have to drink water.

Il faut deux cuillères d'eau pour une cuillère de sucre.

One needs two spoonfuls of water for each spoonful of sugar./You need two spoons of water for each spoon of sugar.

Il faut de la patience!

One must have patience!/You need patience!

PRACTICE 4

You have invited your friend to your home for dinner. In this exercise, use the **tu** form of the imperative to give directions to your friend. Follow the model.

Ex. Il faut descendre l'escalier.
   It's necessary to go down the stairs.

   Descends l'escalier.
   Go down the stairs.

1. D'abord, il faut prendre le grand boulevard.

2. Ensuite, il faut aller tout droit.

3. À la bibliothèque, il faut tourner à gauche au coin de la rue.

4. Puis, il faut continuer jusqu'au bout de la rue et tu arriveras à la maison.

5. Il faut descendre de la voiture.

Discovery activity

Would you like to visit France or another Francophone country? This may turn out to be a reality one day! Before that, start gathering information for your great trip. Create your own personalized travel package. Look for travel websites and check out the places of interest. Consider which airlines may offer the best prices to your destination. Do you want to travel first-class? In what kind of hotel would like to stay? How long would your journey be?

As you continue to learn new vocabulary and more about French culture, add to your travel package so that by the time you have completed this course, you will have everything prepared. Have fun dreaming about your big trip!

ANSWERS

PRACTICE 1: 1. étudie, étudiez, étudions; 2. bâtis, bâtissez, bâtissons; 3. vends, vendez, vendons; 4. prends, prenez, prenons; 5. parle, parlez, parlons

PRACTICE 2: 1. regardons; 2. buvons; 3. réussissons; 4. finissons; 5. dansons

PRACTICE 3: 1. *Give;* 2. *Be;* 3. *Don't blush;* 4. *Fill;* 5. *Let's work;* 6. *Let's speak;* 7. *Let's watch;* 8. *Let's go*

PRACTICE 4: 1. D'abord, prends le grand boulevard. 2. Ensuite, va tout droit. 3. À la bibliothèque, tourne à gauche. 4. Puis, continue jusqu'au bout de la rue et tu arriveras à la maison. 5. Descends de la voiture.

——————— Lesson 23 (sentences) ———————

SENTENCE GROUP 1
DEMANDER LE CHEMIN *(Asking for directions)*

Pouvez-vous m'aider, s'il vous plaît?	*Can you help me, please?*
Je suis perdu/perdue.	*I am lost.*
Où se trouve le musée du Louvre?	*Where is the Louvre Museum?*
Le chemin pour aller à l'opéra?	*Which way to the opera house?*
Où se trouve la station de métro?	*Where is the subway station?*

Où est la station de métro la plus proche?	*Where is the nearest subway station?*
Où se trouve l'arrêt d'autobus?	*Where is the bus stop?*
Avez-vous un plan de la ville?	*Do you have a map of the city?*
Où se trouve le poste de police?	*Where is the police station?*
Il faut aller tout droit.	*You must go straight ahead.*
Où est le bureau de poste?	*Where is the post office?*
Je traverse le pont?	*Do I cross the bridge?*
C'est à combien de kilomètres d'ici?	*It's how many kilometers from here?*
Il y a beaucoup de circulation?	*Is there a lot of traffic?*
Suivez cette route.	*Follow this road.*
C'est loin d'ici?	*Is it far from here?*

NOTES

In France and other European countries, distance is measured in kilometers and meters. A meter is a bit longer than a yard—exactly, 1.09 yards. A kilometer is shorter than a mile—exactly, 0.62 miles.

NUTS & BOLTS 1
THE VERBS POUVOIR *(to be able, can)* AND VOULOIR *(to wish, to want)*

Here are two good verbs to know. They are especially useful in polite expressions.

The first verb is **pouvoir** *(to be able, can).*

je peux	*I can, I am able*	**nous pouvons**	*we can, we are able*
tu peux	*you can, you are able*	**vous pouvez**	*you can, you are able*
il peut	*he can, he is able*	**ils peuvent**	*they can, they are able*
elle peut	*she can, she is able*	**elles peuvent**	*they can, they are able*

Look at some of the ways in which the verb **pouvoir** is used. Often it is used with an infinitive.

Je peux nager.
I can swim.

Je peux chanter.
I can sing.

Peux-tu aller avec moi?
Can you go with me?

Pouvez-vous me dire si . . .
Can you tell me if . . .

Pouvez-vous me dire la route pour aller à . . . ?
Can you tell me the way to . . . ? (lit., Can you tell me the way for to go to . . . ?)

Je peux le faire.
I can do it.

Je ne peux pas.
I can't.

PRACTICE 1

Match the French with the correct English translation.

1. **Tu peux travailler là-bas.**   a. *Can you help me?*
2. **Je ne peux pas entendre.**   b. *She can do it.*
3. **Il ne peut pas attendre.**   c. *We can finish.*
4. **Pouvez-vous m'aider?**   d. *They can cook.*
5. **Pouvez-vous danser?**   e. *You can work over there.*
6. **Ils peuvent faire la cuisine.**   f. *I can't hear.*
7. **Elle peut le faire.**   g. *He can't wait.*
8. **Nous pouvons finir.**   h. *Can you dance?*

Now let's look at the verb **vouloir** *(to wish, to want)*. You will notice that there are similarities between the present tense forms of **pouvoir** *(to be able)*, above, and **vouloir** *(to wish, to want)*, in the table below.

je veux	*I wish, I want*	**nous voulons**	*we wish, we want*
tu veux	*you wish, you want*	**vous voulez**	*you wish you want*
il veut	*he wishes, he wants*	**ils veulent**	*they wish, they want*
elle veut	*she wishes, she wants*	**elles veulent**	*they wish, they want*

Voulez-vous aller au cinéma vendredi soir?
Do you want to go to the movies Friday night?

Il veut conduire sa voiture au parc.
He wants to drive his car to the park.

Qu'est-ce que tu veux pour ton anniversaire?
What do you want for your birthday?

PRACTICE 2
Fill in the blanks with the correct form of the verb **vouloir**.

1. Elle _____ danser.

2. Qu'est-ce qu'ils _____ pour le dîner?

3. Nous _____ visiter les Etats-Unis.

4. Tu _____ aller à la boulangerie.

5. Je _____ boire de l'eau.

SENTENCE GROUP 2
DES EXPRESSIONS POLIES *(Polite requests and expressions)*

Je voudrais acheter . . .	*I would like to buy . . .*
Combien ça coûte, s'il vous plaît?	*How much does that cost, please?*
C'est combien, s'il vous plaît?	*That's how much, please?*
Je prendrai cela.	*I'll take that.*
Je voudrais changer des dollars en euros.	*I'd like to change dollars to euros.*
Avez-vous de la monnaie?	*Do you have change?*
Voici mon passeport.	*Here's my passport.*
Que voulez-vous?	*What do you wish?/What do you want?*
Où puis-je prendre le train pour Paris?	*Where can I get the train for Paris?*
Il faut aller au guichet.	*You must go to the ticket window.*
Je voudrais un billet aller-retour.	*I would like a round-trip ticket.*
Sur quelle voie est le train?	*On which track is the train?*
Sur quel quai doit-on attendre?	*On what platform should we wait?*
Où dois-je descendre?	*Where do I have to get off?*
Quelle est l'heure du départ?	*What is the departure time?*

NUTS & BOLTS 2
ADVERBS

You have already learned several adverbs in earlier units, such as **beaucoup** and **bien,** and in this unit, **ici** and **dessous.** Now let's look at examples of other French adverbs and learn how they are formed. By the way, an adverb is a word that describes or modifies a verb or an adjective.

To form an adverb, add the ending **-ment** to the masculine singular adjective if it ends in a vowel.

ADJECTIVE	ADVERB
facile *(easy)*	**facilement** *(easily)*
poli *(polite)*	**poliment** *(politely)*
probable *(probable)*	**probablement** *(probably)*
vrai *(true, real)*	**vraiment** *(truly, really)*

If the masculine singular form of the adjective ends in a consonant, add the **-ment** to the feminine singular of the adjective to form the adverb.

ADJECTIVE	ADVERB
lent *(slow)*	**lentement** *(slowly)*
certain *(certain)*	**certainement** *(certainly)*
général *(general)*	**généralement** *(generally)*
seul *(alone)*	**seulement** *(only)*
actif *(active)*	**activement** *(actively)*

heureux *(happy, fortunate)*	**heureusement** *(happily, fortunately)*
malheureux *(unhappy, unfortunate)*	**malheureusement** *(unhappily, unfortunately)*
léger *(light)*	**légèrement** *(lightly)*
naturel *(natural)*	**naturellement** *(naturally)*
doux *(sweet)*	**doucement** *(sweetly)*

In the case of simple tenses, the adverb is usually placed after the verb it modifies. If the verb is in the negative form, the adverb follows the complete negative verb.

Elle boit lentement son café.
She drinks her coffee slowly.

La fille répond facilement à la question.
The girl easily responds to the question.

In the past tense and other compound tenses that will be addressed in later units, most adverbs usually follow the past participle.

Elle a bu lentement son café.
She slowly drank her coffee.

La fille a répondu facilement à la question.
The girl easily answered the question.

Note that these sentences can also be formed with the adverb at the end.

There are a few common adverbs, such as **bien** *(well)*, **mal** *(badly)*, **toujours** *(always, still)*, **beaucoup** *(many, a lot)*, **déjà** *(already)*, **vite** *(quickly)*, and **encore** *(again)*, that usually precede the past participle. After having used these for a while in sentences, you will become accustomed to their placement.

Ils n'ont pas beaucoup voyagé.
They haven't traveled much.

Marc a bien travaillé.
Marc worked well.

Nous sommes déjà allés en France.
We already went to France.

PRACTICE 3
Fill in the blanks with the right adverbs.

1. Elles dansent _____. *(well)*

2. La voiture va _____ dans la rue. *(quickly)*

3. Parlez _____, s'il vous plaît. *(slowly)*

4. _____ le train est parti. *(unfortunately)*

5. J'ai appris _____ le poème./J'ai appris le poème _____. *(easily)*

Language link
You may start gathering information on trains for your trip to France. The **TGV** trains, **les trains à grande vitesse** *(the high speed trains),* link most cities in France and elsewhere in Europe. You will need a reservation for this train, and Americans can buy a discount pass in the United States. This exciting site gives you ideas on how to plan for your journey: <u>www.tgv.com/FR/</u>.

ANSWERS

PRACTICE 1: 1. e; 2. f; 3. g; 4. a; 5. h; 6. d; 7. b; 8. c

PRACTICE 2: 1. veut; 2. veulent; 3. voulons; 4. veux; 5. veux

PRACTICE 3: 1. bien; 2. rapidement/vite; 3. lentement;
4. Malheureusement; 5. facilement, facilement

--------- Lesson 24 (conversations) ---------

CONVERSATION 1

Jacques is in Paris for the first time and wants to go to the Orsay Museum. He asks a police officer for directions.

Jacques: Excusez-moi, Monsieur, pouvez-vous m'aider?

Le gendarme: Ah! Vous êtes perdu, n'est-ce pas?

Jacques: Je cherche le chemin pour aller au Musée d'Orsay, s'il vous plaît.

Le gendarme: Eh, bien, Monsieur, vous n'êtes pas sur le bon chemin.

Jacques: Il faut prendre quel chemin?

Le gendarme: Il faut aller le long des quais et puis, vous prenez la première rue et vous tournez à gauche.

Jacques: Est-ce que c'est loin d'ici, Monsieur?

Le gendarme: Non, pas du tout. C'est juste à un kilomètre d'ici.

Jacques: Donc, je vais marcher le long des quais.

Le gendarme: C'est ça. Et quand vous tournez à gauche, il faut continuer tout droit. Le Musée d'Orsay sera juste devant vous.

Jacques: Merci bien, Monsieur!

Le gendarme: Je vous en prie. Passez une bonne journée!

Jacques:	Excuse me, Sir, can you help me?
Police officer:	Ah! You're lost, aren't you?
Jacques:	I'm looking for the way to the Orsay Museum, please.
Police officer:	Well, Sir, you're not on the right road.
Jacques:	Which way do I have to go?
Police officer:	You go along the quay, and then take the first street and turn left.
Jacques:	Is that far from here, Sir?
Police officer:	Not at all. It's just one kilometer from here.
Jacques:	Then I'll walk along the quay.
Police officer:	That's it. And after you turn left, you continue straight ahead. The Orsay Museum will be right in front of you.
Jacques:	Thanks a lot, Sir!
Police officer:	Don't mention it. Have a great day!

NOTES

Le gendarme *(the police officer)* is a term that refers to a local or town guard. **La police** *(the police)* are comparable to state police who enforce the laws.

NUTS & BOLTS 1

THE CONDITIONAL

So far, you have learned how to form the present, past, future, and near future tenses of many different verbs. In this lesson, you'll learn about the conditional form.

Verbs expressing a possibility, a wish, or a necessity are often used in the conditional present when the outcome possibly will not occur. It is understood "as if " it were possible. You actually learned a verb in the conditional form in Unit 4 when you learned **je voudrais** *(I would like)*. The conditional is often used in polite expressions such as this one, and it corresponds to English verbs used with *would*.

The conditional, like the future, uses the full infinitive form of the verb as its stem. In **-re** verbs, the final **-e** of the infinitive is dropped before adding the ending. The endings are as follows.

CONDITIONAL ENDINGS	
je: -ais	nous: -ions
tu: -ais	vous: -iez
il: -ait	ils: -aient
elle: -ait	elles: -aient

Let's take a look at the conditional of the regular verb groups.

danser *(to dance)*	finir *(to finish)*	vendre *(to sell)*
je danserais	je finirais	je vendrais
tu danserais	tu finirais	tu vendrais
il danserait	il finirait	il vendrait
elle danserait	elle finirait	elle vendrait
nous danserions	nous finirions	nous vendrions
vous danseriez	vous finiriez	vous vendriez
ils danseraient	ils finiraient	ils vendraient
elles danseraient	elles finiraient	elles vendraient

Here are some examples of sentences in the conditional. The conditional is often used to make a polite request or express a wish.

Pourriez-vous nous aider?
Could you help us?

Nous voudrions parler français.
We would like to speak French.

Voudriez-vous aller au cinéma?
Would you like to go to the movie theater?

The verb **devoir** *(to have to)* is used in the conditional to express a suggestion or an obligation in a polite way; it corresponds to the English *should*.

Tu devrais voir ce film.
You should see this movie.

Vous devriez venir nous voir.
You should come to see us.

The conditional is also often used to express hypothetical situations.

Nous vendrions la maison pour gagner beaucoup d'argent.
We would sell the house to get a lot of money.

Avec patience, tu apprendrais l'anglais.
With patience, you would learn English.

Verbs that are irregular in the future have the same irregular stems in the conditional.

VERB	CONDITIONAL STEM	
aller	**ir-**	*would go*
avoir	**aur-**	*would have*
être	**ser-**	*would be*
faire	**fer-**	*would make*
devoir	**devr-**	*should, would have to*
pouvoir	**pourr-**	*would be able*
vouloir	**voudr-**	*would like, would want*

PRACTICE 1
Translate the following sentences into English.

1. Vous devriez étudier.

2. Que ferais-tu?

3. Nous pourrions quitter la maison à trois heures.

4. Je voudrais manger.

5. Ils dîneraient dans un bon restaurant français.

6. Où bâtirait-on la nouvelle pharmacie?

7. Il aurait assez de chocolat pour tout le monde.

8. Elle serait à l'hôtel ce soir.

9. J'irais avec vous à la gare.

PRACTICE 2

Replace the present tense verbs in the following sentences with their conditional forms.

1. Il veut aller au cinéma.

2. Avez-vous le temps?

3. Elle prend un bon repas.

4. Je dois réfléchir.

5. Tu choisis la bouteille de vin.

6. Je peux faire du ski.

7. Qu'est-ce qu'elle fait?

8. Ils sont polis.

CONVERSATION 2

Danielle, from the United States, is visiting her friend Martin. She would like to go shopping with Martin, but first, she wants to exchange her dollars for euros. She asks Martin what she needs to do.

Danielle:	Est-ce que nous pouvons aller faire des achats aujourd'hui?
Martin:	Absolument! Tu veux aller au centre commercial ou aux Galeries Lafayette?
Danielle:	J'aimerais aller aux Galeries Lafayette, si c'était possible. C'est très français!
Martin:	Bon. Nous pouvons y aller cet après-midi, si tu veux.
Danielle:	D'abord, il faut changer mes dollars en euros. Qu'est-ce qu'il faut faire?
Martin:	Pour changer de l'argent, il faut aller à la banque. Tu veux changer des chèques de voyage?
Danielle:	Oui. J'ai des chèques et aussi de l'argent.

Martin:	C'est facile. Il faut aller à la banque du quartier. Va au guichet. Montre ton passeport au guichetier.
Danielle:	Tu peux venir avec moi?
Martin:	Bien sûr. On y va tout de suite.

Danielle:	Can we go shopping today?
Martin:	Absolutely! Do you want to go to the mall or Lafayette Galleries?
Danielle:	I would like to go to Lafayette Galleries, if it is possible. It's so French!
Martin:	Good. We can go there this afternoon, if you'd like.
Danielle:	First, I need to change my dollars into euros. What do I have to do?
Martin:	To exchange money, you have to go to the bank. Do you want to exchange traveler's checks?
Danielle:	Yes. I have checks and cash, too.
Martin:	That's easy. You have to go to the bank in town. Go to the teller window. Show your passport to the teller.
Danielle:	Can you go with me?
Martin:	Sure. We'll go right away.

NUTS & BOLTS 2

THE VERB VENIR *(to come)*

Early on in the units, you were briefly introduced to the verb **venir** *(to come)*.

D'où viens-tu?/D'où venez-vous?

Where do you come from?

Je viens des États-Unis.

I come from the United States.

Now let's learn all of its present tense forms.

je viens	*I come*	**nous venons**	*we come*
tu viens	*you come*	**vous venez**	*you come*
il vient	*he comes*	**ils viennent**	*they come*
elle vient	*she comes*	**elles viennent**	*they come*

Here are more examples with the verb **venir.**

Tu viens avec nous?
Are you coming with us?

Il vient à dix heures dix.
He's coming at 10:10.

The verbs **revenir** *(to come back)* and **devenir** *(to become)* are conjugated in exactly the same way as **venir.**

Ils reviennent de vacances dimanche.
They're coming back from vacation on Sunday.

Je reviens.
I'll be back.

L'artiste devient célèbre.
The artist is becoming famous.

Je voudrais devenir professeur.
I'd like to become a teacher.

The verb **venir + de** is used to express the recent past.

Je viens de voir ce film.
I've just seen this movie.

Nous venons d'écouter ce CD.
We've just listened to this CD.

Elle vient de sortir.

She's just left.

PRACTICE 3

Fill in blanks with the correct form of the verb **venir** *(to come)*, **devenir** *(to become)*, or **revenir** *(to return)*.

1. Nous _____ de Washington. (venir)

2. Robert _____ avec nous à la librairie. (venir)

3. Qui _____ au magasin avec moi? (venir)

4. Ils _____ demain soir. (revenir)

5. Elle _____ médecin. (devenir)

Culture note

Money

Traveling to a foreign country is exciting, especially when that country is France! When you travel, the first thing you need to do is exchange currency at **la banque** *(the bank)*. Banks in France are generally open from nine o'clock in the morning until five o'clock in the evening. Some banks may be open on Saturdays. There are also **bureau de change** offices, which stay open later and on weekends.

The rates and fees of exchange vary from one bank to another. Airports and hotels offer the lowest rates. The French **franc** is no longer the currency used in France. On January 1, 2002, the **euro** was introduced throughout France and the other European Union countries. There are eight **pièces** *(coins)*: 1, 2, 5, 10, 20, and 50 **cents** *(cents)*; two of them are 1- and 2-euro coins. One hundred cents equals one **euro. Les billets** *(banknotes)* come in denominations of 5, 10, 20, 50, 100, 200, and 500 euros. The coins have a "European face," common to all of the member countries, and a "national face," with symbols specific to each EU member.

ANSWERS

PRACTICE 1: 1. *You should study.* **2.** *What would you do?* **3.** *We could leave the house at three o'clock.* **4.** *I would like to eat.* **5.** *They would eat dinner in a good French restaurant.* **6.** *Where would we build the new pharmacy?* **7.** *He would have enough chocolate for everyone.* **8.** *She would be at the hotel tonight.* **9.** *I would go with you to the train station.*

PRACTICE 2: 1. Il voudrait aller au cinéma. **2.** Auriez-vous le temps? **3.** Elle prendrait un bon repas. **4.** Je devrais réfléchir. **5.** Tu choisirais la bouteille de vin. **6.** Je pourrais faire du ski. **7.** Qu'est-ce qu'elle ferait? **8.** Ils seraient polis.

PRACTICE 3: 1. venons; **2.** vient; **3.** vient; **4.** reviennent; **5.** devient

UNIT 6 ESSENTIALS

la banque	bank
la boulangerie	bakery
la voiture	car
le métro	subway
Pouvez-vous m'aider?	Can you help me?
Où est la gare?	Where is the train station?
J'y vais.	I'm going there.
Veux-tu venir?	Do you want to come?
Sois sage!	Be good!
Aie patience!	Have patience!
Je finirais.	I would finish.
Je voudrais revenir ici.	I'll like to come back here.
Je voudrais changer mon argent.	I'd like to exchange my money.
Il faut tourner à droite.	You have to turn right.
C'est loin d'ici?	Is it far from here?

UNIT 7
Shopping

In this unit, you will learn vocabulary for clothing and various accessories, as well as numbers up to a million. You will find many useful expressions for shopping.

——————— Lesson 25 (words) ———————

WORD LIST 1
LES VÊTEMENTS *(Clothing)*

les habits *(m.)*	clothes
le complet	suit
le pantalon	pants
le veston	jacket
le manteau	coat
le foulard	scarf
le chapeau	hat
le pull(over), le tricot	sweater
l'imperméable *(m.)*	raincoat
le gant	glove
la chemise	shirt
la jupe	skirt
la blouse, le chemisier	blouse
la chaussette	sock
les chaussures *(f.)*	shoes

NUTS & BOLTS 1
DIRECT OBJECT PRONOUNS

In French, as in English, most sentences have a subject and a verb. The verb is the action word of the sentence, and the subject performs the action. A direct object, on the other hand, is the noun in a sentence that "receives" an action.

Je prends le livre.
I take the book.

The subject of this sentence is **je** *(I)*, the verb is **prends** *(take)*, and the "thing that is taken," or the word receiving the action of taking, is **le livre** *(the book)*, which is the direct object. The direct object pronouns can take the place of the direct objects in sentences.

me (m')	*me*	nous	*us*
te (t')	*you*	vous	*you*
le (l')	*him, it*	les	*them*
la (l')	*her, it*	les	*them*

All direct object pronouns come before the verb in a sentence.

Je vous comprends.
I understand you (fml.).

Je la comprends.
I understand her (it).

Je le comprends.
I understand him (it).

Il ne me comprend pas.
He doesn't understand me.

Je les comprends.
I understand them.

Me comprends-tu?
Do you understand me?

Le prof nous regarde.
The teacher is looking at us.

If the verb after the direct object pronoun begins with a vowel, then **l'** is used instead of **le** or **la**.

J'aime la robe.
I like the dress.

Je l'aime.
I like it.

Il aime le film.
He likes the movie.

Il l'aime.
He likes it.

Aimez-vous les fruits?
Do you like fruit?

Non, je ne les aime pas.
No, I don't like it.

Direct object pronouns must agree in number and gender with the noun they replace.

Elle ferme le livre.
She closes the book.

Elle le ferme.
She closes it.

Elle ferme la porte.
She closes the door.

Elle la ferme.
She closes it.

When a verb is followed by an infinitive, the direct object pronoun comes before the verb of which it is the direct object, which is usually the infinitive.

Vous pouvez nous aider?
Can you help us?

Je vais te téléphoner.
I'm going to call you.

PRACTICE 1
Replace the direct object nouns with the corresponding direct object pronouns. Remember that the direct object pronouns come before the verbs.

1. Nous chantons une chanson.

2. Elle prépare le déjeuner.

3. Le marchand vend les fruits.

4. Aimez-vous les oranges?

5. Ils prennent la voiture.

6. Je n'aime pas le poulet.

WORD LIST 2
LES ACCESSOIRES *(Accessories)*

le mouchoir	*handkerchief*
le sac	*purse, bag*
le bas	*stocking*
le maillot (de bain)	*bathing suit*
le pyjama	*pajamas*
les bijoux *(m.)*	*jewelry*
la montre	*watch*
la boucle d'oreille	*earring*
la bague	*ring*
le bracelet	*bracelet*
le parapluie	*umbrella*
la cravate	*tie*
la casquette	*cap*

les lunettes	glasses
les lunettes de soleil *(f.)*	sunglasses
la serviette	briefcase

NUTS & BOLTS 2
INDIRECT OBJECT PRONOUNS

Indirect object nouns are preceded by the preposition **à** *(to)* and receive the action of the verb indirectly. Indirect object pronouns look similar to the direct object pronouns except for the **lui** and **leur** forms. The word **à** *(to)* is implied in the meaning of these pronouns.

me (m')	*to me*	nous	*to us*
te (t')	*to you*	vous	*to you*
lui	*to him, to her, to it*	leur	*to them*

Like direct object pronouns, indirect object pronouns are placed immediately before the verb of which they are the object (except in affirmative commands).

Je parle à Luc.
I speak to Luc.

Lui is the indirect object pronoun that can replace the expression **à Luc** *(to Luc)*.

It can mean either *to him* or *to her,* depending on the indirect object.

Je lui parle.
I speak to him.

Consider another example with the word **lui,** now meaning *to her.*

Je parle à ma fille.
I speak to my daughter.

Je lui parle.
I speak to her.

Here are some more examples.

Il me parle.
He speaks to me.

Il te parle.
He speaks to you.

Il lui parle.
He speaks to him/to her.

Il nous parle.
He speaks to us.

Il vous parle.
He speaks to you.

Il leur parle.
He speaks to them.

PRACTICE 2
Substitute the indirect objects in the following sentences with indirect object pronouns.

1. Suzanne parle à ses amis.

2. Nous parlons à toi et à Claude.

3. Ils donnent les livres à leurs enfants.

4. Je donne un coup de téléphone à ma mère.

5. Vous parlez à votre ami.

Tip!

There are several verbs that take indirect objects in English but require a direct object in French. We will see them discussed in more detail later in this unit, but for now, these are the ones that are frequently used.

attendre *(to wait for [someone or something])*
regarder *(to look at [someone or something])*

J'attends ma femme.
I'm waiting for my wife.

Je l'attends.
I'm waiting for her.

Je regarde le film.
I'm looking at the movie.

Je le regarde.
I'm looking at it.

Also note that there are several verbs that take direct objects in English but require an indirect object in French.

obéir à *(to obey [someone])*
répondre à *(to answer [someone])*
téléphoner à *(to call [someone])*

Il obéit à son père.
He obeys his father.

Il lui obéit.
He obeys him.

Je réponds à mon ami.
I answer my friend.

Je lui réponds.
I answer him.

> **Je téléphone à mon amie.**
> *I call my friend.*
>
> **Je lui téléphone.**
> *I call him.*

ANSWERS

PRACTICE 1: 1. Nous la chantons. **2.** Elle le prépare. **3.** Le marchand les vend. **4.** Les aimez-vous? **5.** Ils la prennent. **6.** Je ne l'aime pas.

PRACTICE 2: 1. Suzanne leur parle. **2.** Nous vous parlons. **3.** Ils leur donnent les livres. **4.** Je lui donne un coup de téléphone. **5.** Vous lui parlez.

--- Lesson 26 (phrases) ---

PHRASE LIST 1
LES NOMBRES *(Numbers)*

You have already learned the numbers from 1 to 20. The rest of the numbers are not difficult to learn. We count by tens in French from 20 to 99, as we do in English. Note that **un/une** *(one [m./f.])* is joined to the multiples of ten by the word **et** *(and)*. The other units, from **deux** *(two)* to **neuf** *(nine)*, are joined by a hyphen. Let's first look at the numbers from 21 to 100. The list below gives numbers up to 69.

vingt et un	*twenty-one*
vingt-deux	*twenty-two*
trente	*thirty*
trente et un	*thirty-one*
trente-trois	*thirty-three*
quarante	*forty*
quarante et un	*forty-one*
quarante-cinq	*forty-five*
cinquante	*fifty*

cinquante et un	*fifty-one*
soixante	*sixty*
soixante et un	*sixty-one*
soixante-neuf	*sixty-nine*

Remember that **une** is used before a feminine noun.

vingt et une jeunes filles
twenty-one girls

Now let's take a look at the numbers from 70 to 100.

soixante-dix	*seventy*
soixante et onze	*seventy-one*
soixante-douze	*seventy-two*
quatre-vingts	*eighty*
quatre-vingt-un	*eighty-one*
quatre-vingt-dix	*ninety*
quatre-vingt-onze	*ninety-one*
quatre-vingt-dix-neuf	*ninety-nine*
cent	*one hundred*

And let's complete the list with numbers from 101 to 1,000,000.

cent un	*one hundred one*
deux cents	*two hundred*
deux cent six	*two hundred six*
mille	*one thousand*
mille un	*one thousand one*
un million	*one million*

Note the special forms of **soixante-dix** *(seventy)*, **quatre-vingts** *(eighty)*, and **quatre-vingt-dix** *(ninety)*. **Un/Une** is joined by a hyphen, not by **et,** to the number **quatre-vingts** *(eighty)*. Also,

quatre-vingts loses its final **-s** before another number, as in **quatre-vingt-un** *(eighty-one)*.

The round multiples of **cent** *(one hundred)* are written with a final **-s,** but this **-s** is dropped before another number.

trois cents
three hundred

trois cent quatorze
three hundred fourteen

Mille *(one thousand),* on the other hand, does not take an **-s** when multiplied.

deux mille
two thousand

Mille *(one thousand)* and **cent** *(one hundred)* are never preceded by the word **un/une** to say *one thousand* or *one hundred.*

Un million is followed by the word **de** before another noun, except when other numbers come between the word **million** and the noun.

un million de dollars
a million dollars

trois millions cinq cents personnes
three million, five hundred people

NUTS & BOLTS 1
The verb acheter *(to buy)*
Because this unit deals with clothing and shopping, we need to learn to conjugate an important verb, **acheter** *(to buy)*. As we have seen before with certain other **-er** verbs, e.g., **manger** *(to eat)*, there are various spelling changes that help us with pronunciation.

Acheter is another **-er** verb with a simple spelling change that can be easily learned.

j'achète	*I buy, I am buying*	**nous achetons**	*we buy*
tu achètes	*you buy*	**vous achetez**	*you buy*
il achète	*he buys*	**ils achètent**	*they buy*
elle achète	*she buys*	**elles achètent**	*they buy*

Verbs with the mute **e** in the syllable before the infinitive ending change the mute **e** to **è** when the next syllable contains another mute **e**, i.e., before the endings **-e, -es,** and **-ent.** Note that the **nous** and **vous** forms of the verb are spelled without the **è** and are therefore pronounced in the same way as the infinitive, with a silent **e.** Here's a table with other **-er** verbs conjugated like **acheter.**

lever	*to lift, to raise, to pick up*
enlever	*to remove, to take off*
mener	*to lead*
emmener	*to take (someone)*
promener	*to walk*
peser	*to weigh*

Marie achète des bijoux au grand magasin.
Marie buys some jewelry at the department store.

Jean emmène ses amis au restaurant.
Jean takes his friends to the restaurant.

Ils enlèvent leurs manteaux.

They take off their coats.

Take note of the forms of the verb **acheter** in the future and conditional. The **è** is used in all forms in both the future and the conditional. Here is the future of **acheter**.

j'achèterai	*I will buy*	nous achèterons	*we will buy*
tu achèteras	*you will buy*	vous achèterez	*you will buy*
il achètera	*he will buy*	ils achèteront	*they will buy*
elle achètera	*she will buy*	elles achèteront	*they will buy*

Nous achèterons les billets pour la pièce.
We will buy the tickets for the play.

Est-ce que tu achèteras un cadeau pour son anniversaire?
Will you buy a gift for her birthday?

Now look at the conditional of **acheter**.

j'achèterais	*I would/could buy*	nous achèterions	*we would/could buy*
tu achèterais	*you would/could buy*	vous achèteriez	*you would/could buy*
il achèterait	*he would/could buy*	ils achèteraient	*they would/could buy*
elle achèterait	*she would/could buy*	elles achèteraient	*they would/could buy*

J'achèterais de nouveaux vêtements pour notre voyage.
I would buy some new clothes for our trip.

Pour le repas ce soir, vous pourriez acheter du vin.
For the meal tonight, you could buy some wine.

Here are two other verbs with a mute **e** in the syllable before the infinitive ending -**er.** They have a spelling change as well. The verbs are **appeler** *(to call)* and **jeter** *(to throw).* Unlike **acheter,** the verbs **appeler** and **jeter** double the consonant instead of adding an accent on top of the **e.**

j'appelle	*I call*	**nous appelons**	*we call*
tu appelles	*you call*	**vous appelez**	*you call*
il appelle	*he calls*	**ils appellent**	*they call*
elle appelle	*she calls*	**elles appellent**	*they call*

Notice that the **nous** and **vous** forms, like the infinitive, have only one **l.**

je jette	*I throw*	**nous jetons**	*we throw*
tu jettes	*you throw*	**vous jetez**	*you throw*
il jette	*he throws*	**ils jettent**	*they throw*
elle jette	*she throws*	**elles jettent**	*they throw*

J'appelle mon ami.
I call my friend.

Nous appelons le restaurant pour voir s'il y a de la place pour nous.
We call the restaurant to see if there is room for us.

Elle jette les papiers dans la poubelle.
She throws the papers in the garbage.

Vous jetez la pierre dans le lac.
You throw the stone into the lake.

The verbs **appeler** and **jeter** double their consonants in the future and conditional forms as well.

Tu appelleras ton ami demain.
You will call your friend tomorrow.

Tu appellerais ton ami si tu avais un téléphone.
You would call your friend if you had a phone.

Nous jetterons les papiers dans la poubelle.
We will throw the papers in the garbage.

Nous jetterions les papiers dans la poubelle si tu nous aidais.
We would throw the papers in the garbage if you helped us.

The following are other verbs like **appeler** and **jeter**.

rappeler	*to call back*
projeter	*to plan*
rejeter	*to reject*

PRACTICE 1
Fill in the blanks with the correct present tense forms of the verbs with spelling changes found in parentheses.

1. Elle _____ des chaussures. (acheter)

2. _____-ils les chaussettes? (jeter)

3. Tu _____ la balle. (jeter)

4. Vous _____ l'institut de beauté. (appeler)

5. Elles _____ des blouses. (acheter)

6. Je _____ le papier. (jeter)

7. Ils _____ des bijoux. (acheter)

8. Nous _____ la police. (appeler)

9. Est-ce qu'il _____ un complet? (acheter)

10. Comment t'_____-tu? (appeler)

PHRASE LIST 2
LES ALIMENTS *(m.) (Foods)*
Here are more vocabulary words for some foods found in the marketplaces.

la moutarde de Dijon	*Dijon mustard*
un morceau de fromage	*a piece of cheese*
une tranche de saucisson	*a slice of salami*
la crème de marrons	*chestnut paste*
une boîte de marrons glacés	*a box of sugar-coated chestnuts*
le sirop de cassis	*black currant syrup*
un panier de fraises	*a basket of strawberries*
une botte d'asperges	*a bunch of asparagus*
les gauffres	*waffles*
la galette	*puff pastry*

NOTES

The French enjoy eating chestnuts and quite often will use the paste to create various desserts or fillings for pastries. **Les marrons glacés** are sweet, candy-coated confections served with dessert. **Le cassis** *(black currant)* is grown in France and is used in drinks for both adults and children. While the liqueur is imported to the United States, it is quite difficult to find the syrup. This makes a unique souvenir!

NUTS & BOLTS 2
The verb PRÉFÉRER *(to prefer)*

Verbs with **é** in the syllable before the infinitive ending in **-er**, like **préférer** *(to prefer)*, change **é** to **è** in the **je, tu, il/elle,** and **ils/elles** forms. Here's the verb **préférer** *(to prefer)*.

je préfère	*I prefer*	nous préférons	*we prefer*
tu préfères	*you prefer*	vous préférez	*you prefer*
il préfère	*he prefers*	ils préfèrent	*they prefer*
elle préfère	*she prefers*	elles préfèrent	*they prefer*

Here are some other common verbs with **é** in the stem.

célébrer	*to celebrate*
compléter	*to complete*
espérer	*to hope*
posséder	*to own*
protéger	*to protect*
répéter	*to repeat*

Notice that the **nous** and **vous** forms have the same stem as the infinitive.

Qu'est-ce que vous préférez, le café ou le thé?
Which do you prefer, coffee or tea?

Je préfère l'eau.
I prefer water.

Il espère aller en France.
He hopes to go to France.

Nous célébrons les fêtes avec notre famille.
We celebrate the holidays with our family.

The future and conditional remain unchanged.

Vous préférerez le chocolat.
You will prefer chocolate.

Vous préféreriez le chocolat.
You would prefer chocolate.

PRACTICE 2

Rewrite the following sentences using a form of the verb **préférer** in place of the verbs being used in the following sentences.

Ex. Tu choisis la robe bleue.
    Tu préfères la robe bleue.

1. Elle aime la blouse blanche.

2. Je mange des croissants.

3. Elles vendent les chaussures.

4. Il adore la cravate.

5. Nous choisissons les gants noirs.

Discovery activity

You would be surprised to find out how many French phrases and expressions concerning the world of fashion and beauty appear in our American magazines and newspapers. Try looking closely at the various advertisement sections next time you have the opportunity to flip through a magazine. Cut out the ads containing the French expressions you find, and keep them in a file for supplemental vocabulary building.

ANSWERS

PRACTICE 1: 1. achète; **2.** jettent; **3.** jettes; **4.** appelez; **5.** achètent; **6.** jette; **7.** achètent; **8.** appelons; **9.** achète; **10.** appelles

PRACTICE 2: 1. Elle préfère la blouse blanche. **2.** Je préfère des croissants. **3.** Elles préfèrent les chaussures. **4.** Il préfère la cravate. **5.** Nous préférons les gants noirs.

———————— Lesson 27 (sentences) ————————

SENTENCE GROUP 1

LES EXPRESSIONS POUR FAIRE DU SHOPPING *(Expressions for shopping)*

Je voudrais acheter des vêtements.	*I would like to buy some clothes.*
Qu'est-ce que vous avez?	*What do you have?*
C'est combien?	*It's how much?*
C'est trop cher.	*It's too expensive.*
C'est bon marché.	*That's inexpensive./It's a good buy.*
Y a-t-il une remise?	*Is there a discount?*
Est-ce que je peux l'essayer?	*May I try it on?*
Où sont les cabines d'essayage?	*Where are the dressing rooms?*
Quelle taille?	*What size?*
Je préfère ceci.	*I prefer this.*
Je préfère cela.	*I prefer that.*
C'est un bon choix.	*It's a good choice.*
Je le trouve joli.	*I think it's pretty.*
Il/Elle est en solde.	*It's on sale.*
Je vais le/la prendre.	*I'll take it.*

NOTES

Note that the equivalent of the English *on sale* is the French **en solde.** Don't confuse the English *sale* with the French adjective **sale,** which means *dirty.*

NUTS & BOLTS 1

-YER VERBS

Verbs ending in **-yer** change **y** to **i** before a mute **e**. Let's look at the verb **employer** *(to use)*.

j'emploie	*I use*	nous employons	*we use*
tu emploies	*you use*	vous employez	*you use*
il emploie	*he uses*	ils emploient	*they use*
elle emploie	*she uses*	elles emploient	*they use*

Here are some other verbs conjugated like **employer**.

ennuyer	*to bore, to annoy*
nettoyer	*to clean*

Le jeudi, je nettoie la maison.
On Thursdays, I clean the house.

Estelle emploie le téléphone pour son travail.
Estelle uses the phone for her work.

Le programme à la télé m'ennuie.
The program on television bores me.

Now let's learn a verb that is essential when shopping. It's the verb **payer** *(to pay)*. The verb **payer** has two alternative present tense forms—one where **y** changes to **i** and one where it doesn't.

je paye/je paie	*I pay*	nous payons	*we pay*
tu payes/tu paies	*you pay*	vous payez	*you pay*
il paye/il paie	*he pays*	ils payent/ ils paient	*they pay*
elle paye/elle paie	*she pays*	elles payent/ elles paient	*they pay*

Note that **payer** takes a direct object rather than an object preceded by the preposition (as in the English *to pay for*).

Je paye les billets.
I pay for the tickets.

Mes amies payent l'addition au restaurant.
My friends are paying the bill at the restaurant.

The verb **essayer** *(to try on)* is conjugated like **payer**.

J'essaie de parler français.
I'm trying to speak French.

PRACTICE 1
Put the verbs in the following sentences in the correct form of the present tense. Remember the spelling changes that apply.

1. Il _____ l'ordinateur. (employer)

2. Nous _____ la maison. (nettoyer)

3. Est-ce que tu _____ l'addition? (payer)

4. Vous _____ le pantalon. (essayer)

5. Ils _____ à l'avance. (payer)

SENTENCE GROUP 2
ENCORE DES EXPRESSIONS POUR FAIRE DU SHOPPING *(More shopping expressions)*

Je voudrais acheter des souvenirs.	*I would like to buy some souvenirs.*
Je voudrais acheter du parfum pour ma petite amie.	*I'd like to buy some perfume for my girlfriend.*
Je voudrais acheter de l'eau de cologne pour mon petit ami.	*I'd like to buy some cologne for my boyfriend.*
Je voudrais acheter un foulard.	*I would like to buy a scarf.*
Vous n'avez rien d'autre?	*You don't have anything else?*
Avez-vous quelque chose de moins cher?	*Do you have something less expensive?*
Avez-vous quelque chose dans le même genre?	*Do you have something of the same kind?*
Ça coûte cher.	*That costs a lot.*
Ça coûte trois euros la paire.	*That's three euros per pair.*
Excusez-moi, mais où est la caisse?	*Excuse me, but where is the register?*
Il faut payer à la caisse.	*You must pay at the register.*

NUTS & BOLTS 2
DEMONSTRATIVE ADJECTIVES
A demonstrative adjective points out a specific person or thing—e.g., *this book, that house, these people,* or *those cars.*

MASCULINE SINGULAR	FEMININE SINGULAR	MASCULINE AND FEMININE PLURAL
ce, cet *(this, that)*	**cette** *(this, that)*	**ces** *(these, those)*

Here are some examples of demonstrative adjectives.

Ce pullover est jaune.
This/That sweater is yellow.

Cette blouse est parfaite.
This/That blouse is perfect.

Ces chaussures sont marron.
These/Those shoes are brown.

Note that before a masculine singular noun beginning with a vowel or mute **h,** the form **cet** is used.

Cet homme est beau.
This/That man is handsome.

Cet imperméable est joli.
This/That raincoat is pretty.

To distinguish between *this* and *that,* **-ci** is added to a noun to mean *this* or *these,* and **-là** is attached to the noun to mean *that* or *those.*

Tu voudrais ce manteau-ci ou ce manteau-là?
Do you want this coat or that coat?

J'achète cette robe-ci. Je n'aime pas cette robe-là.
I'm buying this dress. I don't like that dress.

Ces chaussettes-ci sont plus confortables que ces chaussettes-là.
These socks are more comfortable than those socks.

PRACTICE 2

Fill in the blanks with the correct demonstrative adjective—**ce, cette, cet,** or **ces.**

1. _____ montre est très chère.

2. J'aime _____ gants.

3. _____ mouchoir est fait en France.

4. Je trouve _____ pyjama très confortable.

5. Est-ce que tu aimes _____ pantalon?

PRACTICE 3

Pretend that you work in a department store. Using the demonstrative pronouns followed by the ending **-ci** or **-là,** ask the customer specifically which item he or she wants. Follow this example.

Ex. Je voudrais acheter cette robe.
I would like to buy that dress.

Cette robe-ci ou cette robe-là?
This dress or that dress?

1. Je voudrais le pantalon, s'il vous plaît.

2. Les chaussures que vous avez derrière vous m'intéressent.

3. Je voudrais essayer la robe, s'il vous plaît.

4. Ce tee-shirt est super.

5. J'aime les sandales que vous portez.

Language link

If you are looking for French fashion in the United States, have fun browsing the Marketplace section of the following website: www.francetoday.com.

ANSWERS

PRACTICE 1: 1. emploie; **2.** nettoyons; **3.** payes/paies;
4. essayez; **5.** payent/paient

PRACTICE 2: 1. Cette; **2.** ces; **3.** Ce; **4.** ce; **5.** ce

PRACTICE 3: 1. Ce pantalon-ci ou ce pantalon-là? **2.** Ces
chaussures-ci ou ces chaussures-là? **3.** Cette robe-ci ou cette
robe-là? **4.** Ce tee-shirt ou ce tee-shirt-là? **5.** Ces sandales-ci ou
ces sandales-là?

——————— Lesson 28 (conversations) ———————

CONVERSATION 1

Ms. Martin is at the **marché** *(farmer's market)* in town shopping
for the items that she needs in order to make **poireaux pommes
de terre** *(potato leek soup)*.

Madame Martin:	Bonjour, Monsieur. Est-ce que vous avez des poireaux aujourd'hui?
Le marchand:	Bien sûr, Madame. Combien en voulez-vous?
Madame Martin:	Combien coûtent les poireaux?
Le marchand:	Deux euros la livre.
Madame Martin:	Donnez-moi une livre, s'il vous plaît.
Le marchand:	Voilà. Il vous faut autre chose, Madame?
Madame Martin:	Ah, oui. Je fais une bonne soupe ce soir—aux poireaux et aux pommes de terre, donc il me faut des pommes de terre.
Le marchand:	Combien en voulez-vous, Madame?
Madame Martin:	Je voudrais trois livres, s'il vous plaît.
Le marchand:	Et voilà, de belles pommes de terre. Et avec ça?
Madame Martin:	Ça suffit, pour le moment. Je vous dois combien, Monsieur?
Le marchand:	Ça fait cinq euros, Madame.

Ms. Martin:	Good day, Sir. Do you have any leeks today?
Merchant:	Certainly, Madam. How much do you want?
Ms. Martin:	How much are the leeks?
Merchant:	Two euros a pound.
Ms. Martin:	Give me one pound, please.
Merchant:	There you go. Do you need anything else, Madam?
Ms. Martin:	Yes. I'm making a good soup tonight—with potatoes and with leeks—so I need some potatoes.
Merchant:	How many would you like, Madam?
Ms. Martin:	I would like three pounds, please.
Merchant:	There you go—some beautiful potatoes. And with that?
Ms. Martin:	That's it for the moment. How much do I owe you, Sir?
Merchant:	That will be five euros, Madam.

NUTS & BOLTS 1
Comparison of adjectives

We've learned how to form adjectives, how to make them agree with the subject in number and gender, and where to place them in a sentence. Now, let's take a look at how to construct the comparative forms of adjectives. One object or person may be seen as having more, less, or the same degree of a characteristic than or as another object or person. To express this, comparative constructions are used. There are three ways to make a comparison. Look at the following examples.

plus + adjective + **que**	*more . . . than*
moins + adjective + **que**	*less . . . than*
aussi + adjective + **que**	*as . . . as*

It is easy to form the comparative of an adjective.

Il est plus actif que moi.
He is more active than I am.

Il est moins actif que moi.
He is less active than I am.

Il est aussi actif que moi.
He is as active as I am.

To make comparisons of superiority, French uses the construction **plus** + adjective + **que**. Note that the adjective must agree in gender and number with the noun it is modifying.

Robert est plus grand que Michel.
Robert is taller than Michel.

Jeanne est plus grande que Robert.
Jeanne is taller than Robert.

Les robes sont plus jolies que les jupes.
The dresses are prettier than the skirts.

To make comparisons of inferiority, French uses the construction **moins** + adjective + **que**.

Robert est moins actif que Pierre.
Robert is less active than Pierre.

Jeanne est moins active que Robert.
Jeanne is less active than Robert.

Les adultes sont moins actifs que les enfants.
Adults are less active than children.

To make a comparison of equality, French uses the construction **aussi** + adjective + **que**.

Le boulevard est aussi large que l'avenue.
The boulevard is as wide as the avenue.

Mon mari est aussi grand que son père.
My husband is as tall as his father.

Les garçons sont aussi grands que les filles.
The boys are as tall as the girls.

In French, as in English, the second noun being compared can be also omitted.

La robe est plus longue.
The dress is longer.

Les parents sont plus gentils.
The parents are kinder.

Les excercices sont plus faciles.
The exercises are easier.

L'appartement est aussi cher.
The apartment is just as expensive.

Il est plus grand.
It's bigger.

PRACTICE 1
Complete the sentences by translating the words in parentheses into French.

1. Es-tu _____ attentif _____ possible? *(as . . . as)*

2. Le livre est _____ intéressant _____ le film. *(more . . . than)*

3. André est _____ petit _____ Gérard. *(less . . . than)*

4. Les gants sont _____ beaux _____ les sacs. *(more . . . than)*

5. Le manteau est _____long _____ l'imperméable. *(as . . . as)*

A few adjectives have irregular comparisons. **Bon/bonne** *(good [m./f.])* has a comparative form **meilleur/meilleure** *(better [m./f.]).*

Le vin est bon, mais le champagne est meilleur.
The wine is good, but the champagne is better.

The adjectives **mauvais** *(bad)* and **petit** *(small)* have both regular and irregular comparative forms. For instance, the comparative form of **mauvais** may be **plus mauvais** or **pire** *(worse).*

Ce restaurant est pire/plus mauvais que l'autre.
This restaurant is worse than the other.

The two comparative forms of the adjective **petit** *(small)* have different meanings. **Plus petit** means *smaller (in size).* Its irregular comparative form, **moindre,** means *less (important)*; it is also used in common expressions.

C'est un accident de moindre importance.
This is an accident of minor importance.

Il n'a pas la moindre idée de cette surprise.
He does not have the slightest idea about this surprise.

Ce chapeau est à moindre prix.
This hat is (sold) at a modest price.

C'est la moindre des choses!
It's the least you can do!

To make a comparison using an adverb, the same rules apply. Here are the three possible comparative forms of the adverb **poliment** *(politely).*

plus poliment que	more politely than
moins poliment que	less politely than
aussi poliment que	as politely as

Here are more examples of comparatives with adverbs.

Marc parle plus lentement que Joseph.
Marc speaks more slowly than Joseph.

Le train va moins vite que l'avion.
The train goes less quickly than the plane.

L'autobus va aussi vite que la voiture.
The bus goes as quickly as the car.

The adverbs **bien** *(well)* and **mal** *(bad)* have irregular comparative forms, **mieux** *(better)* and **pire** *(worse)*. **Pire** is rare as an adverb; **plus mal** is normally used instead. The comparative form of **beaucoup** *(many)* is **plus** *(more)*, and the comparative of **peu** *(little)* is **moins** *(less)*.

Marie parle bien, mais Jean parle mieux.
Mary speaks well, but John speaks better.

When the adverb **beaucoup** modifying a verb is compared, **autant** replaces **aussi** in comparisons of equality.

Je travaille beaucoup.
I work a lot.

Je travaille autant que toi.
I work as much as you do.

When **beaucoup** modifies a noun, **autant de** is used before the noun in the comparison of equality.

Il a beaucoup de problèmes.
He has many problems.

Il a autant de problèmes que nous.
He has as many problems as we do.

We can also compare amounts of things using the expressions **plus de** + noun + **que** *(more than)* and **moins de** + noun + **que**.

Il y a plus de baguettes dans la boulangerie que dans la pâtisserie.
There are more baguettes in the bakery than in the pastry shop.

Il y a moins de choix dans le magasin que dans le centre commercial.
There's less choice in the store than at the mall.

PRACTICE 2
Complete the sentences by supplying the missing words.

1. M. Martin parle _____ Mme Martin.

   Mr. Martin speaks better than Ms. Martin.

2. Il conduit _____ moi.

   He drives worse than I do.

3. Je travaille _____ mon mari.

   I work less than my husband.

4. Nos parents conduisent _____ nous.

   Our parents drive more slowly than we do.

5. Tu parles _____ moi.

   You speak more quickly than I do.

CONVERSATION 2

Cheyann and Jeanne are shopping for a special event next Saturday evening.

Cheyann: Je voudrais acheter une nouvelle paire de chaussures pour la soirée de samedi prochain.

Jeanne: Et moi, je vais regarder les robes. Il y a un bon choix ici.

Cheyann: Regarde ces belles chaussures rouges! Je les aime! Qu'est-ce que tu penses?

Jeanne: Elles sont très belles, mais je pense que les chaussures noires sont plus belles et plus chic. Essaye-les.

Cheyann: Voici ma pointure ... Je les aime beaucoup! Tu as raison. Les chaussures noires sont les plus belles.

Jeanne: Et maintenant, qu'est-ce que tu penses, la robe bleue ou la robe noire?

Cheyann: La robe bleue est la plus jolie. J'adore la couleur. Essaye-la.

Jeanne: Regarde cette belle robe que je porte!

Cheyann: Oh là là! Elle te va à ravir.

Jeanne: À mon avis, nous serons les plus jolies femmes de la soirée.

Cheyann: De toute façon, nous serons bien habillées!

Cheyann: *I'd like to buy a new pair of shoes for the party next Saturday.*

Jeanne: *And me, I'm going to look at the dresses. There's a good selection here.*

Cheyann: *Look at these beautiful red shoes! I love them! What do you think?*

Jeanne: *They're very beautiful, but I think that the black shoes are more beautiful and stylish. Try them on.*

Cheyann: *Here's my size ... I really like them! You're right. The black shoes are the most beautiful.*

Jeanne: And now, what do you think, the blue dress or the black dress?

Cheyann: The blue dress is the prettiest. I love the color. Try it on.

Jeanne: Look at this beautiful dress that I'm wearing.

Cheyann: Wow! It looks great on you.

Jeanne: In my opinion, we'll be the most beautiful women at the party.

Cheyann: At any rate, we'll be well dressed!

NUTS & BOLTS 2

SUPERLATIVES

Superlatives express the idea of the most, the best, or the least. The superlative of an adjective is formed by placing the definite article—**le, la, le,** or **les**—before **plus** or **moins,** followed by the adjective.

le plus beau	*the most handsome*
la plus belle	*the most beautiful*
les plus beaux	*the most handsome*
les plus belles	*the most beautiful*

To express inferiority, use **le (la, les)** + **moins** + adjective.

le moins joli	*the least pretty*
la moins jolie	*the least pretty*
les moins jolis	*the least pretty*
les moins jolies	*the least pretty*

When the adjective follows the noun, the definite article appears both before the noun and before **plus** or **moins**.

Où est le restaurant le plus cher?
Where is the most expensive restaurant?

Les restaurants les plus célèbres sont à New York.
The most famous restaurants are in New York.

After a superlative, the word *in* is translated by the word **de** in French.

Henri est le meilleur élève de la classe.
Henry is the best pupil in the class.

C'est la ville la plus riche du monde.
It's the richest city in the world.

Culture note

The French world of fashion

Along with Milan, New York, and London, Paris has a reputation for being the center of fashion, which is one of the most important industries in France. French **haute couture** *(high fashion)* includes many famous names of **couturiers** *(designers)* from the past and the present, such as Coco Chanel, Yves Saint Laurent, Christian Dior, Pierre Cardin, and Karl Lagerfeld, known throughout the world. Besides being famous for designing clothes, they also have luxury items, such as accessories, perfumes, and colognes.

If you are interested in high fashion, the **rive droite** *(right bank)*, between the **Opéra** and **Place Charles de Gaulle,** or the neighborhood near **Saint-Germain-des Prés** on the **rive gauche** *(left bank)*, is where you need to go. Shopping in Paris is a wonderful experience for anyone. There are many small boutiques, as well as large department stores, such as **les Galeries Lafayette, Au Printemps** and **le Bon Marché.** They stay open all day long. Small shops often close at lunchtime. There are also various new shopping malls, like **la Tour Montparnasse, le Palais des Congrès,** and **la Grande Arche.**

French sizes, **la taille** (*clothing size*) and **la pointure** (*shoe size*), are different from those in the United States. The following chart will give you an approximation of the conversion of sizes that will help when you are shopping for clothing.

Women's dresses and tops							
USA	4	6	8	10	12	14	16
France	36	38	40	42	44	46	48
Men's suits							
USA	35	36	37	38	39	40–41	42
France	33	36	40	42	44	46–48	50
Men's shirts							
USA	14	15	15½	16	16½	17	18
France	37	38	39	40	41	42	43

UNIT 7 ESSENTIALS

les vêtements	*clothing*
Je paye les bijoux.	*I'm paying for the jewelry.*
C'est bon marché.	*That's a good buy.*
Je le prends.	*I'll take it.*
Je les achète.	*I'm buying them.*
Je lui parle.	*I'm talking to him/to her.*
Les gants sont plus chers que le chapeau.	*The gloves are more expensive than the hat.*
Cette bague est la plus chère.	*This ring is the most expensive.*
Cette montre est moins chère que le bracelet.	*This watch is less expensive than the bracelet.*
Ce pantalon-ci est aussi chic que ce pantalon-là.	*These pants are as stylish as those pants.*
vingt et un	*twenty-one*
quatre-vingts	*eighty*
quatre-vingt-un	*eighty-one*
mille dollars	*one thousand dollars*
un million de dollars	*one million dollars*

Unit 8
Work and school

In this unit, you will learn some of the essential vocabulary needed to talk about jobs and the workplace. You will also be introduced to new vocabulary concerning school life in France as compared to the American school system.

An essential past tense called the imperfect will also be presented. Knowing this tense, along with the other verb tenses that you have already learned, will ensure that you are well on your way to excellent communication skills in French.

─────────────── Lesson 29 (words) ───────────────

WORD LIST 1
LES PROFESSIONS ET L'EMPLOI *(Professions and employment)*

le comptable/la comptable	*accountant (male/female)*
l'employé de banque/ l'employée de banque	*bank clerk (male/female)*
le fonctionnaire/ la fonctionnaire	*civil servant (male/female)*
le pharmacien/ la pharmacienne	*pharmacist (male/female)*
l'homme au foyer/ la femme au foyer	*homemaker (male/female)*
l'ouvrier en bâtiment/ l'ouvrière en bâtiment	*construction worker (male/female)*
l'auteur/l'auteure	*author (male/female)*
l'écrivain/l'écrivaine	*writer (male/female)*
l'informaticien/ l'informaticienne	*computer programmer, systems analyst (male/female)*

le dentiste/la dentiste	*dentist (male/female)*
l'infirmier/l'infirmière	*nurse (male/female)*
l'acteur/l'actrice	*actor/actress*
le plombier	*plumber*
le fermier/la fermière	*farmer (male/female)*
le charpentier	*carpenter*
le policier/la femme policier, l'agent/l'agente de police	*policeman/policewoman*
le secrétaire/la secrétaire	*secretary (male/female)*
l'homme d'affaires/ la femme d'affaires	*businessman/businesswoman*
l'esthéticien/l'esthéticienne	*beautician, beauty advisor (male/female)*

NOTES

Note that some professions have a masculine form and a feminine form, while others are used in their masculine form for both men and women.

NUTS & BOLTS 1

THE IMPERFECT TENSE

The formation of imperfect tense is quite simple. Take the **nous** form of the present tense and drop the ending **-ons** from the **nous** form—e.g., **parlons** has the stem **parl-**. This goes for all verbs except **être** *(to be)*, which uses the stem **ét-** to form the imperfect. Here is the list of endings added to the verb stems.

IMPERFECT TENSE ENDINGS	
je: -ais	**nous: -ions**
tu: -ais	**vous: -iez**
il: -ait	**ils: -aient**
elle: -ait	**elles: -aient**

You will notice that the endings for the imperfect are the same as those for the conditional, but they are added to different verb stems—the present tense stem for the imperfect and the infinitive for the conditional.

The imperfect tense is used for two kinds of actions in the past: continuous or ongoing past actions and habitual or repeated past actions. In English, this tense usually corresponds to the past progressive (e.g., *I was talking*) and *used to* + verb. Here are examples of three verbs, one for each verb group, in the imperfect. An example of a Group 1 verb is **parler** *(to speak)*, below.

je parlais	*I was speaking, I used to speak*	**nous parlions**	*we were speaking, we used to speak*
tu parlais	*you were speaking, you used to speak*	**vous parliez**	*you were speaking, you used to speak*
il parlait	*he was speaking, he used to speak*	**ils parlaient**	*they were speaking, they used to speak*
elle parlait	*she was speaking, she used to speak*	**elles parlaient**	*they were speaking, they used to speak*

An example of a Group 2 verb is **finir** *(to finish)*. The **nous** form of the present tense is **nous finissons**. By dropping the **-ons,** we obtain the stem **finiss-**.

je finissais	*I was finishing, I used to finish*	**nous finissions**	*we were finishing, we used to finish*
tu finissais	*you were finishing, you used to finish*	**vous finissiez**	*you were finishing, you used to finish*
il finissait	*he was finishing, he used to finish*	**ils finissaient**	*they were finishing, they used to finish*

elle finissait	she was finishing, she used to finish	elles finissaient	they were finishing, they to used finish

An example of a Group 3 verb is **vendre** *(to sell)*. The stem **vend-** is obtained by dropping the **-ons** from the **nous** form, **nous vendons**.

je vendais	I was selling, I used to sell	nous vendions	we were selling I used to sell
tu vendais	you were selling, you used to sell	vous vendiez	you were selling, you used to sell
il vendait	he was selling, he used to sell	ils vendaient	they were selling, they used to sell
elle vendait	she was selling, she used to sell	elles vendaient	they were selling, they used to sell

As mentioned earlier, all verbs form the imperfect tense in the same way, except for the verb **être** *(to be)*. Remember that the stem for **être** is **ét-**.

j'étais	I was, I used to be	nous étions	we were, we used to be
tu étais	you were, you used to be	vous étiez	you were, you used to be
il était	he was, he used to be	ils étaient	they were, they used to be
elle était	she was, she used to be	elles étaient	they were, they used to be

Now let's take a look at some examples to see how the imperfect is used in everyday conversation.

Elle jouait du piano et nous dansions.
She was playing the piano and we were dancing.

Je lui parlais tous les jours.
I used to talk to him/her every day.

Quand j'étais jeune, je dansais bien.
When I was young, I used to dance well.

When the English *would* means *used to*, it is translated with the imperfect tense.

Quand j'étais jeune, ma mère me chantait une chanson tous les soirs.
When I was young, my mother would/used to sing a song to me every night.

The imperfect of the verb **avoir** *(to have)* is usually translated as *had, was having,* or *used to have.*

j'avais	*I had, I was having, I used to have*	**nous avions**	*we had, we were having, we used to have*
tu avais	*you had, you were having, you used to have*	**vous aviez**	*you had, you were having, you used to have*
il avait	*he had, he was having, he used to have*	**ils avaient**	*they had, they were having, they used to have*
elle avait	*she had, she was having, she used to have*	**elles avaient**	*they had, they were having, they used to have*

Hier, j'avais un problème avec ma voiture.

Yesterday, I had/was having a problem with my car.

Quand j'étais jeune, j'avais un cheval.

When I was young, I had/used to have a horse.

Remember that in the expression **il y a** *(there is, there are)* is the verb **avoir.** In the imperfect, this expression is **il y avait** *(there was, there were).*

Il y a un concert samedi soir.

There is a concert on Saturday evening.

Il y avait un concert samedi soir.

There was a concert on Saturday night.

PRACTICE 1
Use the correct imperfect tense forms of the verbs in parentheses to fill in the blanks.

1. Elle _____ tous les matins. (jouer)

2. Où _____-vous? (aller)

3. Qu'est-ce qu'il _____? (boire)

4. Mon mari et moi, nous _____ tous les soirs. (marcher)

5. Je ____ vendre la maison. (devoir)

6. L'enfant ne _____ pas ses légumes. (finir)

7. Louis _____ les meubles. (vendre)

8. Il _____ froid en janvier. (faire)

9. J'____ des questions. (avoir)

10. Tu _____ bien. (danser)

PRACTICE 2
Change the following sentences from the present to the imperfect tense.

1. Nous aimons la musique.
2. Il fait beau.
3. Où marchez-vous?
4. Qu'est-ce que tu regardes?
5. Mes amis sont heureux.
6. Il vend des bijoux.
7. Je suis furieux.
8. Elle a une nouvelle voiture.
9. Tu prépares un sandwich.
10. Vous habitez à Paris.

WORD LIST 2
LE TRAVAIL *(Work)*

le boulot, le travail	*job, work*
le collègue/la collègue	*colleague (male/female)*
la comptabilité	*accounting*
l'informatique	*computer science*
l'ordinateur	*computer*
le télécopieur	*fax machine*
le logiciel	*software*
la société	*company*
la réunion	*meeting*
la gestion	*management*
le personnel	*the staff*
l'expérience	*experience*

l'usine	factory
le patron/la patronne	boss (male/female)
le salaire	salary

NUTS & BOLTS 2

THE IMPERFECT TENSE OF SOME VERBS WITH SPELLING CHANGES

Verbs with a spelling change in the **nous** form of the present tense, such as **manger** *(to eat)* and **commencer** *(to begin)* have the spelling change before imperfect endings that begin with the vowel **a** as well. However, the **nous** and **vous** forms in the imperfect do not keep that spelling change. Here is the imperfect of **manger** *(to eat)* as an example.

je mangeais	I was eating, I used to eat	nous mangions	we were eating, we used to eat
tu mangeais	you were eating, you used to eat	vous mangiez	you were eating, you used to eat
il mangeait	he was eating, he used to eat	ils mangeaient	they were eating, they used to eat
elle mangeait	she was eating, she used to eat	elles mangeaient	they were eating, they used to eat

Here is the imperfect of **commencer** *(to begin)*.

je commençais	I was beginning, I used to begin	nous commencions	we were beginning, we used to begin
tu commençais	you were beginning, you used to begin	vous commenciez	you were beginning, you used to begin

il commençait	he was beginning, he used to begin	ils commençaient	they were beginning, they used to begin
elle commençait	she was beginning, she used to begin	elles commençaient	they were beginning, they used to begin

Let's look at some examples.

Je mangeais tout ce que ma mère préparait pour notre famille.
I used to eat everything my mom would/used to prepare for our family.

Elles commençaient à parler quand il est entré dans la salle.
They were beginning to speak when he entered the room.

Note that a verb like **étudier,** which already has an **i** in its stem, has two **i**'s in the **nous** and **vous** forms of the imperfect.

Nous étudiions.
We were studying.

Vous étudiiez.
You were studying.

PRACTICE 3
Put the verbs in parentheses in the imperfect tense to complete the sentences.

1. Suzanne _____ au restaurant au coin de la rue. (manger)

2. Nous _____ à la bibliothèque avec nos amis samedi. (étudier)

3. Beaucoup de jeunes filles _____ à faire des exercices. (commencer)

4. Vous _____ à travailler quand le patron est arrivé. (commencer)

5. Je _____ de la viande. (manger)

Discovery activity

Write a short composition or story in French entitled **Quand j'étais plus jeune** *(When I was younger)*. Pick an event or a special moment, something that you used to do that made you laugh, made you feel happy, or perhaps even embarrassed you! Use the imperfect tense to describe this event. If you created a family album in French, which was suggested in Unit 2, you may want to include this story along with a picture that reminds you of the memory. Here is a sample to get you started.

Quand j'étais jeune, j'avais un petit chien. Il était brun et adorable. Il aimait aller se promener avec mes amis et moi. Nous jouions toujours ensemble.

When I was young, I used to have a little dog. He was brown and adorable. He liked to take walks with my friends and me. We used to always play together.

ANSWERS

PRACTICE 1: 1. jouait; **2.** alliez; **3.** buvait; **4.** marchions; **5.** devais; **6.** finissait; **7.** vendait; **8.** faisait; **9.** avais; **10.** dansais

PRACTICE 2: 1. Nous aimions la musique. **2.** Il faisait beau. **3.** Où marchiez-vous? **4.** Qu'est-ce que tu regardais? **5.** Mes amis étaient heureux. **6.** Il vendait des bijoux. **7.** J'étais furieux. **8.** Elle avait une nouvelle voiture. **9.** Tu préparais un sandwich. **10.** Vous habitiez à Paris.

PRACTICE 3: 1. mangeait; **2.** étudiions; **3.** commençaient; **4.** commenciez; **5.** mangeais

——————— Lesson 30 (phrases) ———————

PHRASE LIST 1
VOCABULAIRE POUR LE TRAVAIL *(Vocabulary for work)*

au travail	*at work*
au bureau	*in (at) the office*

gagner de l'argent	*to earn money*
travailler dur	*to work hard*
le directeur du personnel	*personnel manager*
faire une demande d'emploi	*to apply for a job*
avoir une entrevue	*to have an interview*
à plein temps	*full-time*
à temps partiel	*part-time*
à la retraite	*retired*
le chômage	*unemployment*
être sans emploi (sans travail)	*to be unemployed*
l'emploi saisonnier	*summer job*
être occupé/occupée	*to be busy*
être en pleine expansion	*to be growing*

NUTS & BOLTS 1
THE IMPERFECT AND THE COMPOUND PAST TENSE

The imperfect and the compound past tense are both tenses expressing past actions and work well together. The imperfect is often used to set the scene for an action expressed in the compound past tense.

While the compound past tense is used to refer to *completed* actions, the imperfect is used to refer to those that were *continuous* or *habitual* and *repetitive*. The imperfect may describe the weather, the time of the day, the condition or state of something, or what someone was in the process of doing when something else occurred. (Remember that the English words *was, were,* and *used to* always correspond to the French imperfect.)

Note the contrast between the two tenses in the following sentence.

Il faisait froid quand j'ai quitté la maison ce matin.
It was cold when I left the house this morning.

The first part of the sentence, **il faisait froid** *(it was cold),* is in the imperfect because it describes the weather, which is a condition or a state. The second half of the sentence, **j'ai quitté la maison** *(I left the house),* tells of a completed action and uses the compound past tense.

Here are more examples of sentences using both tenses.

Il était minuit quand je suis revenu(e).
It was midnight when I returned.

J'ai entendu la chanson que tu chantais.
I heard the song that you were singing.

Je prenais un bain quand le téléphone a sonné.
I was taking a bath when the phone rang.

PRACTICE 1
Translate the following sentences from French into English.

1. Je n'étais pas à la maison quand tu m'as téléphoné.

2. Tout le monde parlait quand le prof est entré.

3. Il faisait beau quand ils sont allés au parc dimanche.

4. Qui vendait la maison?

5. Quelqu'un nous regardait.

6. Nous chantions beaucoup.

PRACTICE 2
In the following paragraph, Carol is telling her friends what she did during the weekend. Decide whether the verbs in the passage should be in the compound past tense (completed action) or the imperfect (habitual, continuous, or interrupted action). Rewrite the passage with the correct forms of the verbs in parentheses.

Pendant le week-end, je _____ (être) très occupée. Mon mari et moi, nous _____ (décider) d'aller au parc parce qu'il _____ (faire) très beau. Nous _____ (arriver) au parc vers midi. Quand nous _____ (marcher) dans le jardin, nous _____ (regarder) toutes les roses. Ce _____ (être) si joli! Au parc, il y _____ (avoir) beaucoup de monde. À deux heures, nous _____ (quitter) le parc et nous _____ (aller) au musée. Il y _____ (avoir) une exposition des impressionnistes que je _____ (vouloir) voir. Nous _____ (regarder) les belles sculptures quand nous _____ (rencontrer) nos amis Joelle et Robert. Après la visite au musée, nous _____ (dîner) dans un bon restaurant en ville.

PHRASE LIST 2
VOCABULAIRE POUR L'ÉCOLE *(Vocabulary for school)*

à l'école	*at school*
au collège, au lycée	*at (in) middle school, at (in) high school*
à l'université	*in college*
la salle de classe	*classroom*
enseigner	*to teach*
le diplôme	*diploma*
la licence	*bachelor's degree*
la maîtrise	*master's degree*
l'année scolaire	*academic year*
la rentrée	*back-to-school*
les matières difficiles	*difficult subjects*
écrire une dictée	*write a dictation*
la littérature	*literature*
la langue étrangère	*foreign language*
la gymnastique	*gym*
le bulletin scolaire	*report card*

Besides teaching new vocabulary and grammar, such as conjugations of verbs, French schools utilize the technique of **la dictée** *(dictation)* to teach spelling. This is one of the techniques used to teach writing skills in a foreign language. Students must carefully listen to and write down what the teacher is saying in the target language.

NUTS & BOLTS 2

THE VERBS ÉCRIRE *(to write)*, LIRE *(to read)*, AND DIRE *(to say)*

To talk about schools and education, we need to learn how to use the verbs **écrire** *(to write)*, **lire** *(to read)*, and **dire** *(to say)*, which, in French, are all irregular. Here is the verb **écrire** first.

j'écris	*I write*	**nous écrivons**	*we write*
tu écris	*you write*	**vous écrivez**	*you write*
il écrit	*he writes*	**ils écrivent**	*they write*
elle écrit	*she writes*	**elles écrivent**	*they write*

J'écris une lettre à mes amis à l'université.
I'm writing a letter to my friends in college.

Les étudiants écrivent une dictée pour l'examen.
The students are writing a dictation for their test.

The past participle of the verb **écrire** is **écrit/écrite** *(wrote, written [m./f.])*.

Le petit garçon a écrit une lettre au Père Noël.
The little boy wrote a letter to Santa Claus.

Here is the present tense of the verb **lire** *(to read)*.

je lis	*I read*	**nous lisons**	*we read*
tu lis	*you read*	**vous lisez**	*you read*
il lit	*he reads*	**ils lisent**	*they read*
elle lit	*she reads*	**elles lisent**	*they read*

Here are some examples with the verb **lire.**

Nous lisons le journal chaque soir.
We read the newspaper every night.

Les enfants lisent une bonne histoire.
The children are reading a good story.

The past participle for the verb **lire** is **lu/lue** *(read [m./f.]).*

Pendant le voyage, nous avons lu beaucoup de livres.
During the trip, we read a lot of books.

Here is the verb **dire** *(to say).*

je dis	*I say*	**nous disons**	*we say*
tu dis	*you say*	**vous dites**	*you say*
il dit	*he says*	**ils disent**	*they say*
elle dit	*she says*	**elles disent**	*they say*

Here is the verb used with some example sentences.

Ils disent la vérité.
They speak the truth.

Qu'est-ce que vous dites?
What are you saying?

The past participle for the verb **dire** *(to say)* is **dit/dite** *(said [m./f.])*.

J'ai dit qu'elle avait une jolie robe.
I said she had a pretty dress.

The future and conditional stems of **écrire, lire,** and **dire** are formed regularly by dropping the final **-e** from the infinitive and adding the appropriate endings.

PRACTICE 3
Fill in the blanks with the correct present tense forms of the verbs in parentheses.

1. Qu'est-ce que tu _____? (lire)

2. Avant d'aller au supermarché, j'_____ une liste. (écrire)

3. Ma femme _____ un livre au sujet de Marie Antoinette. (lire)

4. Tu n'_____ pas en français. (écrire)

5. Ils _____ très bien. (lire)

6. Vous _____ à votre mère que je suis là. (dire)

7. Tu _____ toujours cela. (dire)

Culture note

French schools

School life in France begins with **l'école maternelle,** the equivalent of kindergarten, nursery school, or preschool. It continues with **l'école primaire** *(elementary* or *primary school)* and **l'enseignement secondaire** *(secondary education).* **Le collège** is the equivalent of the American middle school or junior high school, followed by **le lycée** *([senior] high school).*

French children attend school on Mondays, Tuesdays, Thursdays, and Fridays, and only sometimes on Saturday mornings. Wednesdays and Sundays are days off, although some schools require half days on Wednesdays. The school day begins around 8 or 8:30 a.m. and finishes around 5 p.m., with a two-hour break for lunch. Children may join their families at home or eat in the cafeteria. Participation in various sports and on athletic teams is generally not part of the school day, and students therefore join the various sports teams and clubs available in their towns. It may be a surprising fact to Americans that cheerleaders do not exist in France, nor do pep rallies!

In the first level, or **classe terminale,** of high school, a student wishing to continue his or her education at a higher level must take a special exam called **le baccalauréat.** Upon successful completion of this rigorous exam, a student then has free access to any of more than eighty fine universities in France.

L'Université de Paris, founded in the 12th century by King Philippe-Auguste, is the oldest French university. The university attracted students from all over the world speaking Latin, the language of education and learned scholars; hence, the name of the area where the university campus is located is **le Quartier Latin** (*the Latin Quarter*).

ANSWERS
PRACTICE 1: 1. *I wasn't home when you called.* **2.** *Everyone was talking when the teacher entered.* **3.** *It was beautiful when they went to the park on Sunday.* **4.** *Who was selling the house?* **5.** *Somebody was looking at us.* **6.** *We used to sing a lot.*

PRACTICE 2: Pendant le week-end, j'étais très occupée. Mon mari et moi, nous avons décidé d'aller au parc parce qu'il faisait très beau. Nous sommes arrivés au parc vers midi. Quand nous marchions dans le jardin, nous regardions toutes les roses. C'était si joli! Au parc, il y avait beaucoup de monde. À deux heures, nous avons quitté le parc et nous sommes allés au musée. Il y avait une exposition des impressionnistes que je voulais voir. Nous regardions les belles sculptures quand nous avons rencontré nos amis Joelle et Robert. Après la visite au musée nous avons dîné dans un bon restaurant en ville.

PRACTICE 3: 1. lis; **2.** écris; **3.** lit; **4.** écris; **5.** lisent; **6.** dites; **7.** dis

---
Lesson 31 (sentences)

SENTENCE GROUP 1
EXPRESSIONS AU SUJET DU TRAVAIL (*Expressions about work*)

Je travaille très dur.	*I work very hard.*
Je m'entends bien avec mon patron/patronne.	*I get along well with my boss.*
Je travaille quarante heures par semaine.	*I work forty hours a week.*
C'est une compagnie dynamique.	*It's a dynamic company.*
Les gens où je travaille sont super.	*The people where I work are great.*
Je vous présente mon collaborateur.	*I present to you my coworker (collaborator).*
L'ambiance est relaxe.	*The atmosphere is relaxed.*
Je travaille pour cette société depuis deux mois.	*I've been working for this company for two months.*
J'ai travaillé pour cette société pendant deux ans.	*I worked for that company for two years.*

Voici mon bureau.	*Here is my office.*
Voici mon cubicule.	*Here is my cubicle.*
Je suis vendeur/vendeuse.	*I'm a salesman/saleswoman.*
Je voudrais parler au gérant/ gérante, s'il vous plaît.	*I'd like to speak to the store manager, please.*
Je suis en vacances.	*I'm on vacation.*
Vivement la fin de la journée!	*I can't wait for the end of the day!*

NOTES

Remember that the articles are not used in French in front of professions. The article has to be used if the noun of profession is preceded by an adjective.

Luc est vendeur.

Luc is a salesman.

Jeanne est vendeuse.

Jeanne is a saleswoman.

Luc est un bon vendeur.

Luc is a good salesman.

Jeanne est une bonne vendeuse.

Jeanne is a good saleswoman.

NUTS & BOLTS 1
USING DEPUIS *(since)*, POUR *(for)*, AND PENDANT *(during, for)*
Pour *(for)* is used to express a length of time taken to perform an action.

Je vais travailler pour cette société pour un an.

I'm going to work for this company for one year.

If a situation or action that began in the past is still ongoing, use **depuis** *(since)* to express the time elapsed in combination with the present tense. For instance, if someone asks if you are working at a company and you are still there, you might use the following sentence.

Je travaille pour cette société depuis un an.
I've been working for this company for a year. (And I am still there.)

If you no longer work there, use **pendant** *(for, during)* and keep the verb in the past tense.

J'ai travaillé pour cette société pendant un an.
I worked for that company for one year.

Note also the expression **depuis combien de temps**; it means *for how long,* and it is answered with the verb in the present tense.

Depuis combien de temps attend-il?
How long has he been waiting?

Il attend depuis dix minutes.
He's been waiting for ten minutes.

The expression **depuis quand** *(since when)* is also answered using the present tense.

Depuis quand travaillez-vous ici?
Since when have you been working here?

Je travaille ici depuis janvier.
I've been working here since January.

PRACTICE 1
Insert **depuis, pour,** or **pendant** as you consider appropriate.

1. Nous sommes ici _____ trois heures.

We've been here since three o'clock.

2. Mes amis vont aller au Canada _____ trois semaines.

My friends are going to Canada for three weeks.

3. J'étais en France _____ un mois.

I was in France for a month.

4. _____ combien de temps est-ce que tu habites à New York?

How long have you been living in New York?

5. Il travaille en ville _____ deux ans.

He's been working in town for two years.

6. _____ l'hiver, nous sommes allés en Floride.

During the winter, we went to Florida.

SENTENCE GROUP 2
LES EXPRESSIONS AU SUJET DE L'ÉCOLE *(Expressions about school)*

J'ai fait mes devoirs.	*I did my homework.*
J'ai fait une faute d'orthographe.	*I made a spelling mistake.*
J'assiste à un cours.	*I'm taking a class.*
Je vais à la cantine.	*I'm going to the cafeteria.*
Les enfants jouent dans la cour de récréation.	*The children play in the school yard/playground.*
Elle fait partie du cercle français.	*She's a member of the French club.*
Il faut apprendre le poème par cœur.	*It's necessary to learn the poem by heart.*
Je réussis à mes études.	*I'm doing well in my studies.*
Je passe mon examen de calcul.	*I'm taking my calculus test.*
J'ai réussi à mon examen.	*I did well on my test.*
J'ai échoué à mon examen.	*I failed my test.*
J'ai raté.	*I failed.*

Le football est une activité parascolaire.	*Soccer is an extracurricular activity.*
Il est doué pour les langues.	*He's gifted in languages.*
Je suis licencié/licenciée d'éducationphysique et sportive.	*I'm a graduate in physical education.*

NOTES

Be mindful of the false cognate **passer** in the expression **passer un examen;** it means *to take a test,* not *to pass a test.*

Les devoirs means *the homework,* one duty the students must fulfill to succeed! When used with another verb in the infinitive form, **devoir** is also a verb used to say what one must, should, or has to do. You learned its present tense forms earlier. The past participle of **devoir** is **dû/due** *(had to, owed [m./f.]).*

J'ai dû acheter une nouvelle voiture.

I had to buy a new car.

NUTS & BOLTS 2
THE SST VERBS

We have studied several important irregular verbs. There are certain other irregular verbs that may look like regular second group **-ir** verbs in the infinitive form but have certain irregularities. They are called SST verbs because they end in **-s,** **-s,** and **-t** in the singular forms of the present tense. Here are some common SST verbs.

dormir	*to sleep*
partir	*to leave*
sentir	*to feel*
servir	*to serve*
sortir	*to go out*

To obtain the **je, tu,** and **il/elle** forms of the present tense from an SST verb, the rule is to drop the last three letters of the infinitive form of the verb and add the *(silent)* endings **-s, -s,** or **-t.** For the **nous, vous,** and **ils/elles** forms, we take off the infinitive ending **-re** and add the usual plural present tense endings **-ons, -ez-,** and **-ent.** Look at the verb **partir** *(to leave).*

je pars	*I leave*	**nous partons**	*we leave*
tu pars	*you leave*	**vous partez**	*you leave*
il part	*he leaves*	**ils partent**	*they leave*
elle part	*she leaves*	**elles partent**	*they leave*

Now let's look at the verb **dormir** *(to sleep).*

je dors	*I sleep*	**nous dormons**	*we sleep*
tu dors	*you sleep*	**vous dormez**	*you sleep*
il dort	*he sleeps*	**ils dorment**	*they sleep*
elle dort	*she sleeps*	**elles dorment**	*they sleep*

Here is the verb **servir** *(to serve).*

je sers	*I serve*	**nous servons**	*we serve*
tu sers	*you serve*	**vous servez**	*you serve*
il sert	*he serves*	**ils servent**	*they serve*
elle sert	*she serves*	**elles servent**	*they serve*

Here are some examples of SST verbs in sentences.

Le samedi soir, je sors avec mes amis.
On Saturday night, I go out with my friends.

Quand partez-vous en vacances?
When are you leaving on vacation?

Elle sert les hors-d'œuvre.
She's serving the hors d'œuvres.

Il se sent un peu triste.
He feels a bit sad.

Mon mari dort toujours devant la télévision.
My husband always sleeps in front of the television.

The past participle of an SST verb ends in **-i**, e.g., **parti/partie**
(left) or **dormi/dormie** *(slept)*. Remember that **partir** *(to leave)* and
sortir *(to go out)* also form the compound past tense with the verb
être *(to be)*.

Marie est sortie avec Jean.
Marie went out with Jean.

Ils sont partis de bonne heure.
They left early.

The other SST verbs are conjugated with **avoir** in the past tense.

Vous avez bien dormi hier soir?
Did you sleep well last night?

J'ai servi le dessert avec le café.
I served the dessert with coffee.

PRACTICE 2

Conjugate the verbs in the following sentences in the present tense. Note which verbs may be SST verbs.

1. Les filles _____ dans leur chambre. (dormir)

2. À quelle heure est-ce que nous _____? (partir)

3. Ils _____ le livre. (finir)

4. Marie, _____-elle avec Jean? (sortir)

5. Vous _____ le dîner. (servir)

6. Je _____ à mes examens. (réussir)

Another irregular verb, similar to the **-re** and SST verbs, is **mettre** *(to put, to put on)*. However, note that there is only one **t** in the singular forms of the verb.

je mets	*I put*	**nous mettons**	*we put*
tu mets	*you put*	**vous mettez**	*you put*
il met	*he puts*	**ils mettent**	*they put*
elle met	*she puts*	**elles mettent**	*they put*

Je mets les cahiers sur mon bureau.

I put the notebooks on my desk.

Les élèves mettent leurs devoirs sur le bureau du professeur.

The pupils put their homework on the teacher's desk.

The past participle of **mettre** is **mis/mise** *(put)*.

Hier soir il faisait froid, alors j'ai mis mon manteau.

Last night it was cold, so I put on my coat.

Nous avons mis les livres sur l'étagère à la bibliothèque.
We put the books on the shelf at the library.

PRACTICE 3

Fill in the blanks with the correct present tense forms of the verb **mettre** *(to put)*.

1. Où _____-vous vos notes?

2. Tu ne _____ pas ton pull-over.

3. Est-ce qu'elle _____ le couvert?

4. Mes enfants _____ leurs devoirs sur la table.

5. Je _____ ma composition dans mon cahier.

Language link

If you are looking to further your knowledge of the French culture, there are several magazines to which you can subscribe that provide current information about the Francophone world. *France Magazine* is a publication that comes out four times a year with in-depth articles and striking photographs providing authoritative coverage of life in France. You can go to the website for more information: www.francemagazine.org. Another interesting magazine is *France Today*, the magazine of French culture and travel. You can find more information at www.francetoday.com.

ANSWERS

PRACTICE 1: 1. depuis; **2.** pour; **3.** pendant; **4.** Depuis; **5.** depuis; **6.** Pendant

PRACTICE 2: 1. dorment; **2.** partons; **3.** finissent; **4.** sort; **5.** servez; **6.** réussis

PRACTICE 3: 1. mettez; **2.** mets; **3.** met; **4.** mettent; **5.** mets

CONVERSATION 1

Two friends, Denise and Natalie, haven't seen each other in more than a year. They meet at a café in town to catch up on each other's lives.

Natalie: Quel plaisir de te revoir! Qu'est-ce qui se passe dans ta vie?

Denise: Bonjour, ma chérie! J'ai beaucoup de choses à te dire! Je viens de commencer un nouveau travail comme hôtesse de l'air.

Natalie: Ah bon, je croyais que tu travaillais aux Galeries Lafayette.

Denise: J'étais au magasin pendant un an, et j'ai changé de carrière.

Natalie: C'est formidable! Probablement tu as l'occasion de voyager un peu partout, n'est-ce pas?

Denise: Oui, et la compagnie est fantastique. Les gens sont sympathiques. Eh bien, dis-moi ce que tu fais en ce moment. Tu travaillais dans un restaurant du quartier, je crois.

Natalie: Oui j'ai travaillé au restaurant pendant deux ans et maintenant, je suis le chef du restaurant!

Denise: C'est vrai! Tu aimais toujours faire la cuisine. Tu faisais toutes sortes de plats superbes pour nous!

Natalie: Voici ma carte de visite. La prochaine fois que tu es ici, viens dîner!

Natalie: *How great to see you again! What's going on in your life?*

Denise: *Hi, sweetie! I have so much to tell you! I just started a new job as a flight attendant.*

Natalie:	Ah, I thought you were working at the Galeries Lafayette.		
Denise:	I was working at the store for a year, and then I changed careers.		
Natalie:	That's wonderful! You probably have the opportunity to travel everywhere, don't you?		
Denise:	Yes, and the company is fantastic. The people are friendly. So, tell me what you're doing these days. You were working in a restaurant in the area, I believe.		
Natalie:	Yes, I worked at the restaurant for two years, and now I am the chef of the restaurant!		
Denise:	That's right! You always liked to cook. You used to make all kinds of great dishes for us!		
Natalie:	Here's my business card. Next time you're here, come have dinner!		

NUTS & BOLTS 1
THE VERBS SAVOIR (*to know*) AND CONNAÎTRE (*to know; to be acquainted with*)

Here is the verb **savoir**.

je sais	*I know*	**nous savons**	*we know*
tu sais	*you know*	**vous savez**	*you know*
il sait	*he knows*	**ils savent**	*they know*
elle sait	*she knows*	**elles savent**	*they know*

The past participle of savoir is **su** *(known)*.

Comment a-t-il su?
How did he know?

Elle a su répondre aux questions.
She knew how to answer all questions.

Here is the verb **connaître** in the present tense. The verb **paraître** *(to appear)* is conjugated the same way.

je connais	*I know*	nous connaissons	*we know*
tu connais	*you know*	vous connaissez	*you know*
il connaît	*he knows*	ils connaissent	*they know*
elle connaît	*she knows*	elles connaissent	*they know*

Note the accented **î** in the infinitive form and **il/elle** form. The past participle of **connaître** is **connu/connue**.

Est-ce que tu as connu cet homme?
Did you know this man?

The verbs **savoir** and **connaître** both mean *to know*. However, they are used in different ways. The verb **savoir** is used to mean the possession of any kind of knowledge, and it appears by itself, in front of a verb or a subordinate sentence.

Je ne sais pas.
I don't know.

Il sait nager.
He knows how to swim.

Je sais où il est.
I know where he is.

Je sais pourquoi j'ai raté.
I know why I failed.

The verb **connaître,** on the other hand, expresses familiarity with a person or thing.

Je connais bien Denise.
I know Denise well.

Je connais les chansons d'Edith Piaf.
I know the songs of Edith Piaf.

Elle connaît très bien ce nouveau restaurant.
She knows this new restaurant very well.

PRACTICE 1
Select the verb that best completes the sentence.

1. Est-ce que tu (connais, sais) pourquoi il est en retard?

2. Ils (savent, connaissent) jouer au football.

3. Je ne (sais, connais) pas la sœur de Marie.

4. (Savez-vous, Connaissez-vous) l'histoire de Cendrillon?

5. Je ne (sais, connais) pas si nous irons en France.

CONVERSATION 2
Christophe and Claude are college roommates discussing their studies.

Christophe:	**Je suis crevé ce soir! J'avais un tas de devoirs à faire pour mon cours d'histoire ancienne. Tu es sorti avec ta petite amie ce soir?**
Claude:	Franchement non. Pendant que tu faisais tes devoirs, nous étions à la bibliothèque en train d'étudier pour notre examen de biologie demain matin.
Christophe:	**Je croyais que tu avais ton examen de biologie ce matin.**
Claude:	Non, ce matin, j'avais des difficultés à réussir à mon examen de maths.
Christophe:	**Tu as reçu une bonne note?**

Claude:	Non, je pense que j'ai raté! Tous ces examens, je n'en peux plus. Ma pauvre tête!
Christophe:	Tu peux le dire! Dis, tu veux aller prendre un café avec moi?
Claude:	Non, je reste ici au dortoir pour continuer à étudier. Je vais voir si je peux repasser l'examen un autre jour.
Christophe:	Bon courage, mon cher ami. Encore un examen. Tu es un homme brave!
Claude:	Zut alors, je déteste les examens!

Christophe:	*I am beat tonight! I had tons of homework for my ancient history course. Did you go out with your girlfriend tonight?*
Claude:	*Frankly, no. While you were doing your homework, we were at the library, in the midst of studying for our biology exam tomorrow morning.*
Christophe:	*I thought you had your bio exam this morning.*
Claude:	*No, this morning I had trouble trying to pass my math test.*
Christophe:	*Did you receive a good grade?*
Claude:	*No, I think that I failed. All these exams—I can't take it anymore. My poor head!*
Christophe:	*You can say that again! Hey, you want to go get a coffee with me?*
Claude:	*No, I'm staying in the dorm to continue studying. I'm going to see if I can retake the test another day.*
Claude:	*Have courage, my dear friend. Another test. You are a brave man!*
Christophe:	*Darn it; I hate tests!*

NUTS & BOLTS 2
POSITIONS OF CERTAIN ADJECTIVES

We know that most adjectives in French follow the noun, except for the BAGS adjectives. Other adjectives can stand either before or after the noun they modify. Their position, however, affects their meaning. Here are some examples.

un cher ami
a dear friend

un complet cher
an expensive suit

l'ancien patron/patronne
the former boss

une table ancienne
an old (antique) table

mon vieil ami
my old friend

mon ami vieux
my friend who is old

une pauvre amie
an unfortunate friend

une personne pauvre
a poor person

ma propre voiture
my own car

ma voiture propre
my clean car

un brave homme
a good man

un homme brave
a courageous man

PRACTICE 2
Write the letter that corresponds to the number.

1. **ma maison propre**	a. *my former husband*
2. **les pays pauvres**	b. *a good woman*
3. **ma propre maison**	c. *my expensive car*
4. **ma chère voiture**	d. *my clean house*
5. **ma voiture chère**	e. *a brave, courageous woman*
6. **une femme brave**	f. *my dear car*
7. **mon ancien mari**	g. *my own house*
8. **ma chaise ancienne**	h. *my old chair*
9. **les pauvres gens**	i. *the poor countries*
10. **une brave femme**	j. *the poor, unfortunate people*

Tip!

Writing is a good way to reinforce vocabulary. To help you remember the vocabulary related to work and jobs, make a list in French of the professions that you and your family members have or may have had in the past. If you put together a family album, as was suggested in Unit 2, you may want to include this list there as well.

Next, for fun, write down a list in French of the professions or jobs that you and your family members would prefer or consider doing instead.

ANSWERS
PRACTICE 1: 1. sais; **2.** savent; **3.** connais; **4.** Connaissez-vous; **5.** sais

PRACTICE 2: 1. d; **2.** i; **3.** g; **4.** f; **5.** c; **6.** e; **7.** a; **8.** h; **9.** j; **10.** b

au travail	*at work*
au bureau	*in (at) the office*
gagner de l'argent	*to earn money*
travailler dur	*to work hard*
l'homme au foyer/ la femme au foyer	*homemaker (male/female)*
Je réussis à mes études.	*I'm doing well in my studies.*
Je passe mon examen.	*I'm taking my test.*
J'ai réussi à mon examen.	*I did well on my test.*
J'étais en France pendant un mois.	*I was in France for a month.*
J'attends depuis dix minutes.	*I've been waiting for ten minutes.*
Je vais en France pour deux semaines.	*I'm going to France for two weeks.*
Je sors avec mes amis.	*I'm going out with my friends.*
Quand j'étais jeune, j'avais un chat.	*When I was young, I used to have a cat.*
Je mangeais.	*I was eating.*
Je sais./Je connais.	*I know.*

UNIT 9
Sports and leisure

Vocabulary for **les sports** (sports) and **les loisirs** (leisure activities) will be presented in this unit so that you will be able to talk about some of the things that you enjoy doing in your free time.

———————— Lesson 33 (words) ————————

LES SPORTS (Sports)

le football	soccer
le football américain	football
le hockey sur glace	ice hockey
le patinage sur glace	ice-skating
la natation	swimming
la gymnastique	gymnastics
l'athlétisme	track
l'équitation	horseback riding
l'alpinisme	mountain climbing
la pêche	fishing
la musculation	bodybuilding, strength training
le golf	golf
le cyclisme	cycling
la chasse	hunting
le ski, le ski nautique	skiing, water-skiing
le surf, le surf sur neige	surfing, snowboarding

NUTS & BOLTS 1
USES OF THE VERB JOUER (to play)

The verb **jouer** is followed by either the preposition **de** or the preposition **à**. **Jouer à** is used with sports and games, while **jouer**

de is used with musical instruments. Here are some examples of expressions with **jouer à.**

Tu joues au base-ball.
You play baseball.

Mon mari joue au golf.
My husband plays golf.

Nous jouons aux cartes avec nos voisins.
We play cards with our neighbors.

Je joue au tennis.
I play tennis.

Here are examples with **jouer de.**

Elle joue du piano.
She plays the piano.

Jouez-vous de la guitare?
Do you play the guitar?

Ma mère jouait du violon.
My mother used to play the violin.

PRACTICE 1
Use the correct form of the verb **jouer** followed either by the preposition **de** or **à** according to the context. (Be mindful of the verb tense needed, and remember the rule for contractions with **à** and **de.**)

1. Tu _____ base-ball aujourd'hui?

2. Mes amis _____ guitare ce soir.

3. Quand j' étais jeune, je _____ basket-ball.

4. Il _____ piano quand il avait six ans.

5. Nous _____ tennis maintenant.

WORD LIST 2
LES LOISIRS *(Leisure time activities)*

les passe-temps *(m.)*	*hobbies*
les échecs *(m.)*	*chess*
les dames	*checkers*
le divertissement	*entertainment*
la pièce	*play*
le théâtre	*theater*
le ballet	*ballet*
le cinéma	*movies*
la couture	*sewing*
le tricot	*knitting*
les vacances *(f.)*	*vacation*
le camping	*camping*
le yoga	*yoga*
le cours de danse	*dance class*
la lecture	*reading*
la peinture	*painting*

NUTS & BOLTS 2
THE VERBE POUVOIR *(can, to be able)*
Here is a good verb to use when talking about things you can and cannot do.

je peux	*I can*	nous pouvons	*we can*
tu peux	*you can*	vous pouvez	*you can*
il peut	*he can*	ils peuvent	*they can*
elle peut	*she can*	elles peuvent	*they can*

Note that the verb **pouvoir** is quite often used with an infinitive to express things that one is able to do.

Je peux jouer de la guitare.
I can play guitar.

Marc peut parler trois langues.
Marc can speak three languages.

Tu peux danser.
You can dance.

Pouvez-vous aller au cinéma avec nous?
Can you go to the movies with us?

PRACTICE 2
Translate the following sentences into French.

1. *She can sing.*
2. *They are able to go with us.*
3. *Can you play tennis today?* (Tip: Use inversion.)
4. *I can't sleep.*
5. *We can hear the music.*

Language link

Horseback riding in France

Horseback riding is a rather popular sport in France. The Camargue region in the south of France is famous for its beautiful wild horses that run through the marshes. French cowboys and cowgirls **(les gardians/les gardiennes)** will often capture some of these horses and train them. If you love horses, you may want to check out videos about Camargue, its horses, and the **randonnées à cheval en Camargue** *(horseback riding tours in Camargue)* at www.dailymotion.com.

ANSWERS

PRACTICE 1: 1. joues au; **2.** jouent de la; **3.** jouais au; **4.** jouait du; **5.** jouons au

PRACTICE 2: 1. Elle peut chanter. **2.** Ils/Elles peuvent aller avec nous. **3.** Peux-tu/Pouvez-vous jouer au tennis aujourd'hui? **4.** Je ne peux pas dormir. **5.** Nous pouvons entendre la musique.

––––––––––––– Lesson 34 (phrases) –––––––––––––

Here are some useful phrases when you want to talk about sports.

PHRASE LIST 1
DES PHRASES POUR LES SPORTS *(Phrases for sports)*

jouer un match	*to play a game*
faire du sport	*to play a sport*
gagner un match	*to win a game*
perdre un match	*to lose a game*
le spectateur/la spectatrice	*spectator*
la fin du match	*end of the game*
le score final	*the final score*
donner un coup de pied	*to kick*
la première/deuxième/troisième base	*first/second/third base*
l'équipe de rugby	*rugby team*
plonger dans la piscine	*to dive in the pool*
courir le marathon	*to run the marathon*
sauter une haie	*to jump a hurdle*
monter à cheval	*to go horseback riding*
la planche à roulettes, le skateboard	*skateboard*
la course automobile	*car racing*

NUTS & BOLTS 1
COMPOUND TENSES: FUTURE PERFECT

In Unit 9, you will learn three new compound tenses. You have already learned one compound tense, the compound past tense, which is formed with the present tense forms of a helping verb, either **avoir** *(to have)* or **être** *(to be)*, followed by the past participle. The three other compound tenses you will learn in this unit are formed in the same way, but the helping verbs **avoir** and **être** are in different tenses. Let's begin with the future perfect.

The future perfect is formed with the future tense forms of the helping verb followed by the past participle. Notice how we form the future perfect of the verb **parler** *(to speak)*.

j'aurai parlé	*I will have spoken*	**nous aurons parlé**	*we will have spoken*
tu auras parlé	*you will have spoken*	**vous aurez parlé**	*you will have spoken*
il aura parlé	*he will have spoken*	**ils auront parlé**	*they will have spoken*
elle aura parlé	*she will have spoken*	**elles auront parlé**	*they will have spoken*

Here are the future perfect forms of the **-ir** verb **finir** *(to finish)*.

j'aurai fini	*I will have finished*	**nous aurons fini**	*we will have finished*
tu auras fini	*you will have finished*	**vous aurez fini**	*you will have finished*
il aura fini	*he will have finished*	**ils auront fini**	*they will have finished*
elle aura fini	*she will have finished*	**elles auront fini**	*they will have finished*

Now, look at an example of the **-re** verb **vendre** *(to sell)*.

j'aurai vendu	*I will have sold*	**nous aurons vendu**	*we will have sold*
tu auras vendu	*you will have sold*	**vous aurez vendu**	*you will have sold*
il aura vendu	*he will have sold*	**ils auront vendu**	*they will have sold*
elle aura vendu	*she will have sold*	**elles auront vendu**	*they will have sold*

Here is the irregular verb **faire** *(to do)* in the future perfect.

j'aurai fait	*I will have made (done)*	**nous aurons fait**	*we will have made (done)*
tu auras fait	*you will have made*	**vous aurez fait**	*you will have made*
il aura fait	*he will have made*	**ils auront fait**	*they will have made*
elle aura fait	*she will have made*	**elles auront fait**	*they will have made*

Remember that verbs of motion and change of state are formed with **être** as the helping verb. Here is an example of the future perfect of the verb **aller** *(to go)*.

je serai allé/e	*I will have gone*	**nous serons allés/es**	*we will have gone*
tu seras allé/e	*you will have gone*	**vous serez allé/es**	*you will have gone*
il sera allé	*he will have gone*	**ils seront allés**	*they will have gone*
elle sera allée	*she will have gone*	**elles seront allées**	*they will have gone*

Remember that past participles of verbs conjugated with **être** must agree in number and gender with the subject.

The future perfect is used to speak of an action or state of being in the future that will precede another action in the future. Here's one of the best examples: You are planning a party. The guests are late and you keep picking at the hors d'œuvres. By the time your guests arrive, you "will have eaten all of the food when they arrive."

Tu auras mangé toute la nourriture quand j'arriverai.
You will have eaten all of the food when I arrive.

Here are more examples of sentences in the future perfect.

Tu auras commencé la leçon quand j'entrerai dans la classe.
You will have begun the lesson when I enter the classroom.

Nous aurons pris le livre avant rentrer à la maison.
We will have taken the book before coming home.

Elles auront fini leurs devoirs avant de regarder la télévision.
They will have finished their homework before they watch television.

Il sera parti quand la police sera là.

He will have left when the police get there.

PRACTICE 1

Fill in the blanks with the correct future perfect form of the verbs in parentheses.

1. Mes amis _____ avant six heures. (finir)

2. J'_____ dans le jardin quand il fera beau. (jouer)

3. Nous n'_____ pas _____ plusieurs jours. (attendre)

4. Tu _____ déjà _____ quand mon père viendra. (partir)

PHRASE LIST 2

DES EXPRESSIONS AVEC LES PASSE-TEMPS *(Expressions with leisure time activites)*

Here are some phrases that you will need when talking about hobbies and leisure time activities.

les activités de plein air	*outdoor activities*
aller à la plage	*to go to the beach*
prendre un bain de soleil	*to sunbathe*
faire un château de sable	*to make a sand castle*
faire de la plongée sous-marine	*to go scuba diving*
faire du jogging	*to go jogging*
rester en forme	*to stay in shape*
faire un pique-nique	*to go on a picnic*
faire du vélo d'appartement	*to ride the stationary bike*
écouter le lecteur de CD	*to listen to the CD player*
jouer à cache-cache	*to play hide and seek*
lancer les dés	*to roll the dice*
la comédie de situation	*sitcom*

| le feuilleton télévisé | *TV series* |
| passer du temps avec des amis | *to spend time with friends* |

NUTS & BOLTS 2
THE PAST CONDITIONAL

The past conditional is formed in the same way as the future perfect, except that the conditional of the helping verb is used with the past participle. Here is an example of a Group 1 verb in the past conditional: **parler** *(to speak)*.

j'aurais parlé	*I would have spoken*	nous aurions parlé	*we would have spoken*
tu aurais parlé	*you would have spoken*	vous auriez parlé	*you would have spoken*
il aurait parlé	*he would have spoken*	ils auraient parlé	*they would have spoken*
elle aurait parlé	*she would have spoken*	elles auraient parlé	*they would have spoken*

Here is an example of a Group 2 verb in the past conditional: **finir** *(to finish)*.

j'aurais fini	*I would have finished*	nous aurions fini	*we would have finished*
tu aurais fini	*you would have finished*	vous auriez fini	*you would have finished*
il aurait fini	*he would have finished*	ils auraient fini	*they would have finished*
elle aurait fini	*she would have finished*	elles auraient fini	*they would have finished*

Here is an example of a Group 3 verb in the past conditional:
vendre *(to sell).*

j'aurais vendu	*I would have sold*	nous aurions vendu	*we would have sold*
tu aurais vendu	*you would have sold*	vous auriez vendu	*you would have sold*
il aurait vendu	*he would have sold*	ils auraient vendu	*they would have sold*
elle aurait vendu	*she would have sold*	elles auraient vendu	*they would have sold*

Here is the verb **faire** *(to do, to make)* in the past conditional.

j'aurais fait	*I would have done*	nous aurions fait	*we would have done*
tu aurais fait	*you would have done*	vous auriez fait	*you would have done*
il aurait fait	*he would have done*	ils auraient fait	*they would have done*
elle aurait fait	*she would have have done*	elles auraient fait	*they would have done*

Remember that verbs of motion and change of state are formed with **être** as the helping verb. Here is an example of the past conditional of the verb **aller** *(to go).*

je serais allé/e	*I would have gone*	nous serions allés/es	*we would have gone*
tu serais allé/e	*you would have gone*	vous seriez allé/es	*you would have gone*
il serait allé	*he would have gone*	ils seraient allés	*they would have gone*
elle serait allée	*she would have gone*	elles seraient allées	*they would have gone*

Here are some examples of sentences using the past conditional tense.

Nous aurions joué au tennis si nous avions eu le temps.
We would have played tennis if we had had the time.

J'aurais fait un gâteau pour son anniversaire si j'avais été à la maison.
I would have made a cake for his birthday if I had been home.

Ils seraient entrés s'ils avaient eu la clé.
They would have entered if they had had the key.

Vous seriez resté à la maison si elle avait été là.
You would have stayed home if she had been there.

Note that the tense used in the subordinate clauses is called the pluperfect. You'll learn more about this tense in the next lesson.

PRACTICE 2
Translate the following sentences from English into French.

1. She would have gone.
2. We would have finished.

3. I should have studied.

4. You *(infml.)* should have waited.

5. They would have understood.

Tip!

To help you reinforce the new compound tenses, you may want to create a study chart with the compound past tense as your starting point. For other compound tenses, then you only need to change the tense of the helping verbs **avoir** or **être**. The past participle remains the same.

ANSWERS

PRACTICE 1: 1. auront fini; **2.** aurai joué; **3.** aurons attendu; **4.** seras parti

PRACTICE 2: 1. Elle serait allée. **2.** Nous aurions fini. **3.** J'aurais dû étudier. **4.** Tu aurais dû attendre. **5.** Ils/elles auraient compris.

—————— Lesson 35 (sentences) ——————

SENTENCE GROUP 1
DES PHRASES UTILES POUR LES SPORTS *(Useful sentences for sports)*

Nous allons à une station de sports d'hiver.	*We're going to a ski resort.*
Je porte mes patins à glace.	*I'm wearing my ice skates.*
Je vais à la piste pour débutants.	*I'm going to the bunny slope.*
Les enfants font un bonhomme de neige.	*The kids are making a snowman.*
Je suis un supporteur./ Je suis une supportrice.	*I'm a fan.*

J'aime les publicités de la mi-temps.	*I like the commercials at halftime.*
Ce parcours de golf est difficile.	*This golf course is difficult.*
Je cherche un partenaire.	*I'm looking for a partner.*
Il aime smasher la balle quand il joue au volley-ball.	*He likes to spike the ball when he plays volleyball.*
Je présente mon cheval à un concours.	*I'm showing my horse in a competition.*
Les enfants doivent porter un casque pour monter à bicyclette.	*Children must wear a helmet to go bike riding.*
Ils jouent au ping-pong.	*They are playing table tennis.*
Voici ma raquette.	*Here's my racket.*
Je m'amuse.	*I'm having a good time.*
On ne doit pas tricher.	*You should not cheat.*

NOTES

The expression **je m'amuse** *(I'm having a good time)* is an excellent expression to use. It also can mean *I am enjoying myself* or *I am having fun.* Also note that the verb **porter** means *to wear.*

NUTS & BOLTS 1
THE PLUPERFECT TENSE

In the previous lesson, we learned the future perfect and past conditional tenses. Now, let's take a look at the last compound tense, which is the pluperfect tense. The pluperfect is formed by using the imperfect of the helping verb followed by the past participle. Here is the pluperfect of the verb **parler** *(to speak).*

j'avais parlé	*I had spoken*	nous avions parlé	*we had spoken*
tu avais parlé	*you had spoken*	vous aviez parlé	*you had spoken*

il avait parlé	*he had spoken*	ils avaient parlé	*they had spoken*
elle avait parlé	*she had spoken*	elles avaient parlé	*they had spoken*

Here is the verb **finir** *(to finish)* in the pluperfect.

j'avais fini	*I had finished*	nous avions fini	*we had finished*
tu avais fini	*you had finished*	vous aviez fini	*you had finished*
il avait fini	*he had finished*	ils avaient fini	*they had finished*
elle avait fini	*she had finished*	elles avaient fini	*they had finished*

Here is the verb **vendre** *(to sell)* in the pluperfect.

j'avais vendu	*I had sold*	nous avions vendu	*we had sold*
tu avais vendu	*you had sold*	vous aviez vendu	*you had sold*
il avait vendu	*he had sold*	ils avaient vendu	*they had sold*
elle avait vendu	*she had sold*	elles avaient vendu	*they had sold*

Here is the irregular verb **faire** *(to do, to make)* in the pluperfect.

j'avais fait	*I had done*	**nous avions fait**	*we had done*
tu avais fait	*you had done*	**vous aviez fait**	*you had done*
il avait fait	*he had done*	**ils avaient fait**	*they had done*
elle avait fait	*she had done*	**elles avaient fait**	*they had done*

Remember that the verbs of motion and change of state need the verb **être** in compound tenses.

j'étais allé/e	*I had gone*	**nous étions allés/es**	*we had gone*
tu étais allé/e	*you had gone*	**vous étiez allé/e/es**	*you had gone*
il était allé	*he had gone*	**ils étaient allés**	*they had gone*
elle était allée	*she had gone*	**elles étaient allées**	*they had gone*

In English, this tense is translated by the word *had* followed by the past participle. The pluperfect is used in sentences referring to two actions in the past. The one action that has been completed or finished first is in the pluperfect tense.

Le train était parti quand nous sommes arrivés à la gare.
The train had left when we arrived at the station.

In the example above, two actions took place in the past. The first action, the leaving of the train, occurred before the action of our arrival. Here are more examples of sentences in the pluperfect.

Le garçon avait gardé la monnaie.
The waiter had kept the change.

Ils avaient fini un bon match.
They had finished a good game.

Aviez-vous pu le faire?
Had you been able to do it?

Nous avions eu un rendez-vous.
We had had an appointment.

Elle était partie à midi.
She had left at noon.

PRACTICE 1
Fill in the blanks with the right forms of the missing helping verbs.

1. j'_____ pris *(I had taken)*

2. il _____ sorti *(he had gone out)*

3. vous _____ été *(you had been)*

4. ils _____ partis *(they had left)*

5. tu _____ retourné *(you had returned)*

6. elles _____ répondu *(they had answered)*

7. nous _____ fait *(we had done)*

8. elle _____ bu *(she had drunk)*

9. j'_____ voulu *(I had wanted)*

10. vous _____ mangé *(you had eaten)*

PRACTICE 2

Practice all three compound tenses by choosing the correct translation from the choices below.

1. il était resté

   a. *he stayed*

   b. *he had stayed*

   c. *he will have stayed*

2. j'aurai marché

   a. *I will have walked*

   b. *I had walked*

   c. *I should have walked*

3. vous aviez fini

   a. *you finished*

   b. *you should have finished*

   c. *you had finished*

4. ils seraient entrés

   a. *they will have entered*

   b. *they would have entered*

   c. *they had entered*

5. nous aurons préparé

   a. *we will have prepared*

   b. *we could have prepared*

   c. *we had prepared*

6. tu avais connu

   a. *you had known*

   b. *you will have known*

   c. *you should have known*

7. il avait dansé

   a. *he will have danced*

   b. *he should have danced*

   c. *he had danced*

8. j'aurai fait

   a. *I should have made*

   b. *I will have made*

   c. *I had made*

SENTENCE GROUP 2
ENCORE DES EXPRESSIONS POUR LES PASSE-TEMPS (*More expressions related to hobbies and leisure activities*)

J'adore les tableaux des impressionnistes.	*I love the impressionist paintings.*
Nous allons à l'opéra de temps en temps.	*We go to the opera from time to time.*
Mon neveu est danseur classique (de ballet).	*My nephew is a ballet dancer.*
Je suis maître nageur.	*I'm a lifeguard.*
Ils aiment les excursions en autocar.	*They like bus tours.*
Nous avons visité les châteaux de la Loire.	*We visited the castles of the Loire Valley.*

J'aime bien passer du temps avec des amis.	I like to spend time with friends.
J'aime bien bricoler.	I like to tinker.
Je collectionne les papillons.	I collect butterflies.
Elle porte un bikini.	She's wearing a bikini.
Il fait du surf sans planche.	He's bodysurfing.
J'aime bien me reposer.	I like to relax.

NOTES

You may use the verb **visiter** *(to visit)* to refer to visiting places, cities, monuments, and so on.

Je visite l'Arc de Triomphe.
I'm visiting the Arc de Triomphe.

However, when you wish to say that you are visiting someone, you must use the verb **rendre visite** *(to pay a visit)* followed by the preposition **à** *(to).*

Je rends visite à ma tante Nancy.
I'm visiting my aunt Nancy.

NUTS & BOLTS 2
THE VERB VOIR *(to see)*

The verb **voir** is an irregular verb. See its present tense forms below.

je vois	*I see*	**nous voyons**	*we see*
tu vois	*you see*	**vous voyez**	*you see*
il voit	*he sees*	**ils voient**	*they see*
elle voit	*she sees*	**elles voient**	*they see*

The expression **je vois** *(I see)* is used very commonly in French conversation in the same way as in English.

The past participle of the verb **voir** is **vu/e** *(seen)*. The future and conditional stem for **voir** is irregular: **verr-**. Here are some examples with the verb **voir** *(to see)*.

Je vois le score du match.
I see the score for the match.

Hier soir, j'ai vu un film extraordinaire.
Last night I saw an extraordinary film.

Je te verrai demain.
I'll see you tomorrow.

PRACTICE 3
Fill in the blanks with the correct form of the verb **voir.**

1. Nous _____ le problème.

2. Elle _____ Paul le vendredi.

3. Ils _____ beaucoup de sculptures au musée.

4. _____-tu ce que je vois?

5. Vous _____ les acteurs sur la scène.

Culture note

Must-see places

If you have the opportunity to travel abroad, and France is one of your destinations, here is some background information on Paris and the surrounding area with some of the suggested highlights that should be on your list of places to see.

Paris, originally known as **Lutèce** *(Lutetia)*, received its name from an ancient Gaelic tribe called the **Parisi.** It was originally settled more than 2,000 years ago on the **île de la Cité** *(city island)*, known as "the cradle of Paris." **La Ville Lumière** *(the City of Lights)* is the political, economic, and cultural center of France.

Here's a sampling of some of the most popular tourist sites.

La Tour Eiffel *(The Eiffel Tower)* was constructed of steel by Alexandre Gustave Eiffel for the World's Fair of 1889. It is approximately 1,109 feet high and serves as a radio and television transmitter. It is also a world-known tourist site open to visitors every day of the year with long hours. You can climb the stairs or take the glass elevator to the top. There are three levels open to visitors. For exciting photos, information, and a virtual tour, go to www.tour-eiffel.fr/teiffel/fr/.

L'Arc de Triomphe *(The Arc of Triumph)*, built to commemorate the victories of **Napoléon** *(Napoleon)*, is situated at the **Place Charles de Gaulle.** This public square formerly had the name of the **Place de l'Étoile** *(Square of the Star)* because twelve avenues converge under the Arc. The Arc stands 162 feet tall. The Tomb of the Unknown Soldier lies beneath the Arc, where the first eternal flame burns in honor of all departed soldiers.

Le Musée du Louvre *(The Louvre Museum)*, initially a fortress, was built and expanded over the centuries into a glorious residence of the French kings. Today it is the largest museum in the world, with masterpieces such as **La Joconde** *(The Mona Lisa)*, the **Vénus de Milo** *(Venus de Milo)*, and the Winged Victory of Samothrace. In 1989, a glass pyramid designed by the Chinese-American architect Ieoh Ming Pei was built to serve as new entrance to the always crowded museum.

Le Centre National d'Art et de Culture Georges-Pompidou *(George Pompidou National Art and Culture Center)*, also known as **Centre Pompidou** or **Centre Beaubourg,** after the district of Paris it is located in, is a futuristic industrial-style structure housing a museum of modern art, a large library, a center for industrial creation, and an institute for musical experimentation. It opened its doors in 1977.

Across the Seine river from the Louvre is **Le Musée d'Orsay** *(The Orsay Museum)*, a former train station transformed into a museum in 1986. It houses many of the realist and impressionist works of famous artists, such as Manet, Degas, Van Gogh, and Monet.

When visiting Paris, don't miss **La Cathédrale Notre-Dame de Paris** *(The Notre Dame Cathedral)*, built on **La Île de la Cité** *(The City Island)* on the Seine, in the center of Paris. The construction of the cathedral was begun in 1163 and took more than 100 years to complete. It is famous for its stained-glass windows and beautiful gothic architecture.

There are also many parks and gardens to visit in Paris if you like to spend time outdoors.

If you care to venture beyond Paris, there are excursions to the Loire Valley, where you will find more than one hundred **châteaux** *(castles)* with beautiful views and historic sites.

ANSWERS

PRACTICE 1: 1. avais; 2. était; 3. aviez; 4. étaient; 5. étais; 6. avaient; 7. avions; 8. avait; 9. avais; 10. aviez

PRACTICE 2: 1. b; 2. a; 3. c; 4. b; 5. a; 6. a; 7. c; 8. b

PRACTICE 3: 1. voyons; 2. voit; 3. voient; 4. Vois; 5. voyez

——————— Lesson 36 (conversations) ———————

CONVERSATION 1

Marc and Paul are discussing the Super Bowl football game and the party that was held at Marc's house.

> **Marc:** Tiens, mon mec. Tu n'es pas venu regarder le match de football, le plus important de l'année, le «Super Bowl». Qu'est-ce qui est arrivé?

Paul: Je suis désolé. J'aurais voulu venir si j'avais eu le temps, mais j'ai dû finir du travail chez moi.

Marc: Tu aurais dû voir le match. C'était extraordinaire, surtout quand ils ont marqué le premier but.

Paul: J'ai vu seulement une moitié du match.

Marc: Laquelle?

Paul: La deuxième moitié, quand le joueur a envoyé le ballon très loin et notre équipe a gagné!

Marc: Est-ce que tu avais regardé les publicités à la mi-temps? Elles étaient si drôles!

Paul: Pendant que je travaillais, j'ai vu la publicité qui montrait tous les grands chevaux qui parlaient.

Marc: De toute façon, il y a toujours le match de basket-ball dimanche prochain et cette fois, tout le monde vient chez toi!

Marc: *Hey, buddy. You did not come to see the most important football game of the year, the Super Bowl. What happened?*

Paul: *I'm sorry. I would have wanted to come if I had had the time, but I had to finish work at my house.*

Marc: *You should have seen the game. It was really great, especially when they scored the first touchdown.*

Paul: *I saw one half of the game.*

Marc: *Which one?*

Paul: *The second half, when the player kicked the ball really far and our team won!*

Marc: *Did you see the commercials at halftime? They were really so funny!*

Paul: *While I was working, I saw the commercial with the big horses that were talking.*

Marc: *At any rate, there's always the basketball game next Sunday, and this time, everybody's coming to your house!*

NUTS & BOLTS 1
RELATIVE PRONOUNS

Relative pronouns are words like *who* or *that* in English used to connect two sentences, e.g., *I know the guy who's standing over there.* The most frequently used French relative pronouns are **qui** *(who, which, that)* and **que/qu'** *(whom, which, that)*. Let's look at how they are used.

Qui is used for both people and things and to refer to the noun that is a subject of the verb in the relative clause.

Je vois le pain. Le pain est sur la table.
I see the bread. The bread is on the table.

Je vois le pain qui est sur la table.
I see the bread that is on the table.

Natalie est la fille. Natalie chante bien.
Natalie is the girl. Natalie sings well.

Natalie est la fille qui chante bien.
Natalie is the girl who sings well.

The relative pronoun **que/qu'** refers back to a noun that is the object of the relative clause.

Voilà le livre. J'ai lu le livre.
There is the book. I read the book.

Voilà le livre que j'ai lu.
There's the book that I read.

C'est la voiture. Je conduis la voiture.
That's the car. I drive the car.

C'est la voiture que je conduis.
That's the car that I drive.

Note that in English, relative pronouns can be omitted. They are never omitted in French.

Voici les fleurs que j'adore.

Here are the flowers that I adore.

Tu manges le dessert que j'ai fait.

You're eating the dessert that I made.

The relative pronoun **que** becomes **qu'** before a word beginning with a vowel. Remember that the **i** in the relative pronoun **qui** is never dropped.

Marie est la fille qu'il aime.

Mary is the girl (that) he loves.

Le match de tennis qu'il a vu était passionnant.

The tennis match (that) he saw was exciting.

Qui, when used for persons, can also be preceded by a preposition. Then it is translated as *whom* or *whose*. Here is **qui** preceded by different prepositions.

à qui	*to whom*
avec qui	*with whom*
chez qui	*at whose house*
de qui	*from whom, of whom, about whom*
pour qui	*for whom*

Here are example sentences.

C'est la femme pour qui je travaille.

She's the woman for whom I work.

La dame à qui vous parlez s'appelle Sophie.

The woman to whom you are speaking is named Sophie.

C'est le jeune homme avec qui elle sort.

It's the young man she goes out with (lit., with whom she goes out).

PRACTICE 1

Supply the missing relative pronouns in the following sentences.

1. Il y a beaucoup de neige _____ est tombée.

2. Voilà la jeune fille avec _____ il joue au tennis.

3. Je n'ai pas vu le stylo _____ vous cherchez.

4. Donnez-moi le verre _____ sur la table, s'il vous plaît.

5. Voici la plage _____ est excellente pour le surf.

6. C'est la plage _____ nous préférons.

7. J'accepte la raison _____ tu me donnes.

8. Les joueurs _____ finissent le concours reçoivent un maillot jaune.

9. Voici les cartes _____ j'ai.

10. Voici la pièce _____ tout le monde veut voir.

The relative pronouns **ce qui** and **ce que** are used only for things that do not have a prior reference in the sentence. They are both translated as *what*.

Ce qui is used as the subject of the relative clause.

Je vois ce qui est sur la table.

I see what is on the table.

Ce qui me rend heureux, c'est d'aller à la plage.

What makes me happy is going to the beach.

Ce que is used as the direct object of the relative clause. Here are some examples.

Je comprends ce que tu dis.
I understand what you are saying./I understand that which you are saying.

Voici ce que je fais.
Here's what I am doing.

Marc dit toujours ce qu'il pense.
Mark always says what he's thinking.

PRACTICE 2
Choose the correct relative pronouns to complete the sentences.

1. Je n'aime pas (ce que, ce qui) est arrivé.

2. Elle ne comprend pas (ce que, ce qui) vous dites.

3. J'adore (ce qu', ce qui) il a fait.

4. Ramassez (ce que, ce qui) est sous la chaise.

5. Qu'est-(ce que, ce qui) tu bois?

CONVERSATION 2
Martine and Donna are two friends discussing what they did during the summer vacation.

Martine: **Dis-moi ce que tu as fait pendant les vacances cet été. Je sais bien que tu as fait quelque chose d'extraordinaire, comme toujours!**

Donna: **Tu sais que j'adore voyager avec mes amis mais ils avaient décidé d'aller faire du camping dans les montagnes. Je serais allée avec eux mais franchement, je voulais aller à la plage.**

Martine: **Alors, qu'est-ce que tu as fait?**

Donna: **J'ai fait ce qui me plaît. Je suis allée au Mexique.**

Martine: Avec qui as-tu voyagé?

Donna: J'y suis allée avec Claire et Dominique, les deux sœurs dont le père est le meilleur ami de mon père.

Martine: Ah, oui, les filles qui sont dans tes photos de l'année dernière.

Donna: Il y avait beaucoup à faire; nous avons nagé et nous étions à la plage tous les jours en train de jouer au volley-ball.

Martine: Tu es toute bronzée, ma chère!

Donna: Eh bien, qu'est-ce que tu as fait l'été dernier?

Martine: Mon mari et moi, nous avons préparé un beau séjour en France. Ce qui me rend heureuse, c'est d'être à Paris. C'est la ville que j'adore!

Martine: *Tell me what you did during the summer vacation. I know you must have done something extraordinary, like always!*

Donna: *You know I love to travel with my friends, but they decided to go camping in the mountains. I would have gone with them, but frankly, I wanted to go to the beach.*

Martine: *So, what did you do?*

Donna: *I did what I like. I went to Mexico.*

Martine: *Whom did you go with?*

Donna: *I went with Claire and Dominique, the two sisters whose father is my dad's best friend.*

Martine: *Oh, yes, the girls who are in your pictures from last year.*

Donna: *There was a lot to do; we went swimming and we were at the beach every day, playing volleyball.*

Martine: *You have a nice tan, my dear.*

Donna: *So what did you do this past summer?*

Martine: *My husband and I planned a beautiful trip to France. What makes me happy is to be in Paris. It's the city that I adore!*

NUTS & BOLTS 2

THE RELATIVE PRONOUNS LEQUEL (*which*) AND DONT (*of whom, of which, whose*)

There are four forms of the relative pronoun **lequel,** and they are used after prepositions. They all mean *which,* and they are used for things.

	SINGULAR	PLURAL
MASCULINE	**lequel**	**lesquels**
FEMININE	**laquelle**	**lesquelles**

The relative pronoun **lequel** and its forms agree in gender and number with the nouns to which they refer.

Voici la maison dans laquelle nous habitions.

Here's the house in which we used to live.

Où est le crayon avec lequel j'écrivais?

Where's the pencil with which I was writing?

Sometimes the word **où** *(where)* can be used as a relative pronoun to replace **dans** + a form of **lequel.**

Voici la maison où nous habitions.

Here's the house where we used to live.

The relative pronoun **dont** *(of whom, of which, whose)* is used for both people and things.

Voici le stylo dont j'ai besoin.

Here's the pen I need (lit., of which I have need).

Les enfants dont je parle sont mes enfants.

The children I am talking about are my children.

C'est le mari dont la femme est actrice.
That's the husband whose wife is an actress.

PRACTICE 3
In this exercise, you will practice all of the relative pronouns. Choose the correct relative pronouns to complete the sentences.

1. Marie est la petite fille (dont, de ce qui) je vous ai parlé.

2. Voici la femme pour (qui, qu') il écrit le poème.

3. Il y beaucoup de pièces à New York (que, qui) sont intéressantes.

4. Voici les pages sur (lesquelles, qu') il a écrit.

5. Elle ne comprend pas (ce qui, ce que) nous lisons.

6. Voici le sport (que, qui) j'adore.

Discovery activity

For fun, you may wish to explore information on some of the sports that are popular in both France and the United States and their special events, such as tennis (The French Open), biking **(Le Tour de France)**, and car racing **(Les 24 heures du Mans, le Rallye de Monte Carlo)**. Which sports interest you? See how French and U.S. teams and contestants fare against each other.

ANSWERS
PRACTICE 1: 1. qui; **2.** qui; **3.** que; **4.** qui; **5.** qui; **6.** que; **7.** que; **8.** qui; **9.** que; **10.** que

PRACTICE 2: 1. ce qui; **2.** ce que; **3.** ce qu'; **4.** ce qui; **5.** ce que

PRACTICE 3: 1. dont; **2.** qui; **3.** qui; **4.** lesquelles; **5.** ce que; **6.** que

le football	*soccer*
le football américain	*American football*
Je joue au tennis.	*I play tennis.*
Je joue de la guitare.	*I play guitar.*
Je peux nager.	*I can swim.*
Il sera allé.	*He will have gone.*
Il aura fini.	*He will have finished.*
Elle aurait attendu.	*She would have waited.*
Elle avait vu.	*She had seen.*
Je pense que tu as raison.	*I think that you are right.*
Voici la fille qui chante bien.	*Here's the girl who sings well.*
C'est tout ce que je veux.	*It's all that I want.*
Qu'est-ce qui se passe?	*What's going on?*
C'est le stylo avec lequel j'écris.	*It's the pen with which I am writing.*
C'est la femme dont je vous ai parlé.	*It's the woman I spoke to you about.*

UNIT 10
Doctors and health

In this unit you will learn the vocabulary for the parts of the body as well as useful expressions when talking about health and how you are feeling.

──────────── Lesson 37 (words) ────────────

WORD LIST 1
LES PARTIES DU CORPS *(Parts of the body)*

la tête	*head*
l'œil *(m.)*	*eye*
les yeux	*eyes*
le nez	*nose*
la bouche	*mouth*
l'oreille *(f.)*	*ear*
la dent	*tooth*
le cou	*neck*
l'épaule *(f.)*	*shoulder*
le dos	*back*
le bras	*arm*
la main	*hand*
la jambe	*leg*
le genou	*knee*
le pied	*foot*

NOTES
Notice that the plural of **l'œil** *(eye)* is irregular, **les yeux.** Take note also that in French, when expressing an action with a part of the

body, the definite article is used. In English, the possessive adjective is used.

Elle lève la main.
She raises her hand.

Il baisse les jambes.
He lowers his legs.

NUTS & BOLTS 1
REFLEXIVE VERBS

A reflexive verb express actions where the one who does the action also receives it. The action is performed by the subject to itself. For example, in English we use reflexive verbs when we say *I wash myself* or *I dress myself*. Take a look at the Group 1 verb **laver** *(to wash)*.

je lave	*I wash*	**nous lavons**	*we wash*
tu laves	*you wash*	**vous lavez**	*you wash*
il lave	*he washes*	**ils lavent**	*they wash*
elle lave	*she washes*	**elles lavent**	*they (f.) wash*

Je lave la voiture.
I'm washing the car.

Il lave le chien.
He washes the dog.

Now let's look at the same verb with the addition of the reflexive pronouns that make the verb a reflexive verb.

je me lave	I wash myself	nous nous lavons	we wash ourselves
tu te laves	you wash yourself	vous vous lavez	you wash yourselves
il se lave	he washes himself	ils se lavent	they wash themselves
elle se lave	she washes herself	elles se lavent	they wash themselves

Here are just the reflexive pronouns.

me	myself	nous	ourselves
te	yourself	vous	yourselves
se	himself, herself, itself	se	themselves

Here is a list of some common reflexive verbs. You may already know the definitions of some of the verbs because they were presented in earlier units as regular **-er** verbs. Note that not all French reflexive verbs correspond to reflexive verbs in English.

REFLEXIVE VERBS	
s'amuser	to have a good time, to enjoy onself
s'appeler	to be called
se blesser	to hurt oneself
se brosser	to brush oneself

se coucher	to go to bed, to lie down
se demander	to wonder, to ask oneself
se dépêcher	to hurry
s'ennuyer	to get bored
s'habiller	to dress oneself, to get dressed
se lever	to get up, to rise
se promener	to take a walk
se reposer	to rest
se réveiller	to wake up
se souvenir	to remember
se tromper	to be mistaken, to make a mistake
se trouver	to be situated

Take note of several important rules when conjugating a reflexive verb. First, notice that, like other pronouns, the reflexive pronouns normally precede the verb.

Look at the examples of reflexive verbs in sentences.

Je me couche quand j'ai sommeil.
I go to bed when I'm sleepy.

Nous nous habillons pour la soirée.
We get dressed for the party.

Les garçons se dépêchent.
The boys hurry.

Je me demande si elle peut venir avec nous.
I wonder if she can come with us.

Me, te, and **se** become **m', t',** and **s'** before a verb beginning with a vowel or silent **h.**

Je m'amuse.
I'm having a good time.

Elle s'habille.
She's getting dressed.

Il s'appelle Paul.
His name is Paul. (lit., He calls himself Paul.)

In the affirmative imperative, reflexive pronouns follow the verb and are connected to it with a hyphen. After the verb, **toi** is used instead of **te.**

Dépêche-toi!
Hurry up!

Dépêchons-nous!
Let's hurry!

Amusez-vous bien!
Have a good time! (lit., Entertain yourselves!)

Amuse-toi bien!
Have a good time!

In the negative form, **ne** is placed after the subject pronoun and **pas** comes right after the verb.

Je ne me lève pas tôt le week-end.
I don't get up early on weekends.

Vous ne vous réveillez pas avant midi.
You don't get up before noon.

Tu ne te couches pas de bonne heure.

You don't go to bed early.

Il ne s'habille pas pour la soirée.

He's not getting dressed for the party.

Also notice that the reflexive pronoun is not always used as a direct object. It may be the indirect object in the sentence, while some other word is the direct object.

Je me brosse les dents.

I brush my teeth.

In this sentence, **me** is the indirect object, and **dents** is the direct object.

Il se lave la figure.

He's washing his face.

In this sentence, **se** is the indirect object, and **figure** is the direct object. Remember that a verb that is reflexive in French need not be reflexive in English.

Je ne me dépêche pas.

I do not hurry.

Marie se lève.

Marie gets up.

Remember the spelling changes of certain regular verbs, such as **appeler** *(to call)* and **lever** *(to lift)*. When these verbs become reflexive—**s'appeler** *(to call oneself)* and **se lever** *(to get up)*—the same rules apply for spelling changes.

Je m'appelle Paul.

My name is Paul.

Vous vous appelez Marie.
Your name is Marie.

Ils se lèvent de bonne heure.
They get up early.

Nous nous levons à six heures du matin.
We get up at six o'clock in the morning.

Finally, note that any French verb that takes an object, direct or indirect, may be made reflexive by adding a personal reflexive pronoun object that refers back to the subject.

Quand tu utilises un couteau, fais attention! Tu te couperas.
Be careful when you use a knife! You'll cut yourself.

PRACTICE 1
Fill in the blanks with the correct present tense form of the reflexive verbs in parentheses.

1. Les fermiers _____ de bonne heure chaque matin. (se lever)

2. Nous _____ pour être à l'heure. (se dépêcher)

3. Madame Dumas _____ pour la soirée. (s'habiller)

4. Les enfants _____ quand on regarde les nouvelles à la télé. (s'ennuyer)

5. Comment _____-ils? (s'appeler)

6. Généralement, je _____ très tard le soir. (se coucher)

7. Vous _____ chez vos amis. (s'amuser)

8. _____- elles avant vous? (se réveiller)

9. En vacances, tout le monde _____. (se reposer)

10. Tu _____ la figure. (se laver)

PRACTICE 2

Complete the English translations of the following French sentences.

1. Je me trouvais devant la Tour Eiffel.

   _____ in front of the Eiffel Tower.

2. Tu ne t'ennuies pas en été.

   _____ in the summer.

3. Il se dépêche rarement.

   He rarely _____.

4. Est-ce qu'ils s'amusaient avec leurs amis?

   _____ with their friends?

5. Nous nous brossons les dents.

   _____ our teeth.

6. Elle se levait avant neuf heures.

   _____ before nine o'clock.

7. Lave-toi tout de suite!

   _____ at once!

8. Tu te souviens de moi?

   _____ me?

9. Je me demande ce qui est dans la boîte.

   _____ what is in the box.

10. Ne vous brossez pas vos cheveux dans la cuisine!

    _____ your hair in the kitchen!

WORD LIST 2
LA SANTÉ ET LA MALADIE *(Health and sickness)*

l'examen médical *(m.)*	*medical checkup*
le cabinet médical	*doctor's office*
l'état de santé	*bill of health*
le docteur/la doctoresse	*doctor (male/female)*
le patient/la patiente	*patient (male/female)*
le laboratoire	*laboratory*
la radiographie, la radio	*x-ray*
le diagnostic	*diagnosis*
le rhume	*cold*
la fièvre	*fever*
la grippe	*flu*
le virus	*virus*
l'allergie *(f.)*	*allergy*
l'infection *(f.)*	*infection*
le soin	*care*

NUTS & BOLTS 2
PAST TENSE OF REFLEXIVE VERBS

Reflexive verbs are all formed with the helping verb **être.** Like adjectives, past participles conjugated with **être** agree in gender and number with the subject. Look at the verb **se laver** *(to wash oneself, to get washed)* in the compound past tenses. First is the compound past tense.

je me suis lavé/e	*I washed myself*	nous nous sommes lavé/e/s	*we washed ourselves*
tu t'es lavé/e	*you washed yourself*	vous vous êtes lavé/e/s	*you washed yourselves*

il s'est lavé	*he washed himself*	ils se sont lavés	*they washed themselves*
elle s'est lavée	*she washed herself*	elles se sont lavées	*they washed themselves*

Here is the future perfect of **se laver.**

je me serai lavé/e	*I will have washed myself*	nous nous serons lavé/e/s	*we will have washed ourselves*
tu te seras lavé/e	*you will have washed yourself*	vous vous serez lavé/e/s	*you will have washed yourself*
il se sera lavé	*he will have washed himself*	ils se seront lavés	*they will have washed themselves*
elle se sera lavée	*she will have washed herself*	elles se seront lavées	*they will have washed themselves*

Here is the past conditional of **se laver.**

je me serais lavé/e	*I would have washed myself*	nous nous serions lavé/e/s	*we would have washed ourselves*
tu te serais lavé/e	*you would have washed yourself*	vous vous seriez lavé/e/s	*you would have washed yourself*
il se serait lavé	*he would have washed himself*	ils se seraient lavés	*they would have washed themselves*
elle se serait lavée	*she would have washed herself*	elles se seraient lavées	*they would have washed themselves*

The last compound past tense is the pluperfect.

je m'étais lavé/e	I had washed myself	nous nous étions lavé/e/s	we had washed ourselves
tu t'étais lavé/e	you had washed yourself	vous vous étiez lavé/e/s	you had washed yourself
il s'était lavé	he had washed himself	ils s'étaient lavés	they had washed themselves
elle s'était lavée	she had washed herself	elles s'étaient lavées	they had washed themselves

Note that the past participles of reflexive verbs agree in gender and number with the subject, which is also the object of the action.

Mes amis se sont amusés.
My friends had a good time.

Elle s'est lavée.
She washed herself.

However, when the reflexive pronoun is the indirect object, it doesn't agree with the subject.

Elle s'est lavé la figure.
She washed her face.

In the preceding sentence, **la figure** *(the face)* is the direct object and comes after the past participle. Here is another example of the direct object coming after the past participle.

Ils se sont brossé les dents.
They brushed their teeth.

PRACTICE 3

Choose the correct translation.

1. Elle s'était amusée.

 a. *She had had a good time.*

 b. *She was having a good time.*

 c. *She had a good time.*

2. Je me serais levé.

 a. *I would get up.*

 b. *I would have gotten up.*

 c. *I had gotten up.*

3. Nous nous sommes habillés.

 a. *We had gotten dressed.*

 b. *We were getting dressed.*

 c. *We got dressed.*

4. S'était-elle lavée?

 a. *Did she get washed?*

 b. *Had she gotten washed?*

 c. *Will she have gotten washed?*

5. Ils se seraient souvenus.

 a. *They would have remembered.*

 b. *They had remembered.*

 c. *They remembered.*

Culture note

Over the centuries, France has been a leader and innovator in science and technology, as well as in social sciences, music, arts, and literature. In sciences, take for example Pasteur's contribution to medicine and Pierre and Marie Curie's to physics. French writers have made great contributions to the world of letters, from Molière and Montaigne to Sartre and Camus.

ANSWERS

PRACTICE 1: 1. se lèvent; **2.** nous dépêchons; **3.** s'habille; **4.** s'ennuient; **5.** s'appellent; **6.** me couche; **7.** vous amusez; **8.** Se réveillent; **9.** se repose; **10.** te laves

PRACTICE 2: 1. *I found myself (I was situated);* **2.** *You're not bored;* **3.** *hurries;* **4.** *Were they having fun;* **5.** *We're brushing;* **6.** *She used to get up;* **7.** *Get washed;* **8.** *Do you remember;* **9.** *I wonder;* **10.** *Don't brush*

PRACTICE 3: 1. a; **2.** b; **3.** c; **4.** b; **5.** a

─────────────── Lesson 38 (phrases) ───────────────

PHRASE LIST 1
DES PHRASES POUR L'APTITUDE PHYSIQUE *(Phrases for physical ability)*

se casser le bras/la jambe	*to break one's arm/leg*
se fouler la cheville	*to sprain one's ankle*
marcher avec une canne	*to walk with a cane*
marcher avec des béquilles *(f.)*	*to walk with crutches*
la chaise roulante	*wheelchair*
être handicapé/e	*to be disabled*
avoir la maladie d'Alzheimer	*to have Alzheimer's disease*
avoir la maladie de Parkinson	*to have Parkinson's disease*
être sourd/e	*to be deaf*

utiliser le langage des signes	*to use sign language*
être paralysé/e	*to be paralyzed*
porter des verres (lentilles) de contact	*to wear contact lenses*
être aveugle	*to be blind*
avoir besoin d'un chien d'aveugle	*to need a seeing-eye dog*

NUTS & BOLTS 1
THE EXPRESSIONS AVOIR MAL À *(to have pain in, to ache)* AND FAIRE MAL *(to hurt)*

To express a hurt or pain in a certain part of your body, use the verb **avoir mal à** + the part of the body.

J'ai mal aux dents.
I have a toothache.

Il a mal aux pieds.
He has sore feet. (lit., He has pain in the feet.)

If your pain is caused by someone or something, we use the expression **faire mal à** *(to hurt)* with an indirect object pronoun.

Son dentiste ne lui fait jamais mal.
His dentist never hurts him.

Tu me fais mal.
You're hurting me.

Mes chaussures me font mal.
My shoes hurt me.

PRACTICE 1
Translate the following sentences into English.

1. J'ai une dent qui me fait mal.

2. Il a mal au dos.

3. Ne me fais pas mal!

4. Quand il fait très froid, j'ai mal aux doigts.

5. Mon dentiste ne me fait pas mal.

PHRASE LIST 2
L'EXERCISE *(Exercise)*

le club de remise en forme	*health club*
s'entraîner	*to train*
faire de la musculation	*to do strength training, to lift weights*
le tapis de course, le tapis de jogging	*treadmill*
les abdominaux *(m.)*	*sit-ups*
les pompes *(f.)*	*push-ups*
les tractions *(f.)*	*pull-ups, press-ups*
soulever un haltère	*to lift a dumbell*
le vélo d'appartement, le vélo d'entraînement	*stationary bike*
la séance de mise en forme	*workout session*
l'entraînement *(m.)*	*workout*
être en sueur	*to be sweating*
le battement de cœur	*heartbeat*
se faire une élongation	*to pull a muscle*
être en forme	*to be fit, to be in shape*

NUTS & BOLTS 2
RECIPROCAL VERBS

In the previous lesson, you learned about reflexive verbs. With reflexive verbs, the subjects act on themselves. With reciprocal verbs, the plural subjects act on one another. A plural reflexive pronoun may be used to express *each other*.

Ils se regardent.
They look at each other.

Jennifer et Carol se voient de temps en temps.
Jennifer and Carol see each other from time to time.

Thomas et Nicole se marient dimanche.
Thomas and Nicole are getting married to each other on Sunday.

PRACTICE 2
Translate the following sentences into French.

1. *They speak to each other from time to time.*
2. *We phone each other every day.*
3. *Do you speak to each other often?*
4. *My parents understand each other.*
5. *My friends meet each other at the restaurant.*

Discovery activity

Think of a love story between two people that you may know, such as your parents or grandparents, or perhaps from your own life situation, from a work of fiction, from the lives of celebrities, or from movies or TV. Try to write a short paragraph in French about the couple, using as many reciprocal verbs as possible. Besides the ones mentioned in the *Nuts & bolts 2* section, here are a few more you may want to include in your paragraph.

s'entendre bien (mal)	*to get along well (badly)*
s'embrasser	*to hug (each other), to kiss (each other)*
se fiancer	*to get engaged (to each other)*
se disputer	*to argue (with each other)*
se connaître	*to know (each other)*

ANSWERS

PRACTICE 1: 1. *I have a tooth that hurts me.* **2.** *He has back pain.* **3.** *Don't hurt me!* **4.** *When it's very cold out, my fingers hurt.* **5.** *My dentist doesn't hurt me.*

PRACTICE 2: 1. Ils se parlent de temps en temps. **2.** Nous nous téléphonons tous les jours. **3.** Est-ce que vous vous parlez souvent? **4.** Mes parents se comprennent. **5.** Mes amis se rencontrent au restaurant.

──────────── Lesson 39 (sentences) ────────────

SENTENCE GROUP 1
LES EXPRESSIONS CHEZ LE DOCTEUR *(Expressions at the doctor's office)*

Je voudrais prendre rendez-vous.	*I would like to make an appointment.*
Qu'est-ce qu'il y a?	*What's the matter?*
Qu'est-ce qui vous est arrivé?	*What happened to you?*
Aïe!	*Ouch!*
Je suis malade.	*I am sick.*
Qu'est-ce que je dois faire?	*What should I do?*
Le médecin fait une ordonnance.	*The doctor gives a prescription.*
J'ai du mal à avaler.	*I have trouble swallowing.*
J'ai mal à la gorge.	*I have a sore throat.*
Tu as un chat dans la gorge.	*You have a frog in your throat.*
Il a mal à la tête.	*He has a headache.*
L'enfant va attraper un rhume.	*The child is going to catch a cold.*
J'ai le nez bouché.	*My nose is stuffed up.*
À cause de ses allergies, il tousse.	*Because of his allergies, he coughs.*
Il faut prendre la température.	*You have to take your temperature.*
Je ne suis pas dans mon assiette.	*I'm not myself./I'm not feeling well.*

NUTS & BOLTS 1

THE SUBJUNCTIVE

Speakers can use different moods in French to indicate how the speaker views an event. For instance, the indicative mood is used to talk about objective facts (using different tenses, such as the present, the past tense, the imperfect, or the future). The imperative mood is used to express a command. The conditional states what could, should, or would happen.

The subjunctive is a mood expressing wishes, desires, necessities, emotions, opinions, doubts, uncertainties, grief, and suppositions. Verbs in the subjunctive mood are generally used in dependent clauses introduced by the conjunction **que** *(that)*.

The present subjunctive is formed by adding the endings below to the stem obtained by dropping the **-ent** ending from the **ils/elles** form of the verb.

SUBJUNCTIVE ENDINGS	
je: -e	**nous: -ions**
tu: -es	**vous: -iez**
il: -e	**ils: -ent**
elle: -e	**elle: -ent**

We will discuss in more depth when to use the subjunctive as we continue with this lesson. First, note the formation of the present subjunctive of three regular Group 1, Group 2, and Group 3 verbs.

parler *(to speak)*	**finir** *(to finish)*	**répondre** *(to answer)*
que je parle	**que je finisse**	**que je réponde**

que tu parles	que tu finisses	que tu répondes
qu'il parle	qu'il finisse	qu'il réponde
qu'elle parle	qu'elle finisse	qu'elle réponde
que nous parlions	que nous finissions	que nous répondions
que vous parliez	que vous finissiez	que vous répondiez
qu'ils parlent	qu'ils finissent	qu'ils répondent
qu'elles parlent	qu'elles finissent	qu'elles répondent

Regular -er verbs with spelling changes, such as **acheter, appeler, préférer,** and **nettoyer,** have those changes in the subjunctive as well.

que j'achète
that I buy
que nous achetions
that we buy

qu'elle appelle
that she call

que je nettoie
that I clean

Now let's look at the contexts in which the subjunctive mood has to be used. First, the subjunctive is used after verbs expressing want, preference, need, and imposition of will.

Je veux qu'elle parte.
I want her to leave.

Il exige que tu partes.
He demands that you leave.

Le professeur suggère que vous parliez français.
The teacher suggests that you speak French.

The subjunctive is used after verbs expressing a wish or command.

Sa femme désire qu'il finisse le travail autour de la maison.
His wife wants him to finish the work around the house.

Aimez-vous mieux que je vous attende?
Do you prefer that I wait for you?

The subjunctive is used after expressions of doubt or uncertainty.

Je doute que vous m'écoutiez.
I doubt that you're listening to me.

Je ne pense pas que vous m'écoutiez.
I don't think you're listening to me.

The verbs below are followed by the subjunctive.

aimer mieux que *(to prefer that)*	**ordonner que** *(to order that)*
attendre que *(to wait until)*	**permettre que** *(to allow that)*
avoir besoin que *(to need for)*	**préférer que** *(to prefer that)*
demander que *(to request that, to ask that)*	**recommander que** *(to recommend that)*
désirer que *(to desire that, to want that, to wish that)*	**souhaiter que** *(to wish that)*

empêcher que *(to prevent from, to keep from)*	suggérer que *(to suggest that)*
exiger que *(to demand that, to require that)*	vouloir que *(to want that, to wish that)*

The subjunctive is also used after many impersonal expressions conveying similar concepts of necessity, obligation, wishing, possibility, etc. In the sentences below, note that the subjunctive can sometimes be translated as an infinitive in English.

Il faut que ma nièce vende sa maison.

My niece must sell her house. (lit., It is necessary that my niece sell her house.)

Il est nécessaire que je finisse la lettre.

I have to finish the letter. (lit., It is necessary that I finish the letter.)

Il est urgent que je finisse la lettre.

It is urgent that I finish the letter.

Il est possible que nous travaillions samedi.

It is possible that we will work on Saturday.

Il est important que tu arrives à l'heure.

It is important that you arrive on time.

Il est essentiel que vous arriviez à l'heure.

It is essential that you arrive on time.

The subjunctive is not used after impersonal expressions of certainty or probability. We use the indicative instead.

Il est vrai que tu réussiras.

It is true that you will succeed.

Il est certain que l'enfant obéit à sa mère.

It is certain that the child obeys his mother.

Il est probable que nous voyagerons en France.

It is probable that we will travel to France.

Note that the subjunctive is used only when the subjects of the main clause and the dependent clause are different. If the subjects are the same in both clauses, the infinitive is used.

Je veux qu'il parte.

I want him to leave.

Je veux partir.

I want to leave.

Ils désirent que nous restions.

They want us to stay.

Ils désirent rester.

They want to stay.

The subjunctive is used after expressions of emotion, such as joy, fear, and sorrow.

Je suis content que vous m'aidiez.

I am happy that you are helping me.

Je regrette que tu partes si tôt.

I am sorry you're leaving so soon.

Nous avons peur qu'il ne parte.

We are afraid he may leave.

Note the negation word **ne** in the sentence above. In French, expressions of fear often have **ne** before the verb in the subjunctive. It is not translated into English.

The subjunctive is used after certain conjunctions.

afin que, pour que (in order that, so that)	bien que, quoique (although)
avant que (before)	sans que (without)
à moins que . . . ne (unless)	jusqu'à ce que (until)

Il travaille dur pour que sa famille réussisse.
He works hard so that his family succeeds.

Note that there is no future tense in the subjunctive. The present subjunctive is used for both present and future.

PRACTICE 1
Add the expression **il faut que** *(it is necessary)* before each sentence and make all changes necessary for the subjunctive. Follow the example.

Ex. Tu parles français. *You speak French.*
    Il faut que tu parles français. *You must speak French.*

1. Ils marchent lentement à la pharmacie.

2. Elle répond à la lettre.

3. Nous cherchons l'hôpital.

4. Vous coupez le gâteau.

5. J'attends mes amis.

6. Mon mari finit son travail.

7. Il vend son auto.

8. Tu choisis des fleurs.

PRACTICE 2

Place the verbs in parentheses in the right present subjunctive or present indicative forms as needed.

1. Il est possible que le médecin le _____. (guérir)

2. Il est important que tu _____ de bonne heure. (se lever)

3. Il faut que vous _____ les fenêtres. (fermer)

4. Il est vrai que nous _____ la maison. (vendre)

5. Il est impossible que vous _____ cinq langues! (parler)

SENTENCE GROUP 2
ENCORE DES EXPRESSIONS POUR LA SANTÉ (*More health expressions*)

les cas d'urgence	*emergency situations*
Il faut avoir une trousse de secours.	*It's necessary to have a first-aid kit.*
avoir un accident	*to have an accident*
Appelez le service d'assistance médicale d'urgence.	*Call the emergency medical service.*
L'ambulance arrive.	*The ambulance is arriving.*
Il lui faut une transfusion de sang.	*He needs a blood transfusion.*
C'est une blessure superficielle.	*It's a superficial injury.*
Ce n'est pas grave.	*It's not serious.*
Est-ce que vous avez une assurance?	*Do you have insurance?*
Prenez une pilule (un cachet, une capsule).	*Take a pill (a tablet, a capsule).*
Quelquefois il y a des effets secondaires.	*Sometimes there are side effects.*

C'est une brûlure.	*It's a burn.*
C'est une coupure.	*It's a cut.*
Le dentiste va remplacer le plombage.	*The dentist is going to replace the filling.*
Il faut arracher une dent.	*It's necessary to have a tooth pulled.*

NUTS & BOLTS 2
THE SUBJUNCTIVE OF IRREGULAR VERBS

Most irregular verbs follow the same pattern as the regular verbs in the present subjunctive. For example, here is the verb **écrire** *(to write)* in the subjunctive.

écrire *(to write)*	
que j'écrive	que nous écrivions
que tu écrives	que vous écriviez
qu'il écrive	qu'ils écrivent
qu'elle écrive	qu'elles écrivent

Some irregular verbs, such as the verbs **prendre** *(to take)*, **venir** *(to come)*, and **boire** *(to drink)*, have variations in the present indicative, and therefore, these verbs undergo the same changes in the subjunctive. Remember, we go to the **ils/elles** form and drop the **-ent** ending before adding the subjunctive endings.

prendre *(to take)*	
que je prenne	que nous prenions
que tu prennes	que vous preniez
qu'il prenne	qu'ils prennent
qu'elle prenne	qu'elles prennent

venir *(to come)*	
que je vienne	que nous venions
que tu viennes	que vous veniez
qu'il vienne	qu'ils viennent
qu'elle vienne	qu'elles viennent

boire *(to drink)*	
que je boive	que nous buvions
que tu boives	que vous buviez
qu'il boive	qu'ils boivent
qu'elle boive	qu'elles boivent

Some irregular verbs, like **faire** *(to do)*, **pouvoir** *(can)*, and **savoir** *(to know)*, have a single irregular stem.

faire *(to do)*	
que je fasse	que nous fassions
que tu fasses	que vous fassiez
qu'il fasse	qu'ils fassent
qu'elle fasse	qu'elles fassent

pouvoir *(can, to be able)*	
que je puisse	que nous puissions
que tu puisses	que vous puissiez
qu'il puisse	qu'ils puissent
qu'elle puisse	qu'elles puissent

savoir *(to know)*	
que je sache	que nous sachions
que tu saches	que vous sachiez
qu'il sache	qu'ils sachent
qu'elle sache	qu'elles sachent

Some irregular verbs have two stems in the present subjunctive—that is, one for the **nous** and **vous** forms and one for the other persons.

aller *(to go)*	
que j'aille	que nous allions
que tu ailles	que vous alliez
qu'il aille	qu'ils aillent
qu'elle aille	qu'elles aillent

croire *(to believe)*

que je croie	que nous croyions
que tu croies	que vous croyiez
qu'il croie	qu'ils croient
qu'elle croie	qu'elles croient

devoir *(to have to, to owe)*

que je doive	que nous devions
que tu doives	que vous deviez
qu'il doive	qu'ils doivent
qu'elle doive	qu'elles doivent

envoyer *(to send)*

que j'envoie	que nous envoyions
que tu envoies	que vous envoyiez
qu'il envoie	qu'ils envoient
qu'elle envoie	qu'elles envoient

recevoir *(to receive)*	
que je reçoive	que nous recevions
que tu reçoives	que vous receviez
qu'il reçoive	qu'ils reçoivent
qu'elle reçoive	qu'elles reçoivent

voir *(to see)*	
que je voie	que nous voyions
que tu voies	que vous voyiez
qu'il voie	qu'ils voient
qu'elle voie	qu'elles voient

vouloir *(to wish, to want)*	
que je veuille	que nous voulions
que tu veuilles	que vous vouliez
qu'il veuille	qu'ils veuillent
qu'elle veuille	qu'elles veuillent

The present subjunctive endings are the same for all verbs except **avoir** and **être**.

avoir *(to have)*	
que j'aie	que nous ayons
que tu aies	que vous ayez
qu'il ait	qu'ils aient
qu'elle ait	qu'elles aient

être *(to be)*	
que je sois	que nous soyons
que tu sois	que vous soyez
qu'il soit	qu'ils soient
qu'elle soit	qu'elles soient

Here are some examples of irregular verbs used in the subjunctive mood.

Il faut que tu sois à l'heure.
You have to be on time. (lit., It's necessary that you be on time.)

Je ne crois pas qu'il puisse le faire.
I don't believe he can do it.

Nous doutons qu'elle comprenne.
We doubt she understands.

J'ai peur qu'il ne sache pas la vérité.
I'm afraid he doesn't know the truth.

Penchez-vous un peu à gauche pour que je puisse voir l'écran.

Move a little to the left so I can see the screen.

PRACTICE 3

Translate the following sentences into English.

1. Je voudrais qu'elle vienne demain.

2. Il faut que nous lisions beaucoup.

3. Je suis heureux que tu puisses venir avec nous.

4. Bien qu'il pleuve, elle va sortir.

5. Il ne pense pas que l'avion parte à l'heure.

6. Il est possible que vous fassiez de votre mieux.

7. Ils désirent que nous jouions aux cartes.

8. Parlez plus fort afin que je vous entende mieux.

Tip!

To memorize when to use the subjunctive mood, think of the word *wedding*. Each letter stands for the kind of verb that is followed by the subjunctive and represents an element that surrounds a wedding. Also, just like the outward "sign" of a wedding is a ring, the outward sign of the subjunctive is **que**.

W for *wishing*	(for the perfect wedding and the perfect marriage)
E for *emotion*	(emotions abound at weddings)
D for *doubt*	(sometimes the bride or groom may have doubts)
D for *denial*	(sometimes the bride or groom may be in denial about what they are doing)
I for *in certain special cases*	(certain weddings are really special)
N for *necessity*	(some weddings take place out of necessity)
G for *grief*	(some weddings may create grief)

ANSWERS

PRACTICE 1: 1. Il faut qu'ils marchent lentement à la pharmacie. **2.** Il faut qu'elle réponde à la lettre. **3.** Il faut que nous cherchions l'hôpital. **4.** Il faut que vous coupiez le gâteau. **5.** Il faut que j'attende mes amis. **6.** Il faut que mon mari finisse son travail. **7.** Il faut qu'il vende son auto. **8.** Il faut que tu choisisses des fleurs.

PRACTICE 2: 1. guérisse; **2.** te lèves; **3.** fermiez; **4.** vendons; **5.** parliez

PRACTICE 3: 1. *I would like her to come tomorrow.* **2.** *We should read a lot. (lit., It is necessary that we read a lot.)* **3.** *I am happy that you can come with us.* **4.** *Although it's raining, she's going to go out.* **5.** *He doesn't think the plane is leaving on time.* **6.** *It's possible that you're doing your best.* **7.** *They want us to play cards.* **8.** *Speak louder so I can hear you better.*

––––––––––– Lesson 40 (conversations) –––––––––––

CONVERSATION 1

In this dialogue, Anne and Nancy are discussing diets and the need to lose weight.

Anne: Eh bien, mon mari et moi, nous sommes en train de suivre un régime.

Nancy: Comment? Tu suis un régime? Pourquoi faut-il que tu perdes du poids? Tu ne grossis pas, ma chère. Tu gardes toujours la ligne!

Anne: Merci, Anne. Grâce à Dieu, je suis en bonne forme après tout le chocolat que je mange, mais il est nécessaire que mon mari perde cinq kilos.

Nancy: Je doute que ce soit facile. Tu sais bien que les hommes n'aiment pas manger tout ce qui est bon pour eux.

Anne: Il est important que je fasse des repas plus

légers car, il faut que mon mari maigrisse. C'est plus facile de le faire ensemble, tu sais.

Nancy: Mon docteur voudrait aussi que nous perdions quelques kilos. Mais moi, j'adore les desserts.

Anne: Il est possible que tu puisses manger des desserts s'ils sont faits avec de bons ingrédients, comme les fruits, par exemple.

Anne: Well, my husband and I are in the midst of following a diet.

Nancy: What? You're on a diet? Why do you have to lose weight? You're not gaining weight, my dear. You have always kept your shape!

Anne: Thanks, Anne. Thank God I am in good shape after all the chocolate that I eat, but my husband needs to lose ten pounds.

Nancy: I doubt that it's going to be easy. You know how men are when it comes to eating what's good for them.

Anne: It's important that I make lighter meals because my husband needs to slim down. It's easier to do it together, you know.

Nancy: My doctor would like us to lose a few pounds, too. But I just love desserts.

Anne: It's possible for you to eat desserts if they are made with good ingredients, like fruit, for example.

NOTES
A kilogram is equal to 2.2 pounds.

NUTS & BOLTS 1
THE VERB SUIVRE *(to follow)*
Here are the present tense forms of the verb **suivre** *(to follow)*.

je suis	*I follow*	nous suivons	*we follow*
tu suis	*you follow*	vous suivez	*you follow*
il suit	*he follows*	ils suivent	*they follow*
elle suit	*she follows*	elles suivent	*they follow*

This verb is useful in many expressions.

Nous suivons la route vers la ville.
We follow the road to town.

Suivez les instructions.
Follow the instructions.

Suivez-moi au café du quartier.
Follow me to the neighborhood café.

Pour être en bonne santé, il faut suivre un bon régime.
To be in good health, you must follow a good diet.

S'il vous plaît, faites suivre mon courrier à la nouvelle adresse.
Please forward my mail to the new address.

The past participle of **suivre** is **suivi** *(followed)*.

PRACTICE 1
Fill in the blanks with the correct form of the verb **suivre** *(to follow)*.

1. Marc _____ la route au gymnase.

2. _____-ils les instructions du médecin?

3. Nous _____ un bon régime pour maigrir.

4. Est-ce que vous avez _____ mes instructions?

5. Tu ne _____ pas la route.

CONVERSATION 2

After having eaten too much during the holidays, Joseph and Jonathan have decided to go to the gym for a workout session.

Joseph: Il faut qu'on aille au gymnase cet après-midi.

Jonathan: Absolument. J'ai tellement mangé hier soir. Il faut que je fasse beaucoup d'exercices!

Joseph: Tu peux le dire! Avec tous ces repas lourds que l'on a mangés . . . Je me sens toujours mieux après avoir fait un bon entraînement.

Jonathan: Tu es dingue. J'aime le vélo d'appartement mais ça me fait mal de lever les poids.

Joseph: Écoute, la seule façon de changer la forme du corps, c'est d'utiliser du poids.

Jonathan: Pour que je puisse perdre des kilos, je fais de l'aérobic.

Joseph: Il est nécessaire de bien manger pour que tu perdes des kilos, et l'aérobic c'est bon pour la santé. Mais comme j'ai dit tout à l'heure, pour changer la forme du corps, il faut faire de la musculation avec des poids.

Jonathan: D'accord, commençons avec des abdominaux.

Joseph: Zut alors! J'ai toujours mal au ventre quand je les fais!

Joseph: *We have to go to the gym this afternoon.*

Jonathan: *Absolutely. I ate so much last night. I have got to do a lot of exercising!*

Joseph: *Tell me about it! With all those heavy meals we ate . . . I always feel better after a good workout.*

Jonathan:	You're nuts. I like the stationary bike, but it hurts to lift weights.
Joseph:	Listen, the only way to change the shape of your body is to use weights.
Jonathan:	So that I can lose weight, I do aerobic exercises.
Joseph:	Yes, it's necessary to eat well so that you lose weight, and aerobic exercise is good for your health. But like I said before, to change your body shape, you have to do strength training with weights.
Jonathan:	Okay, let's start with the abdominal exercises.
Joseph:	Darn! It always hurts my stomach when I do them!

NUTS & BOLTS 2

AGREEMENT OF PAST PARTICIPLES

Past participles conjugated with **avoir** agree in gender and number with the preceding direct object if there is one.

J'ai vu Christine.

I saw Christine.

Je l'ai vue.

I saw her.

Il a fait des exercices.

He did some exercises.

Voici les exercices qu'il a faits.

Here are the exercises that he did.

J'ai pris une pilule.

I took a pill.

Voici la pilule que j'ai prise.

Here's the pill that I took.

PRACTICE 2

Decide whether agreement with the past participle is necessary; if needed, rewrite the past participles in the correct form.

1. Où sont les pilules que tu as acheté?

2. Il a pris trois pilules.

3. Voilà la dent que le dentiste a arraché.

4. Voici les cachets que le docteur m'a donné.

5. Le médecin m'a donné ces cachets.

Language link

For more information about health care in France, especially for visitors to the country, go to www.discoverfrance.net and search for *health*.

ANSWERS

PRACTICE 1: 1. suit; **2.** suivent; **3.** suivons; **4.** suivi; **5.** suis

PRACTICE 2: 1. Où sont les pilules que tu as achetées? **2.** Il a pris trois pilules. **3.** Voilà la dent que le dentiste a arrachée. **4.** Voici les cachets que le docteur m'a donnés. **5.** Le médecin m'a donné ces cachets.

le corps	*body*
la tête	*head*
la main	*hand*
Je me réveille à cinq heures et demie.	*I wake up at five thirty.*
Il se couche tard.	*He goes to bed late.*
Ils s'aiment.	*They love each other.*
Ils se sont mariés.	*They got married.*
Il faut que tu fasses de ton mieux.	*You have to do your best.*
Il est vrai que tu fais de ton mieux.	*It's true that you do your best.*
Je suis désolé que tu partes.	*I'm sorry you are leaving.*
Il est nécessaire que tu sois à l'heure.	*It's necessary that you be on time.*
Il faut faire de la musculation.	*It's necessary to do strength training.*
être en bonne santé	*to be in good health*
J'ai mal à la tête.	*I have a headache.*
Je suis les instructions du médecin.	*I'm following the doctor's orders.*

Here are several examples of French language in action, outside of conversations.

1. RECIPE

La recette de crêpes
Pour 6 personnes

200 grammes de farine
1 quart de litre de lait
1 quart de litre d'eau
4 œufs
une demi-cuillère à café de sel
3 cuillères à soupe d'huile
3 cuillères à soupe de rhum (ou un autre parfum)
un zeste de citron
3 cuillères à soupe de sucre

Dans un grand saladier, mettre les œufs, le sel, le sucre et l'huile. Bien mélanger tous les ingrédients. Puis, ajouter petit à petit la farine et le lait. À la fin, ajouter l'eau, le rhum et le zeste de citron. C'est fait! Attendre 20–30 minutes avant de faire les crêpes.

Recipe for crepes
For 6 people

200 grams of flour
1 quarter liter of milk
1 quarter liter of water
4 eggs
one half teaspon of salt
3 tablespoons of oil
3 tablespoons of rum (or another aroma)
a piece of lemon peel
3 tablespoons of sugar

In a large bowl, place the eggs, salt, sugar, and oil. Mix all of the ingredients well. Then slowly add the flour and the milk. Finally, add the water, the rum, and the piece of lemon peel. It's done! Wait 20–30 minutes before making the crepes.

2. PERSONAL E-MAIL

À:	azizam@yahoo.com
De:	elianep@hotmail.com
Objet:	Notre voyage
Cc:	jenb@yahoo.com

Salut, Aziza:

Comme promis, je t'envoie les informations (en pièces jointes) concernant notre voyage. N'hésite pas à les faire suivre aux parents. J'espère que tu vas bien, ainsi que toute ta famille.

Bises,
Eliane

P.S. J'ai reçu les photos que tu m'a envoyées la semaine dernière. Elles sont super! J'ai téléchargé la plus belle—ta fille—sur mon écran . . .

Hi, Aziza:

As promised, I'm sending you the info (in the attachment) about the trip. Don't hesitate to forward it to your parents. I hope you are well, and your family, too.

Love,
Eliane

P.S. I've received the pictures that you sent me last week. They're great! I've downloaded the most beautiful one—your daughter—onto my screen . . .

3. INVITATION TO A WEDDING

Monsieur et madame Pommateau
et
madame Martin, monsieur Petittot
sont heureux de vous annoncer le mariage de leurs enfants
Antoine Pommateau et Marie-Thérèse Petittot
le quatorze avril deux mille huit.
La réception aura lieu à quinze heures au Grand Hôtel du
Casino à Enghien-les-Bains.
R.S.V.P.

Mr. and Ms. Pommateau
and
Ms. Martin, Mr. Pettitot
are happy to announce the wedding of their children
Antoine Pommateau and Marie-Thérèse Petittot
on the fourteenth of April, two thousand eight.
The reception will take place at three o'clock in the afternoon at the
Grand Hôtel du Casino in Enghien-les-Bains.
R.S.V.P.

Notes
Note that **Madame** and **Monsieur** are capitalized when used
without a name; they are written in lowercase letters when a
name follows, e.g., **madame Pommateau. R.S.V.P.** stands for
Répondez, s'il vous plaît *(Please reply).*

4. ADVERTISEMENT

La rentrée au Bon Marché
Des pages d'idées nouvelles pour toute la famille!

Le Bon Marché, Rive Gauche
24, rue de Sèvres, Paris, 7e
Métro: Sèvres-Babylone (lignes 10 et 12)
Service clientèle, tél.: 01–44–39–82–80
www.lebonmarche.fr

Back-to-school sale at the Bon Marché
New ideas for the whole family!

The Bon Marché, Left Bank
40 Sèvres Street, Paris, 7th district
Customer service, tel.: 01–44–39–82–80

5. BUSINESS LETTER

Roger Beaumont
2, rue Chalgrin
17028 La Rochelle

Monsieur le Rédacteur en chef
"Vu"
3, Blvd. des Capucines
75019 Paris

La Rochelle, le 6 novembre 2008

Objet: Abonnement

Monsieur,

Veuillez trouver ci-joint un chèque de 110 euros, montant de mon abonnement d'un an à votre publication.
Veuillez agréer, Monsieur, mes salutations distinguées.

Roger Beaumont

PJ: Chèque

Roger Beaumont
2 Chalgrin Street
17028 La Rochelle

Editor-in-Chief
"Vu"
3 Blvd. des Capucines
Paris 75019
La Rochelle, November 6, 2008

Subject: Subscription

Sir,

Enclosed please find a check for 110 euros to cover a year's subscription to your magazine.

Sincerely,

Roger Beaumont

Encl.: Check

SUPPLEMENTAL VOCABULARY

1. FAMILY AND RELATIONSHIPS

la famille et les liens de parenté	*family and relationships*
la mère	*mother*
le père	*father*
le fils	*son*
la fille	*daughter*
la sœur	*sister*
le bébé	*baby*
le frère	*brother*
le mari	*husband*
la femme	*wife*
la tante	*aunt*
l'oncle	*uncle*
la grand-mère (les grands-mères)	*grandmother*
le grand-père (les grands-pères)	*grandfather*
le cousin/la cousine	*cousin (male/female)*
la belle-mère (les belles-mères)	*mother-in-law*
le beau-père (les beaux-pères)	*father-in-law*
la belle-mère	*stepmother*
le beau-père	*stepfather*
le beau-fils (les beaux-fils)	*son-in-law, stepson*
la belle-fille (les belles-filles)	*daughter-in-law, stepdaughter*
le copain/la copine	*boyfriend/girlfriend*
le fiancé/la fiancée	*fiancé/fiancée (male/female)*
l'ami/l'amie	*friend (male/female)*
le parent	*relative*
aimer	*to like, to love*
connaître (une personne/quelqu'un)	*to know (a person/someone)*

rencontrer (une personne/quelqu'un)	to meet (a person/someone)
épouser (quelqu'un)	to marry (someone)
divorcer de (quelqu'un)	to divorce (someone)
divorcer	to get a divorce
hériter	to inherit

2. PEOPLE

les gens	people
la personne	person
l'homme	man
la femme	woman
l'adulte	adult
l'enfant	child
le garçon	boy
la fille	girl
l'adolescent/l'adolescente	teenager
grand/petit	tall/short
vieux *(m.)*, vieille *(f.)*/jeune	old/young
gros *(m.)*, grosse *(f.)*/mince	fat/thin
amical *(m.)* (amicaux)[1]/peu amical	friendly/unfriendly
heureux *(m.)* (heureux), heureuse *(f.)*/triste	happy/sad
beau *(m.)* (beaux), belle *(f.)*/laid	beautiful/ugly
malade/en bonne santé	sick/healthy
fort/faible	strong/weak
célèbre *(m./f.)*	famous
intelligent	intelligent
talentueux *(m.)* (talentueux), talentueuse *(f.)*	talented

[1] The word in parentheses is the irregular plural form of the masculine form of the adjective.

3. AT HOME

à la maison	at home
la maison	house
l'appartement *(m.)*	apartment
la pièce	room
le salon	living room
la salle à manger (les salles à manger)	dining room
la cuisine	kitchen
la chambre	bedroom
la salle de bain (les salles de bain)	bathroom
le couloir	hall
le placard	closet
la fenêtre	window
la porte	door
la table	table
la chaise	chair
le canapé	sofa, couch
le rideau	curtain
la moquette	carpet
le tapis	rug
la télévision	television
le lecteur de CD	CD player
la lampe	lamp
le lecteur de DVD	DVD player
la chaîne hifi	sound system
la peinture	painting
la photo	photo
l'étagère *(f.)*	shelf
les escaliers	stairs
le plafond	ceiling
le mur	wall
le sol	floor

petit/grand	big/small
nouveau (m.) (nouveaux), nouvelle (f.)/	new/old
vieux (m.) (vieux), vieille (f.)	
en bois	wood, wooden
en plastique	plastic, made of plastic

4. IN THE KITCHEN

dans la cuisine	in the kitchen
le réfrigérateur	refrigerator
l'évier (m.) de la cuisine	(kitchen) sink
le comptoir, le bar	counter
la cuisinière	stove
le four	oven
le micro-onde (les micro-ondes)	microwave
le placard	cupboard
le tiroir	drawer
l'assiette (f.)	plate
la tasse	cup
le saladier	salad bowl
le verre	glass
la cuillère	spoon
le couteau	knife
la boîte de conserve	can
la boîte	box
la bouteille	bottle
la boîte en carton	carton
la cafetière	coffeemaker
la théière	teapot
le mixer	blender
le fer à repasser	iron
la planche à repasser	ironing board
le balai	broom

le lave-vaisselle	*dishwasher*
la machine à laver, le lave-linge	*washing machine*
le sèche-linge	*dryer*
cuisiner	*to cook*
faire la vaisselle	*to do the dishes*
faire la lessive	*to do the laundry*
la lessive vaisselle	*dishwashing detergent*
la lessive	*laundry detergent*
l'eau de javel *(f.)*	*bleach*
propre/sale	*clean/dirty*

5. IN THE BATHROOM

dans la salle de bains	*in the bathroom*
le cabinet de toilette	*toilet*
l'évier (de la salle de bains)	*sink (washbasin)*
la baignoire	*bathtub*
la douche	*shower*
le miroir	*mirror*
l'armoire à pharmacie	*medicine cabinet*
la serviette de bain	*towel*
le papier hygiénique	*toilet paper*
le shampooing	*shampoo*
le savon	*soap*
le gel douche	*bath gel*
la crème à raser	*shaving cream*
le rasoir	*razor*
se laver	*to wash oneself*
prendre une douche	*to take a shower*
prendre un bain	*to take a bath*
se raser	*to shave*
l'eau de cologne *(f.)*	*cologne*
le parfum	*perfume*
le déodorant	*deodorant*

| le bandage, le pansement | bandage |
| la poudre, le talc | powder |

6. IN THE OFFICE

au bureau	in the office
le bureau	office
le bureau	desk
l'ordinateur	computer
le téléphone	telephone
le télécopieur	fax machine
l'étagère/la bibliothèque	bookshelf
le fichier	file
le patron	boss
le collègue/la collègue	colleague (male/female)
l'employé/l'employée	employee (male/female)
le personnel	staff
la société	company
les affaires	business
l'usine	factory
la salle de réunion	meeting room
le rendez-vous	meeting, appointment, date
le salaire	salary
le boulot, le travail	job
occupé	busy
travailler	to work
gagner	to earn

7. AT SCHOOL

à l'école	at school
l'école (f.)	school
l'université (f.)	university
la salle de classe	classroom

le cours	*course*
l'enseignant/l'enseignante	*teacher (male/female)*
le professeur	*teacher, professor*
l'étudiant/l'étudiante	*student (male/female)*
le sujet	*subject*
le cahier	*notebook*
le livre scolaire	*textbook*
les mathématiques	*math*
l'histoire	*history*
la chimie	*chemistry*
la biologie	*biology*
la littérature	*literature*
la langue	*language*
l'art	*art*
la musique	*music*
la gymnastique	*gym*
l'examen	*test*
la note	*grade*
le bulletin scolaire	*report card*
le diplôme	*diploma*
le diplôme universitaire	*college degree*
difficile/facile	*difficult/easy*
étudier	*to study*
apprendre	*to learn*
réussir à un examen	*to pass a test*
râter un examen	*to fail a test*

8. NATURE

la nature	*nature*
l'arbre *(m.)*	*tree*
la fleur	*flower*
la forêt	*forest*

la montagne	mountain
le champ	field
la rivière	river
le fleuve	stream
le lac	lake
l'océan *(m.)*	ocean
la mer	sea
la plage	beach
le désert	desert
le rocher	rock
le sable	sand
le ciel (les cieux)[2]	sky
l'arc-en-ciel	rainbow
le soleil	sun
la lune	moon
l'étoile *(f.)*	star
l'eau *(f.)* (les eaux)	water
la terre	land
la plante	plant
la colline	hill
la mare, l'étang *(m.)*	pond

9. WEATHER

le temps	weather
Il pleut.	It's raining.
Il neige.	It's snowing.
Il grêle.	It's hailing.
Il fait du vent.	It's windy.
Il fait chaud.	It's hot.
Il fait froid.	It's cold.
Il fait soleil./Il fait du soleil.	It's sunny.

[2] The word in parentheses is the irregular plural form of the noun.

C'est nuageux.	*It's cloudy.*
Il fait beau.	*It's beautiful./Nice weather.*
l'orage *(m.)*	*storm*
le vent	*wind*
le soleil	*sun*
le tonnerre	*thunder*
l'éclair *(m.)*	*lightning*
l'ouragan *(m.)*	*hurricane*
la température	*temperature*
le degré	*degree*
la pluie	*rain*
la neige	*snow*
le nuage	*cloud*
le brouillard	*fog*
le parapluie	*umbrella*

10. IN TOWN

en ville	*in town*
la ville	*town, city*
le village	*village*
la voiture	*car*
le bus, l'autocar *(m.)*	*bus*
le train	*train*
le taxi	*taxi*
le métro	*subway, metro*
la circulation	*traffic*
le bâtiment	*building*
l'immeuble *(m.)*	*apartment building*
la bibliothèque	*library*
le restaurant	*restaurant*
le magasin	*store*
la rue	*street*

le parc	*park*
la gare	*train station*
l'aéroport *(m.)*	*airport*
l'avion *(m.)*	*airplane*
l'intersection *(f.)*	*intersection, junction*
le réverbère	*lamppost*
le lampadaire	*streetlight*
la banque	*bank*
l'église *(f.)*	*church*
le temple	*temple*
la mosquée	*mosque*
la synagogue	*synagogue*
le trottoir	*sidewalk*
la boulangerie	*bakery*
la pâtisserie	*pastry shop*
la boucherie	*butcher shop*
la charcuterie	*delicatessen*
la confiserie	*candy store*
le traiteur	*caterer*
le café	*café, coffee shop*
le salon de thé	*tearoom*
la pharmacie	*pharmacy*
le supermarché	*supermarket*
le marché	*market*
le magasin de chaussures	*shoe store*
le magasin de vêtements	*clothing store*
le magasin d'électronique	*electronics store*
la librairie	*bookstore*
le grand magasin	*department store*
le maire	*mayor*
la mairie	*city hall, municipal building*
acheter	*to buy*

faire des courses	*to go food shopping*
près de/loin de	*near/far from*
urbain	*urban*
de banlieue	*suburban*
rural	*rural*

11. ON THE JOB

les professions	*occupations, professions*
le policier/la femme policier	*policeman/policewoman*
l'avocat	*lawyer*
le docteur/la doctoresse	*doctor (male/female)*
l'ingénieur	*engineer*
l'homme d'affaires/	*businessman/businesswoman*
la femme d'affaires	
le vendeur/la vendeuse	*salesman/saleswoman*
l'enseignant/l'enseignante	*teacher (male/female)*
le professeur	*teacher, professor*
le banquier/la banquière	*banker (male/female)*
l'architecte	*architect*
le vétérinaire	*veterinarian*
le dentiste	*dentist*
la femme au foyer/	*stay-at-home mom/stay-at-home dad*
l'homme au foyer	
le charpentier	*carpenter*
l'ouvrier en bâtiment	*construction worker*
le chauffeur de taxi	*taxi driver*
l'artiste	*artist*
l'écrivain	*writer*
le plombier	*plumber*
l'électricien	*electrician*
le journaliste/la journaliste	*journalist (male/female)*
l'acteur/l'actrice	*actor/actress*
le musicien/la musicienne	*musician (male/female)*

le fermier/la fermière	*farmer (male/female)*
le secrétaire/la secrétaire	*secretary (male/ female)*
l'assistant/ l'assistante	*assistant (male/female)*
sans emploi, au chômage	*unemployed*
à la retraite	*retired*
à plein temps	*full-time*
à temps partiel	*part-time*
l'emploi régulier *(m.)*	*steady job*
l'emploi saisonnier	*summer job*

12. COMPUTERS AND THE INTERNET

les ordinateurs et Internet	*computers and the internet*
l'ordinateur *(m.)*	*computer*
le clavier	*keyboard*
l'écran *(m.)*	*monitor, screen*
l'imprimante *(f.)*	*printer*
la souris	*mouse*
le modem	*modem*
la mémoire	*memory*
le CD Rom	*CD-ROM*
le lecteur de CD Rom	*CD-ROM drive*
le fichier	*file*
le dossier	*folder*
le document	*document*
le câble	*cable*
le logiciel	*software*
Internet	*internet*
le site web	*website*
la page web	*webpage*
le mail, l'e-mail, le courrier électronique	*e-mail*
la salle de chat	*chatroom*

le message instantané	*instant message*
la pièce jointe	*attachment*
envoyer un courrier électronique/un mail/un e-mail	*to send an e-mail*
envoyer un fichier	*to send a file*
faire suivre	*to forward*
répondre	*to reply*
supprimer	*to delete*
sauvegarder un document	*to save a document*
ouvrir un fichier	*to open a file*
fermer un fichier	*to close a file*
envoyer en pièces jointes	*to attach a file*
télécharger	*to download*
les outils de recherche	*search engine*

13. SPORTS AND RECREATION

les sports et les loisirs	*sports and recreation*
le football	*soccer*
le basket-ball	*basketball*
le baseball	*baseball*
le football américain	*football*
le hockey	*hockey*
le tennis	*tennis*
le rugby	*rugby*
le match	*game*
l'équipe *(f.)*	*team*
le stade	*stadium*
l'entraîneur *(m.)*	*coach*
le joueur/la joueuse	*player (male/female)*
le champion, la championne	*champion (male/female)*
le ballon, la balle (smaller)	*ball*
faire de la marche	*to go hiking*

camper	to go camping
faire du sport	to play a sport
jouer un match	to play a game
gagner	to win
perdre	to lose
faire match nul	to tie
les cartes	cards
le billard	pool, billiards

14. ENTERTAINMENT

le spectacle	entertainment, show
le film	movie, film
le divertissement	recreation, pastime
aller au cinéma	to go to the movies
voir un film	to see a movie
le théâtre	theater
voir une pièce	to see a play
l'opéra (m.)	opera
le concert	concert
le club	club
le cirque	circus
la place de concert	concert ticket
le musée	museum
la galerie	gallery
la peinture	painting
la sculpture	sculpture
l'émission	television program, radio program
regarder la télévision	to watch television
la comédie	comedy
le documentaire	documentary
le drame	drama
le livre	book

le magazine, la revue	*magazine*
lire un livre	*to read a book*
lire un magazine	*to read a magazine*
écouter de la musique	*to listen to music*
la chanson	*song*
le groupe de musique	*band*
les nouvelles	*the news*
changer de chaîne	*to change channels*
s'amuser	*to have fun*
s'ennuyer	*to be bored*
amusant	*funny*
intéressant	*interesting*
passionnant	*exciting*
effrayant	*scary*
la partie, la soirée	*party*
aller au restaurant	*to go to the restaurant*
aller à une fête	*to go to a party*
organiser une fête	*to have a party*
danser	*to dance*

15. FOOD

la nourriture	*food*
le dîner	*dinner*
le déjeuner	*lunch*
le petit déjeuner	*breakfast*
le repas	*meal*
la viande	*meat*
le poulet	*chicken*
le bœuf	*beef*
le porc	*pork*
l'agneau *(m.)*	*lamb*
le poisson	*fish*

les crevettes	*shrimp*
le homard	*lobster*
le pain	*bread*
l'œuf *(m.)*	*egg*
le fromage	*cheese*
le riz	*rice*
le légume	*vegetable*
la laitue	*lettuce*
la tomate	*tomato*
la carotte	*carrot*
le concombre	*cucumber*
le poivron	*pepper*
le fruit, les fruits	*fruit*
la pomme	*apple*
l'orange *(f.)*	*orange*
la banane	*banana*
la poire	*pear*
le raisin (also, les raisins)	*grapes*
la boisson	*drink*
l'eau *(f.)*	*water*
le lait	*milk*
le jus	*juice*
le café	*coffee*
le thé	*tea*
le vin	*wine*
la bière	*beer*
la boisson sans alcool	*non-alcoholic drink*
la boisson gazeuse	*carbonated drink*
le sel	*salt*
le poivre	*pepper*
le sucre	*sugar*
le miel	*honey*

chaud/froid	*hot/cold*
doux/aigre	*sweet/sour*

16. CLOTHING

les vêtements	*clothing*
la chemise	*shirt*
le pantalon	*pants*
le jean	*jeans*
le T-shirt	*tee shirt*
la chaussure	*shoe*
la chaussette	*sock*
la ceinture	*belt*
la (chaussure de) basket	*sneaker, tennis shoe*
la robe	*dress*
la jupe	*skirt*
le chemisier	*blouse*
le costume	*suit*
le chapeau	*hat*
le gant	*glove(s)*
le foulard, l'écharpe *(f.)*	*scarf*
la veste	*jacket*
le manteau	*coat*
le bijou	*jewel*
les bijoux	*jewelry*
la boucle d'oreille	*earring*
le bracelet	*bracelet*
le collier	*necklace*
les lunettes	*eyeglasses*
les lunettes de soleil	*sunglasses*
la montre	*watch*
la bague	*ring*
les sous-vêtements, le caleçon	*underpants*
le soutien-gorge	*bra*

le slip, la culotte	panties
le string	thong
le tricot de peau	undershirt
le maillot de bain	bathing trunks, bathing suit
le pyjama	pajamas
le coton	cotton
le cuir	leather
la soie	silk
la taille	size
porter	to wear

17. THE HUMAN BODY

le corps	the human body
la tête	head
le visage	face
le front	forehead
l'œil (m.), les yeux	eye, eyes
le sourcil	eyebrow
le cil, les cils	eyelash, eyelashes
l'oreille (f.)	ear
le nez	nose
la bouche	mouth
la dent	tooth
la langue	tongue
la joue	cheek
le menton	chin
les cheveux	hair
le cou	neck
la poitrine	chest, breast
les seins	breasts
les épaules (m.)	shoulders
le bras	arm

le coude	*elbow*
le poignet	*wrist*
la main	*hand*
le doigt	*finger*
l'estomac	*stomach, abdomen*
le foie	*liver*
les fesses	*buttocks*
la jambe	*leg*
le genou, les genoux	*knee, knees*
la cheville	*ankle*
le pied	*foot*
le doigt	*finger*
l'orteil *(m.)*, le doigt de pied	*toe*
la peau	*skin*
le sang	*blood*
le cerveau	*brain*
le cœur	*heart*
les poumons *(m.)*	*lungs*
l'os *(m.)*, les os	*bone, bones*
le muscle	*muscle*
le tendon	*tendon*

18. TRAVEL AND TOURISM

le voyage et le tourisme	*travel and tourism*
le touriste/la touriste	*tourist (male/female)*
l'hôtel *(m.)*	*hotel*
l'auberge *(f.)* de jeunesse	*youth hostel*
la réception	*reception desk*
prendre une chambre	*to check in*
régler sa note	*to check out*

la réservation	*reservation*
le passeport	*passport*
le circuit en bus	*tour bus*
la visite guidée	*guided tour*
l'appareil photo *(m.)*	*camera*
le centre d'informations	*information center*
la carte, le plan	*map*
la brochure	*brochure*
le monument	*monument*
aller visiter	*to go sightseeing*
prendre une photo	*to take a picture*
Pourriez-vous nous prendre en photo, s'il vous plaît?	*Can you take our picture?*

INTERNET RESOURCES

The following is a list of French language websites that you will find interesting and useful.

www.livinglanguage.com	Living Language's site offers online courses, descriptions of supplemental learning material, resources for teachers and librarians, and much more.
www.french-linguistics.co.uk/ dictionary	This site contains a handy French-English/English-French dictionary.
www.francemonthly.com	A travel site (and more) that will give you great ideas about where to travel. Beautiful pictures, and lots of cultural material.
www.yahoo.fr	Yahoo! France. A good way to increase your French vocabulary and learn about life in France.
www.lemonde.fr	Le Monde is a serious daily newspaper covering international and national news, as well as culture, sports, science, and more.
www.monde-diplomatique.fr	A monthly edition of Le Monde.

www.courrierinternational .com	Le Courrier International is a weekly newspaper that collects material from international press sources and translates it in French. A good way to practice French while getting an international perspective on the news.
www.paroles.net	A site that provides the lyrics for most French songs. A great way to practice and learn French, especially if you get the CD and sing along!
www.google.fr	Google in the French language.
www.fnac.com	FNAC is a famous French bookstore chain. This is a great website to learn French as well as order your French books, CDs or DVDs.
http://fr.wikipedia.org/wiki/ Accueil	Wikipedia in French.
www.tv5.org/locaux/usa	A global French language network broadcasting in French 24 hours a day.
www.france5.fr/videos	Educational TV in French with some free videos.
www.frenchculture.org	Everything about the French culture in the USA. Check the TV & Radio tab as well.
www.marmiton.org/recettes	Simple recipes in the French language for the food lover.

SUMMARY OF FRENCH GRAMMAR

1. THE ALPHABET

a	a	*j*	ji	*s*	esse
b	bé	*k*	ka	*t*	té
c	cé	*l*	elle	*u*	u
d	dé	*m*	emme	*v*	vé
e	e	*n*	enne	*w*	double vé
f	effe	*o*	o	*x*	iks
g	gé	*p*	pé	*y*	i grec
h	ache	*q*	ku	*z*	zède
i	i	*r*	erre		

2. THE NUMBERS

0	zéro	11	onze	30	trente
1	un	12	douze	40	quarante
2	deux	13	treize	50	cinquante
3	trois	14	quatorze	60	soixante
4	quatre	15	quinze	70	soixante-dix
5	cinq	16	seize	80	quatre-vingts
6	six	17	dix-sept	81	quatre-vingt-un
7	sept	18	dix-huit	90	quatre-vingt-dix
8	huit	19	dix-neuf	100	cent
9	neuf	20	vingt	101	cent un
10	dix	21	vingt et un	1,000	mille

3. THE APOSTROPHE

Certain one-syllable words ending in a vowel drop, or "elide," the vowel when they come before words beginning with a vowel sound.

This dropping of the vowel, or "elision," is marked by an apostrophe. Common cases are:

3.1 The **a** of **la**:

je l'aime	*I like her (or it)*
l'heure	*the hour*
l'amande	*the almond*

3.2 The vowel **e** in one-syllable words (**le, je, se, me, que,** etc.):

l'argent	*the money*
j'habite	*I live*
j'ai	*I have*

3.3 The vowel **i** in **si** *(if)*, when it comes before **il** *(he)* or **ils** *(they)*:

s'il vous plaît	*please (lit., if it pleases you)*

3.4 **Moi** and **toi** when they come before **en** are written **m'** and **t'**:

Donnez m'en.	*Give me some of it (of them).*

3.5 A few words like:

aujourd'hui	*today*
entr'acte	*interlude*

4. THE DEFINITE ARTICLE

4.1 The forms of the definite article *(the)* are:

	Singular	Plural
Masculine	**le**	**les**
Feminine	**la**	**les**

le garçon	*the boy*
la fille	*the girl*
les garçons	*the boys*
les filles	*the girls*

Le and **la** become **l'** before words beginning with a vowel sound. This contraction takes place before most words beginning with **h** (this **h** is called "mute" **h**). There are a few words where this contraction does not occur (this **h** is called "aspirate" **h**).

l'ami	*the friend*
le héros	*the hero*
l'heure	*the hour*
la hache	*the ax*

4.2 The definite article is used:

a. before a noun used in a general sense, before titles, days of the week, parts of the body, etc.:

l'avion	*the airplane*
le dimanche	*Sunday, Sundays*
le Comte . . .	*Count . . .*
J'aime les livres.	*I like books.*
Le fer est utile.	*Iron is useful.*
L'avarice est un vice.	*Avarice is a vice.*
Je vais me laver les mains.	*I'm going to wash my hands.*

b. with names of languages, unless preceded by **en**:

Le français est difficile.　　　　　*French is difficult.*

Elle raconte l'histoire en français.　　*She tells the story in French.*

Note: The article is usually omitted with the name of a language used immediately after the verb **parler**.

Elle parle français.　　　　　*She speaks French.*

4.3 Unlike English, the definite articles must be repeated before each noun they modify:

les portes et les fenêtres　　　*the doors and windows*

5. THE INDEFINITE ARTICLE

5.1 The forms of the indefinite article *(a/an)* are:

	Singular	Plural
Masculine	**un**	**des**
Feminine	**une**	**des**

un homme　　　　*a man*

une femme　　　　*a woman*

des hommes　　　*men; some men; a few men*

des femmes　　　*women; some women; a few women*

As you can see, **des** is often used to mean *some* or *a few*.

5.2 The indefinite article is used:

a. with an adjective:

C'est un bon médecin.　　　*He is a good doctor.*

b. but <u>not</u> before an unmodified statement of profession, nationality, rank, etc.:

Je suis médecin.	*I am a doctor.*
Elle est américaine.	*She is an American.*
Il est capitaine.	*He is a captain.*

5.3 The indefinite articles are repeated before each noun:

un homme et une femme *a man and a woman*

6. THE POSSESSIVE

Possession is shown in the following way:

State the thing possessed + **de** *(of)* + the possessor:

le livre de Marie	*Marie's book (lit., the book of Marie)*
le stylo de l'élève	*the pupil's pen (lit., the pen of the pupil)*

7. CONTRACTIONS

7.1 The preposition **de** *(of)* combines with the definite articles **le** and **les** as follows. There is no contraction with **la** or **l'**.

a. **de + le = du**:

le livre du professeur *the teacher's book*

b. **de + les = des**:

les stylos des élèves *the pupils' pens*

7.2 The preposition **à** *(to)* combines with the articles **le** and **les** as follows. There is no contraction with **la** or **l'**.

a. **à + le = au**:

Il parle au garçon. *He's talking to the boy.*

b. à + les = aux:

Il parle aux garçons. *He's talking to the boys.*

8. GENDER

All nouns in French, even those that refer to objects, are either masculine or feminine. The gender of each noun must be learned with the noun.

Nouns referring to males are masculine, and nouns referring to females are feminine.

le père	*father*
la mère	*mother*
le roi	*king*
la reine	*queen*

There are exceptions. Here are a few: **la sentinelle** *(sentinel)*, even if male, and **le professeur** *(teacher)* if female or male.

However, you will not often be able to figure out the gender of the noun based on its sex, such as when the noun is an inanimate object or an abstract concept. Nevertheless, there are some general rules that will help you to know the gender of a noun in such cases.

8.1 The following classes of nouns are generally masculine:

a. Nouns ending in a consonant:

le parc	*park*
le tarif	*rate, tariff*
le pont	*bridge*

Exceptions: Nouns ending in **-ion** and **-son** are generally feminine.

l'action	*action*
la raison	*reason*
la conversation	*conversation*

b. Nouns ending in any vowel except "mute" **e**:

le pari	*bet, wager*
le menu	*menu*
le vélo	*bicycle*

Exceptions: Nouns ending in–**age**.

c. Nouns ending in **-ment, -age** and **-ège** (note that **-age** and **-ège** end in "mute" **e**):

le ménage	*household*
le document	*document*
le manège	*riding school*
l'usage	*usage*

d. Names of days, months, seasons, metals, colors, trees, shrubs:

le jeudi	*Thursday*
(le) septembre	*September*
le printemps	*spring*
l'or	*gold*
le plomb	*lead*
le bleu	*blue*
le chêne	*oak*
l'olivier	*olive tree*
le genêt	*broom (a shrub)*

e. The names of parts of speech when used as nouns:

le nom	*noun*
le participe	*participle*
le verbe	*verb*

f. Metric weights and measures.

le mètre	*meter*
le kilogramme	*kilogram*
le litre	*liter*

Note the contrast with a non-metric measure: **la livre** *(pound)*.

g. The names of the cardinal points.

le nord	*north*
le sud	*south*
l'est	*east*
l'ouest	*west*

8.2 The following classes of nouns are generally feminine:

a. Nouns ending in **-te, -son, -ion**:

la détente	*détente*
la conversation	*conversation*
la raison	*reason*

Exceptions:

le camion	*truck*
le million	*million*
l'avion	*airplane*

b. Names of qualities or states of being ending in: **-nce, -esse, -eur, -ude**:

la distance	*distance*
la gentillesse	*niceness*
la largeur	*width*
la douceur	*sweetness*
la gratitude	*gratitude*

Exceptions:

| le bonheur | happiness |
| le malheur | unhappiness, misfortune |

c. Most nouns ending in mute **e**:

| la blague | joke |
| la voiture | car |

d. Names of moral qualities, sciences and the arts:

la bonté	kindness	l'avarice	greed
l'algèbre	algebra	la chimie	chemistry
la peinture	painting	la musique	music

Exceptions: **l'art** *(art)* is masculine.

e. Most names of fruits:

| la pomme | apple |
| la cerise | cherry |

Exceptions:

| le pamplemousse | grapefruit |
| le raisin | grapes |

f. Nouns ending in **-té**:

l'activité	activity
la générosité	generosity
la proximité	proximity
la priorité	priority

9. THE PLURAL OF NOUNS

9.1 Most nouns add **-s** to form the plural:

| la ville | the city | les villes | the cities |
| l'île | the island | les îles | the islands |

9.2 Nouns ending in **-s, -x, -z** do not change:

le fils	*the son*	les fils	*the sons*
la voix	*the voice*	les voix	*the voices*
le nez	*the nose*	les nez	*the noses*

9.3 Nouns ending in **-au** or **-eu** add **-x**:

le chapeau	*the hat*	les chapeaux	*the hats*
l'eau	*water*	les eaux	*waters*
le jeu	*the game*	les jeux	*the games*

9.4 Nouns ending in **-al** and **-ail** form the plural with **-aux**:

l'hôpital	*the hospital*	les hôpitaux	*the hospitals*
le travail	*work*	les travaux	*works*

9.5 Some irregular plurals:

le ciel	*the sky*	les cieux	*the heavens*
l'œil	*the eye*	les yeux	*the eyes*
Madame	*Madam, Mrs., Ms.*	Mesdames	*Madams*
Mademoiselle	*Miss*	Mesdemoiselles	*Misses*
Monsieur	*Sir, Mr.*	Messieurs	*Sirs*
le bonhomme	*the fellow*	les bonshommes	*the fellows*

10. ADJECTIVES

10.1 Adjectives agree with the nouns they modify in gender and number; that is, they are masculine if the noun is masculine, plural if the noun is plural, etc.:

Marie et sa sœur sont grandes.	*Marie and her sister are tall.*
Pierre est grand.	*Pierre is tall.*

10.2 The following adjectives have two forms for the masculine singular:

Masculine		Feminine	
Before a consonant	Before a vowel or "mute" *h*		
beau	bel	belle	*beautiful, handsome*
nouveau	nouvel	nouvelle	*new*
vieux	vieil	vieille	*old*

un beau livre   *a beautiful book*
un bel arbre   *a beautiful tree*
une belle femme   *a beautiful woman*

10.3 The feminine of adjectives is normally formed by adding **-e** to the masculine singular:

un petit garçon   *a little boy*
une petite fille   *a little girl*

a. If the masculine singular already ends in **-e,** the adjective has the same form in the feminine:

un jeune homme   *a young man*
une jeune femme   *a young woman*

b. Adjectives ending in **-er** in the masculine singular change the **e** to **è** and then add **-e:**

Masculine	Feminine	
étranger	étrangère	*foreign*

c. Most adjectives ending in **-eux** in the masculine singular change this ending to **-euse**:

Masculine	Feminine	
heureux	**heureuse**	*happy*
sérieux	**sérieuse**	*serious*

d. Some adjectives double the final consonant of the masculine singular form and add **-e**:

Masculine	Feminine	
bon	**bonne**	*good*
ancien	**ancienne**	*former, ancient*
gentil	**gentille**	*nice*
gros	**grosse**	*fat*

e. Adjectives ending in **-eau** in the masculine singular change the **-au** to **-lle**:

Masculine	Feminine	
beau	**belle**	*beautiful*
nouveau	**nouvelle**	*new*

f. There are also a number of irregular feminines:

Masculine	Feminine	
actif	**active**	*active*
blanc	**blanche**	*white*
doux	**douce**	*sweet, gentle, soft*
faux	**fausse**	*false*
long	**longue**	*long*
vieux	**vieille**	*old*

10.4 The plural of adjectives is regularly formed by adding **-s** to the singular:

	Singular		Plural	
Masculine	**un petit garçon**	*a little boy*	**deux petits garçons**	*two little boys*
Feminine	**une petite fille**	*a little girl*	**deux petites filles**	*two little girls*

a. But if the the adjective ends in **-s** or **-x** in the masculine singular, the masculine plural stays the same:

un mauvais garçon	*a bad boy*
deux mauvais garçons	*two bad boys*

b. Adjectives ending in **-au** add **-x**:

un nouveau livre	*a new book*
des nouveaux livres	*new books*

c. Adjectives ending in **-al** change to **-aux**:
un homme loyal   *a loyal man*
des hommes loyaux   *loyal men*

10.5 An adjective that modifies nouns of different gender is in the masculine plural:
Marie et Jean sont petits.   *Marie and Jean are little.*

11. POSITION OF ADJECTIVES

11.1 Adjectives usually follow the noun:
un livre français   *a French book*
un homme intéressant   *an interesting man*
une idée excellente   *an excellent idea*

11.2 There are some common adjectives, however, that usually precede the nouns they modify. These are often known as the "BAGS" adjectives because they are the adjectives that deal with Beauty, Age, Good (and Bad), and Size.

beau	*beautiful*	joli	*pretty*
bon	*good*	long	*long*
court	*short*	mauvais	*bad*
gentil	*nice, pleasant*	nouveau	*new*
gros	*big, fat*	petit	*small, little*
jeune	*young*	vieux	*old*

11.3 The following common adjectives differ in meaning depending on whether they come before or after the noun:

	Before the Noun	After the Noun
ancien	*former*	*ancient*
grand	*great*	*tall*
brave	*worthy*	*brave*
cher	*dear (beloved)*	*expensive*
pauvre	*poor (wretched)*	*poor (impoverished)*
propre	*own*	*clean*
même	*same*	*himself, herself, itself, very*

12. COMPARISON OF ADJECTIVES

12.1 Most adjectives form the comparative with **plus** *(more)* and **moins** *(less)*, using **que** where English uses *than*. To express *as . . . as,* use **aussi** and **que**.

difficile	*difficult*
plus difficile (que)	*more difficult (than)*
moins difficile (que)	*less difficult (than)*
aussi difficile (que)	*as difficult (as)*

Note that the adjective still has to agree with the noun it is modifying.

Jeanne est plus grande que Robert.   *Jeanne is taller than Robert.*

12.2 To express the superlative of something, use **le (la, les)** + **plus** + adjective to express superiority *(the most, -est)* and **le (la, les)** + **moins** + adjective to express inferiority *(the least)*.

la plus belle	*the most beautiful*	la moins belle	*the least beautiful*
le plus joli	*the prettiest*	le moins joli	*the least pretty*

12.3 Certain common adjectives have irregular forms in comparison:

bon	*good*	mauvais	*bad*
meilleur	*better*	plus mauvais, pire	*worse*
le meilleur	*the best*	le plus mauvais, le pire	*the worst*

13. POSSESSIVE ADJECTIVES

13.1. Possessive adjectives agree in gender and number with the thing possessed:

Before Singular Nouns		Before Plural Nouns	
Masculine	Feminine	Masculine and Feminine	
mon	ma	mes	*my*
ton	ta	tes	*your (fam.)*
son	sa	ses	*his, her, its*
notre	notre	nos	*our*
votre	votre	vos	*your*
leur	leur	leurs	*their*

mon chien	*my dog*
sa mère	*his (or her) mother*
ma robe	*my dress*
votre livre	*your book*
leurs crayons	*their pencils*

13.2 Notice that these adjectives agree in gender not with the possessor as in English, but with the noun they modify. For example, **son** could mean *his, her,* or *its.*

| Jean parle à son père. | *Jean is talking to his father.* |
| Marie parle à son père. | *Marie is talking to her father.* |

13.3 Possessive adjectives are repeated before each noun they modify:

| mon père et ma mère | *my father and mother* |
| leurs livres et leurs stylos | *their books and pens* |

13.4 Before a feminine word beginning with a vowel or "mute" **h,** the forms **mon, ton,** and **son** are used instead of **ma, ta,** and **sa.**

| son histoire | *his/her story, his/her history* |
| son école | *his/her school* |

13.5 In speaking of parts of the body, the definite article is usually used instead of the possessive adjective (except where it might be ambiguous):

| Elle lève la main. | *She raises her hand.* |

14. DEMONSTRATIVE ADJECTIVES

14.1 The demonstrative adjective in French stands for both *this* and *that* (plural *these* and *those*). Demonstrative adjectives agree with the nouns they modify in gender and number:

a. Masculine singular: **ce** or **cet**
ce: before a consonant
cet: before a vowel or "mute" **h**

ce livre	*this (that) book*
cet arbre	*this (that) tree*
cet homme	*this (that) man*

b. Feminine singular: cette

| cette femme | *this (that) woman* |

c. Plural: ces

| ces hommes | *these (those) men* |
| ces femmes | *these (those) women* |

14.2 Demonstrative adjectives must be repeated before each noun:

| cet homme et cette femme | *this man and this woman* |

14.3 When it is necessary to distinguish between *this* and *that*, -**ci** and -**là** are added to the noun.

Donnez-moi ce livre-ci.	*Give me this book.*
Voulez-vous cette robe-là?	*Do you want that dress (over there)?*
J'aime ce livre-ci mais je n'aime pas ce livre-là.	*I like this book but I don't like that book.*

15. DEMONSTRATIVE PRONOUNS

A demonstrative pronoun replaces a demonstrative adjective and its noun. Like demonstrative adjectives, they agree in gender and number with the nouns they are replacing.

Masculine singular	**celui**	*this one, that one, the one*
Feminine singular	**celle**	*this one, that one, the one*
Masculine plural	**ceux**	*these, those, the ones*
Feminine plural	**celles**	*these, those, the ones*

As with demonstrative adjectives, -ci and -là can be added to the pronoun to make a distinction between the two nouns.

Préférez-vous celui-ci ou celui-là?	*Do you prefer this one or that one?*
J'aime celui-ci.	*I like this one.*
Donne-moi celle de ton frère.	*Give me your brother's. (calculator [la calculatrice], for example).*
Ceux qui sont sur cette étagère sont en solde.	*Those that are on this shelf are on sale.*

16. Y AND EN

Y and en are two important adverbial pronouns in French.

16.1 Y

a. Y is a pronoun meaning *there* which always refers to things or places.

It usually replaces à + noun but may also replace other prepositions such as dans *(in)*, sur *(on)*, or chez *(at)* + noun.

It can be used to replace a location when the location has already been referenced and in English it commonly also means *to it/them, in it/them, on it/them.* Sometimes the equivalent is not expressed in English.

It is placed before the verb.

Elle va à Paris au printemps.	*She's going to Paris in the spring.*
Elle y va.	*She's going there.*

b. Y also forms part of the very common and useful expression il y a, which means *there is* or *there are:*

Il y a un train à 10 heures.	*There is a train at 10 a.m.*
Il y a trois chats.	*There are three cats.*
Il n'y a pas de chats.	*There are no cats.*

16.2 En

En is a pronoun that generally means *some*. It is used to replace the partitive article (or **de**) + a noun. For more on partitives, see section 24.

When **en** replaces a quantity, the quantity expression remains. Also note that in an inversion, **en** comes before the verb.

Nous buvons du thé.	*We drink tea.*
Nous en buvons.	*We drink some.*
Je mange beaucoup de fromage.	*I eat a lot of cheese.*
J'en mange beaucoup.	*I eat a lot of it.*
Je voudrais une livre et demie de champignons.	*I would like a pound and a half of mushrooms*
J'en voudrais une livre et demie.	*I would like a pound and a half.*
Vous en voulez un kilo.	*You want a kilo.*
En voulez-vous un kilo?	*Do you want a kilo?*

17. PERSONAL PRONOUNS

The forms of the pronouns depend on how they are used in a sentence:

17.1 Subject pronouns:

je/j'	*I*
tu	*you (infml.)*
il	*he, it*
elle	*she, it*
on	*we, one, people, you, they*
nous	*we*

vous	*you*
ils	*they*
elles	*they*

Je suis heureuse.	*I am happy.*
Nous allons au cinéma.	*We're going to the movie theater.*

a. **Vous** and **tu**

Vous is the pronoun normally used in talking to several people; the plural form of *you*. It is also used in talking to someone you don't know very well or someone who is older than you **(vous** is more polite or formal and shows respect).

Tu is the familiar form that is used only when addressing people you know very well (a member of one's family or a close friend; also a child, pet, etc.).

b. **Il, elle, ils,** and **elles** are used as pronouns referring to things as well as to persons. They agree with the nouns they refer to in gender and number:

Où est le livre?	*Where's the book?*
Il est sur la table.	*It's on the table.*
Où est la lettre?	*Where's the letter?*
Elle est sur la table.	*It's on the table.*
Où sont les livres et les lettres?	*Where are the books and letters?*
Ils sont sur la table.	*They're on the table.*

Notice that **ils** is used when referring to multiple nouns of different genders (**les livres** [*m.*] **et les lettres** [*f.*]). This applies to people as well as to things. For example, if you are talking about a group of three girls and one boy, you would use **ils**.

Les trois filles et le garçon,   *The three girls and the boy,*
ils regardent la télévision.   *they're watching television.*

17.2 DIRECT OBJECT PRONOUNS

The direct object pronoun takes the place of the direct object in a sentence. Direct object pronouns must agree in gender and number with the noun they replace. They come before the verb.

me/m'	*me*
te/t'	*you (infml.)*
le/l'	*him, it*
la/l'	*her, it*
nous	*us*
vous	*you*
les	*them*

Je te comprends.   *I understand you (infml.).*
J'aime la robe.   *I like the dress.*
Je l'aime.   *I like it.*

17.3 INDIRECT OBJECT PRONOUNS

An indirect object is the person to whom or for whom an action is done. It is linked to the verb by the preposition **à** and receives the action of the verb indirectly. It comes before the verb. Indirect object pronouns look similar to the direct object pronouns except in the third persons singular and plural. The word *to* is always included in the definition.

me/m'	*to me*
te/t'	*to you (infml.)*
lui	*to him, to her*
nous	*to us*
vous	*to you*
leur	*to them*

Je parle à ma fille.	*I speak to my daughter.*
Je lui parle.	*I speak to her.*

17.4 DISJUNCTIVE (STRESSED) PRONOUNS

These pronouns are emphatic and call attention to a person or to what that person is doing or saying.

They are used: to emphasize a subject pronoun, after prepositions, in comparisons, after **c'est** or **ce sont,** in response to questions (when used alone), and in certain expressions, such as **Moi non plus** *(Neither do/am I, Me neither)* and **Moi aussi** *(Me too, So do/am I).*

moi	*I, me*
toi	*you (infml.)*
soi	*himself, herself, oneself, itself*
lui	*he, him*
elle	*she, her*

nous	we, us
vous	you
eux	they, them (m.)
elles	they, them (f.)

Moi, j'ai six ans!	I'm six! (lit., Me, I'm six!)
Je viens avec toi.	I'm coming with you.
Elle est plus intelligente que toi.	She is smarter than you.
C'est toi sur la photo?	It's you in the picture?
-Qui est là? -Moi.	-Who's there? -Me.

17.5 Reflexive pronouns

In a reflexive verb, the person or thing does the action to himself, herself or itself. In other words, the one who does the action also receives it. For example: *I dress myself.* Reflexive pronouns normally precede the verb to turn that verb into a "reflexive" one.

me	myself
te	yourself (infml.)
se	himself, herself, itself, oneself
nous	ourselves
vous	yourself, yourselves
se	themselves

Je lave la voiture.	I wash the car.
Je me lave.	I wash myself, I get washed.
J'appelle Paul.	I'm calling Paul.
Je m'appelle Paul.	My name is Paul. (I am called Paul.)

Note that many reflexive verbs in French are not reflexive in English.

Reflexive pronouns in the affirmative imperative follow the verb and are connected to it with a hyphen. After the verb, **toi** is used instead of **te.**

Tu t'amuses.	*You are having fun.*
Amuse-toi bien!	*Have fun!*

18. POSITION OF PRONOUNS

Apart from disjunctive pronouns (see 17.4 above), personal pronouns, as well as **y** and **en,** generally precede the verb except in affirmative commands and requests. Pronouns <u>do</u> precede the verb in negative commands and requests.

18.1 When there are multiple pronouns before a verb, they are placed in the following order:

subject pronoun	me te se nous vous	le la l' les	lui leur	y	en	verb

Il me le donne.	*He gives it to me.*
Il le lui donne.	*He gives it to him (to her, to it).*
Je l'y ai vu.	*I saw him (her, it) there.*
Je leur en parlerai.	*I'll speak to them about it.*
Il y en a trois.	*There are three of them.*

18.2 In affirmative commands and requests (positive imperative), pronouns are placed after the verb and connected by hyphens. The direct object pronoun precedes the indirect:

positive imperative form of verb	le la les	me (moi) te (toi) lui nous vous leur	y	en

Donnez-le-lui.	*Give it to him.*
Donnez-leur-en.	*Give them some.*
Allez-vous-en.	*Go away./Get out of here.*
Donnez-moi le livre.	*Give me the book.*
Donnez-le-moi.	*Give it to me.*
Montrez-moi des pommes.	*Show me apples.*
Montrez-m'en.	*Show me some.*
Écrivez-lui la lettre.	*Write him the letter.*
Écrivez-la-lui.	*Write it to him.*

Note that when **moi** or **toi** are used with **en,** they become **m'** and **t'** and precede **en.**

Va t'en.	*Go away./Get out of here.*

18.3 The pronoun objects precede **voici** and **voilà**:

Où est le livre?	*Where's the book?*
Le voici.	*Here it is.*
Les voilà.	*There they are.*

19. RELATIVE PRONOUNS

Relative pronouns link the dependent part of a sentence to the main clause. For example, in the sentence, *This is the book that I read, that* is the relative pronoun that connects the main clause *(This is the book)* with the dependent clause *(that I read)*.

Although we sometimes omit the relative pronoun in English *(You're eating the dessert [that] I made)*, it must be used in French.

Relative pronouns can be the subject or direct object of the verb, or the object of a preposition, in the dependent clause.

19.1. As the subject of a verb (can be used for both persons and things):

qui	who, which, that

L'homme qui est là . . .   *The man who is there . . .*
Voici la dent qui me fait mal.   *Here's the tooth that hurts me.*

19.2. As the object of a verb (can be used for both persons and things):

que/qu'	whom, which, that

L'homme que tu vois . . .   *The man whom you see . . .*
Voici la dent que le dentiste   *Here's the tooth that the dentist is*
va m'arracher.   *going to pull out.*

19.3 As the object of a preposition:

a. For a person

qui	whom

C'est la femme pour qui je   *She's the woman for whom I work.*
travaille.
La dame à qui vous parlez   *The woman to whom you are*
                                  speaking
s'appelle Sophie.   *is named Sophie.*

b. For a thing

lequel *(m. sg.)* **laquelle** *(f. sg.)* **lesquels** *(m. pl.)* **lesquelles** *(f. pl.)*	*which*

Voici la maison dans laquelle nous habitons.	*Here is the house in which we live.*

As you can see, the relative pronoun *lequel* and its forms agree in gender and number with the nouns to which they refer.

19.4 Sometimes the word **où** *(where)* is used as a relative pronoun. It can be used with both places and time.

Connaissez-vous l'endroit où il habite?	*Do you know the place where he lives?*
Le jour où je suis partie en vacances . . .	*The day (that, when) I left for vacation . . .*

19.5 The relative pronoun **dont** can take on two meanings:

a. dont *(whose)*

Dont can take on the possessive meaning of *whose*.

C'est le mari dont la femme est actrice.	*That's the husband whose wife is an actress.*

b. dont *(of whom, of which)*

Dont is used with verbs or expressions that use the preposition **de,** such as **parler de** *(to talk about)*, **avoir besoin de** *(to need)*, **se souvenir de** *(to remember)*, etc.

J'ai besoin du stylo./Voici le stylo dont j'ai besoin.	I need the pen./Here's the pen I need (lit., of which I have need).
Les enfants dont je parle sont mes enfants.	The children of whom I am talking are my children.

20. INDEFINITE RELATIVE PRONOUNS

ce qui ce que	what

Ce qui and **ce que** are only used for things (not people) that do <u>not</u> have a prior reference in the sentence. **Ce qui** is used as the subject of the dependent clause and **ce que** is used as the direct object of the dependent clause.

Je vois ce qui est sur la table.	I see what is on the table.
Je comprends ce que tu dis.	I understand what you are saying./ I understand that which you are saying.

21. INDEFINITE PRONOUNS

Indefinite pronouns refer to no one or nothing in particular. Some indefinite pronouns in French include:

quelque chose	something
quelqu'un	someone
chacun	each (one)
un/une autre	another
plusieurs	several
on	one, people, they, you

ne . . . rien	*nothing*
ne . . . personne	*no one*
n'importe quoi/qui/où	*anything/anyone/anywhere*

Quelqu'un t'a téléphoné.	*Somebody called you.*
Chacun ses goûts.	*To each his own.*
Pendant l'été, on peut nager.	*During the summer, you can swim/ one can swim/people can swim.*
Il fait n'importe quoi pour gagner de l'argent.	*He does anything to make money.*

22. NOUNS USED AS INDIRECT OBJECTS

A noun used as an indirect object is always preceded by the preposition **à**:

Je donne un livre à la jeune fille.	*I'm giving the girl a book.*

23. REPETITION OF PREPOSITIONS

The prepositions **à** and **de** must be repeated before each of their objects:

Je parle au deputé et à son secrétaire.	*I'm speaking to the deputy and his secretary.*
Voici les cahiers de Jean et ceux de Marie.	*Here are Jean's and Marie's notebooks.*

24. THE PARTITIVE

24.1 When a noun is used in such a way as to express or imply an unspecified quantity, it is preceded by the partitive article. The partitive very often translates the English *some* or *any*. In French, **du, de l', de la,** and **des** are the partitive articles.

The partitive is formed in the following way:

Masculine singular	**de + le = du**
Feminine singular	**de + la = de la**
Masculine and feminine singular	**de + l' = de l'**
Masculine and feminine plural	**de + les = des**

J'ai de l'argent.	*I have some money.*
Il a des amis.	*He has some friends.*

In many cases, however, the partitive article is used where we don't use *some* or *any* in English:

A-t-il des amis ici?	*Does he have friends here?*

24.2 De (or **d'**) is used, instead of the partitive article, when:

a. an expression of quantity is used:

J'ai beaucoup d'argent.	*I have a lot of money.*
Combien de livres avez-vous?	*How many books do you have?*
Ça coûte plus/moins de dix euros.	*That costs more/less than ten euros.*

Exceptions: **bien** *(much, many)* and **la plupart** *(most, the majority)*:

bien des hommes	*many men*
la plupart des hommes	*most men*

b. the noun is preceded by an adjective:

J'ai acheté de belles cravates.	*I bought some nice ties.*

24.3 The negative of the partitive is **pas de/d'** + noun.

Il n'a pas d'amis.	*He has no friends.*
Mon ami n'a pas d'argent.	*My friend hasn't any money.*

25. NEGATION

25.1 A sentence is made negative by placing **ne** before the verb and **pas** after it:

Je sais.	*I know.*
Je ne sais pas.	*I don't know.*
Je ne l'ai pas vu.	*I haven't seen it.*

When placed before a vowel or mute **h**, **ne** becomes **n'**.

Also note that multiple object pronouns are placed before the verb in negative sentences (and negative commands), following the same order as discussed in 18.1:

Vous le leur donnez.	*You give it to them.*
Vous ne le leur donnez pas.	*You don't give it to them.*
Ne le leur donnez pas.	*Don't give it to them.*

25.2 Other negative expressions include:

ne . . . guère	*hardly*
ne . . . point	*not (at all) (literary)*
ne . . . rien	*nothing*
ne . . . nul, nulle	*no one, no*
ne . . . jamais	*never*
ne . . . personne	*nobody*
ne . . . plus	*no longer*
ne . . . ni . . . ni	*neither . . . nor*
ne . . . que	*only*
ne . . . aucun, aucune	*no one, none*

Il ne travaille jamais le vendredi.	*He never works on Fridays.*
Je ne mange rien le matin.	*I eat nothing in the morning.*
Il n'y a ni chauffage ni eau chaude.	*There is neither heat nor hot water.*

25.3 Although both **oui** and **si** mean *yes*, **si** is used to contradict a negative statement:

Vous buvez du vin?	*You drink wine?*
Oui.	*Yes.*
Vous ne buvez pas de vin?	*You don't drink wine?*
Si.	*Yes, I do.*

26. QUESTIONS

In spoken French, questions are often formed simply by raising your voice to indicate that the sentence is a question. There is no change in sentence form.

Vous êtes libre?	*Are you free?/You're free?*

There are several other ways to ask a question in French:

26.1 QUESTIONS WITH PRONOUN SUBJECTS:

There are two ways of asking a question with a pronoun subject:

a. Place the pronoun after the verb:

Parlez-vous français?	*Do you speak French?*

b. Place **est-ce que** *(is it that)* before the sentence:

Est-ce que je parle trop vite?	*Am I talking too fast?*
Est-ce que vous parlez français?	*Do you speak French?*

26.2 QUESTIONS WITH NOUN SUBJECTS:

When a question begins with a noun, the pronoun is repeated after the verb. The letter t is inserted between the subject pronoun and the verb in the 3rd person singular form when the verb ends with an–e and after the verb a (has).

Votre frère parle-t-il français?   *Does your brother speak French?*

Votre sœur a-t-elle quitté la maison?   *Has your sister left the house?*

26.3 QUESTIONS INTRODUCED BY INTERROGATIVE WORDS:

The common interrogative words are:

combien	*how many/how much*
quand	*when*
comment	*how*
où	*where*
pourquoi	*why*
que	*what*
qui	*who/whom*

a. In questions which begin with an interrogative word, the order is usually interrogative word + verb + pronoun subject:

Comment allez-vous payer?   *How are you going to pay?*

Que désirez-vous?   *What would you like?*

b. However, in everyday, informal speech, French speakers will often simply place the question word at the end of the sentence and raise their voice to indicate that it is a question.

Vous allez où?   *Where are you going?*

c. A question word can also be used with **est-ce que**:

Comment est-ce que vous allez payer?   *How are you going to pay?*

27. ADVERBS

Adverbs are usually placed after verbs in the present and other simple tenses. In the **passé composé** and other compound tenses, adverbs of quality (**bien**), quantity (**beaucoup**), and frequency (**toujours**) are placed between the auxiliary verb and the past participle. For more on verbs, see sections 28–34.

Il marche lentement.	*He walks slowly.*
On a bien mangé dans ce restaurant.	*We ate well in this restaurant.*

27.1 Most adverbs are formed from the adjectives by adding **-ment** to the feminine form. If the adjective ends in **e** in the masculine form, just add **-ment** to the adjective.

froid	*cold*	**froidement**	*coldly*
certain	*certain*	**certainement**	*certainly*
naturel	*natural*	**naturellement**	*naturally*
facile	*easy*	**facilement**	*easily*

27.2 Adjectives that end in **-ent** and **-ant** add **-emment** or **-amment** to form the adverbs.

intelligent	*intelligent*	**intelligemment**	*intelligently*
constant	*constant*	**constamment**	*constantly*

27.3 However, there are many adverbs which must be learned separately. See 27.5–8 for some lists of common adverbs.

vite	*quickly*	**mal**	*badly*

27.4 Adverbs are compared like adjectives (see section 12):

loin	*far*	plus loin	*farther*	le plus loin	*the farthest*
bien	*well*	mieux	*better*	le mieux	*the best*
mal	*badly*	pire	*worse*	le pire	*the worst*

27.5 Some common adverbs of place include:

ici	*here*
là	*there*
à côté	*at the side*
de côté	*aside*
devant	*before, in front of*
derrière	*behind*
dessus	*on top*
dessous	*underneath*
dedans	*inside*
dehors	*outside*
partout	*everywhere*
nulle part	*nowhere*
loin	*far*
près	*near*
où	*where*

y	*there*
ailleurs	*elsewhere*
là-haut	*up there*
là-bas	*over there*

27.6 SOME COMMON ADVERBS OF TIME:

aujourd'hui	*today*
demain	*tomorrow*
hier	*yesterday*
avant-hier	*the day before yesterday*
après-demain	*the day after tomorrow*
maintenant	*now*
alors	*then*
avant	*before*
autrefois	*once, formerly*
tôt	*early*
bientôt	*soon*
tard	*late*
souvent	*often*
ne . . . jamais	*never*
toujours	*always, ever*

longtemps	long, for a long time
encore	still, yet
ne . . . plus	no longer, no more
à nouveau	again

27.7 ADVERBS OF MANNER:

bien	well
mal	ill, badly
ainsi	thus, so
de même	similarly
autrement	otherwise
ensemble	together
fort	much, very
volontiers	willingly
surtout	above all, especially
exprès	on purpose, expressly

27.8 ADVERBS OF QUANTITY OR DEGREE:

beaucoup	much, many
assez	enough
ne . . . guère	not much, scarcely
peu	little

plus	*more*
ne . . . plus	*no more*
moins	*less*
encore	*more*
bien	*much, many*
trop	*too, too much, too many*
tellement	*so much, so many*

28. AUXILIARY OR HELPING VERBS

In French, the auxiliary verbs are **avoir** *(to have)* and **être** *(to be)*, although they are both also used as main verbs. Auxiliary verbs are used with other verbs to help express tenses or moods of verbs.

Elle est americaine.	*She is American.*
Elle est allée chez le médecin.	*She went to the doctor's.*
Nous avons le livre.	*We have the book.*
Nous avons lu le livre.	*We read the book.*

Avoir and **être** are conjugated in the present indicative as follows:

	avoir	être
je/j'	ai	suis
tu	as	es
il/elle/on	a	est
nous	avons	sommes
vous	avez	êtes
ils/elles	ont	sont

29. THE INFINITIVE

French verbs are divided into three groups depending on their ending in the infinitive form or the form they appear in the dictionary. The infinitive is expressed in English with *to: to do, to be, to have, to want*, etc.

Group	Verb Ending:	Example:
First Conjugation (I)	-er	**parler** *(to speak)*
Second Conjugation (II)	-ir	**finir** *(to finish)*
Third Conjugation (III)	-re	**vendre** *(to sell)*

30. PARTICIPLES

30.1 THE PRESENT PARTICIPLE:

The present participle indicates an action closely related to the action of the main verb of the sentence.

a. It is formed by adding **-ant** to the stem of the verb at the first person plural.

nous finissons	**finissant**	*finishing*
nous allons	**allant**	*going*
nous buvons	**buvant**	*drinking*

Some verbs have irregular present participles, such as **être (étant)** and **avoir (ayant)**.

b. The present participle can be used as an adjective or verb. When used as an adjective, it must agree with the noun it is modifying.

However, the present participle is most commonly used with **en.** In this sense, it describes two actions taking place simultaneously or how something is done.

une histoire intéressante	*an interesting story*
Sachant cela, je ne fume plus.	*Knowing this, I don't smoke anymore.*
Il dîne en regardant la télévision.	*He is having dinner while watching the television.*
C'est en apprenant ces verbes par cœur que vous les saurez.	*It's by memorizing these verbs that you'll know them.*

30.2 THE PAST PARTICIPLE:

a. The past participle of regular verbs is formed the following ways:

	Infinitive	Past Participle
I	**parler**	**parl-é**
II	**finir**	**fin-i**
III	**vendre**	**vend-u**

b. However, many past participles are irregular and have to be memorized. For example:

Infinitive	Past Participle
avoir *(to have)*	**eu**
être *(to be)*	**été**
savoir *(to know)*	**su**
faire *(to do)*	**fait**
pouvoir *(can, to be able)*	**pu**
vouloir *(to want)*	**voulu**

c. Agreement (in gender and number):

When a verb is conjugated with **avoir,** there is usually no agreement:

J'ai couru.	*I ran.*
Ils ont vendu la maison.	*They sold the house.*

However, if a direct object pronoun precedes the verb, the past participle must agree in gender and number with direct object pronoun:

La pièce que j'ai vue hier était mauvaise.	*The play I saw yesterday was bad.*
Avez-vous vu le livre qu'il a acheté?	*Have you seen the book he bought?*
Avez-vous donné la chemise à Charles?	*Did you give the shirt to Charles?*
Non, je l'ai donnée à Claire.	*No, I gave it to Claire.*

When using **être** to conjugate verbs, such as with reflexive (**se laver**) and intransitive verbs expressing movement (**aller, venir**), the past participle agrees with the subject:

Marie est arrivée hier.	*Marie arrived yesterday.*
Jean et Pierre se sont levés.	*Jean and Pierre got up.*
Ils sont arrivés.	*They arrived.*
Nous sommes rentrés très tard.	*We came back very late.*
Elle s'est lavée.	*She washed herself.*

31. THE INDICATIVE

Note that the following points describe regular conjugations. There, however, are a number of verbs with irregular present (and other) tense conjugations. For more information on irregular verbs, please see the verb charts at the end of this summary.

31.1 PRESENT TENSE (PRÉSENT)

For regular verbs, the present tense is formed by taking the **-er**, **-ir**, or **-re** off the infinitive and adding the following endings:

-er verbs	-ir verbs	-re verbs
-e	-is	-s
-es	-is	-s
-e	-it	- (no ending added)
-ons	-issons	-ons
-ez	-issez	-ez
-ent	-issent	-ent

parler *(to speak)*	finir *(to finish)*	vendre *(to sell)*
parle	finis	vends
parles	finis	vends
parle	finit	vend
parlons	finissons	vendons
parlez	finissez	vendez
parlent	finissent	vendent

This tense has several English translations:

je parle	*I speak, I am speaking, I do speak*
ils finissent	*they finish, they are finishing, they do finish*

31.2 The imperfect tense (**imparfait**) is formed by dropping the **-ons** of the present **nous** form and adding **-ais, -ais, -ait, -ions, -iez, -aient.**

The imperfect expresses a continued or habitual action in the past. It also indicates an action that was happening when something else happened:

Je me levais à sept heures.	*I used to get up at seven o'clock.*
Il dormait quand Jean est entré.	*He was sleeping when Jean entered.*
Il parlait souvent de cela.	*He often spoke about that.*

31.3 The future tense (**futur simple**) is formed by adding the endings **-ai, -as, -a, -ons, -ez, -ont** to the full infinitive (or the irregular future stem) of the verb. It indicates a future action:

Je me lèverai tôt.	*I'll get up early.*
Il arrivera demain.	*He'll arrive tomorrow.*
Je le vendrai demain.	*I'll sell it tomorrow.*

31.4 The simple past tense (**passé simple**), or past definite, is used only in formal written French. It expresses an action begun and ended in the past. It is formed by adding to the root the endings -ai, -as, -a, -âmes, -âtes, -èrent for -er verbs; the endings -is, -is, -it, -îmes, -îtes, -irent for -ir verbs; and for all other verbs either these last or -us, -us, -ut, -ûmes, -ûtes, -urent.

Le roi fut tué.	*The king was killed.*
Les soldats entrèrent dans la ville.	*The soldiers entered the city.*

31.5 The past tense (**passé composé**) is formed by adding the past participle to the present indicative of **avoir** or **être**. Most verbs use **avoir** to form the **passé composé**. Intransitive verbs that express movement and reflexive verbs use **être**.

Some common intransitive verbs that use **être** include:

aller *(to go)*	**partir** *(to leave)*	**rester** *(to stay)*
venir *(to come)*	**sortir** *(to go out)*	**retourner** *(to go back)*
monter *(to go up)*	**naître** *(to be born)*	**revenir** *(to come back)*
descendre *(to go down)*	**mourir** *(to die)*	**tomber** *(to fall)*
arriver *(to arrive)*	**entrer** *(to enter)*	

The **passé composé** is used to indicate a past action which has been completed.

Je me suis levé tôt.	*I got up early.*
Il ne m'a rien dit.	*He didn't tell me anything.*
J'ai fini mon travail.	*I finished my work/I have finished my work.*
L'avez-vous vu?	*Have you seen him?/Did you see him?*
Ils sont arrivés.	*They arrived.*

31.6 The pluperfect or past perfect tense (**plus-que-parfait**) is formed by adding the past participle to the imperfect of **avoir** or **être**. It translates the English past perfect, and it refers to an action that happened before another point of reference in the past.

Il l'avait fait. *He had done it.*

Lorsque je suis revenu, il était parti. *When I came back, he had gone.*

31.7 The past anterior tense (**passé antérieur**) is formed by adding the past participle to the simple past of **avoir** or **être**. It is used for an event that happened just before another event. It is used mostly in literary style.

Dès qu'il eut dîné, il sortit. *As soon as he had eaten, he went out.*

Quand il eut fini, il se leva. *When he had finished, he got up.*

31.8 The future perfect tense (**futur antérieur**) is formed by adding the past participle to the future of **avoir** or **être**. It translates the English future perfect and indicates an action that will happen before another point of reference in the future:

Il aura bientôt fini. *He will soon have finished.*

Sometimes it indicates probability:

Il le lui aura sans doute dit. *No doubt he must have told him.*

Il aura été malade. *He probably was sick.*

Je me serai trompé. *I must have been mistaken.*

32. THE CONDITIONAL

The conditional is used to express hypothetical states or actions. Sometimes it expresses probability or conjecture.

32.1 The conditional is formed by adding the endings **-ais, -ais, -ait, -ions, -iez, -aient** to the infinitive. It translates the English *would* or *should*:

| Je le prendrais si j'étais à votre place. | *I would take it if I were you.* |
| Je ne ferais jamais une chose pareille. | *I would never do such a thing.* |

Verbs that are irregular in the future tense have the same irregular stems in the conditional, such as **aller** *(ir-)* or **être** *(ser-)*.

32.2 The conditional perfect is formed by adding the past participle to the conditional of **avoir** or **être.** It translates the English *would have:*

| Si j'avais su, je n'y serais jamais allé. | *If I had known, I would never have gone there.* |
| Si j'avais eu assez d'argent, je l'aurais acheté. | *If I had had the money, I would have bought it.* |

33. THE IMPERATIVE

The imperative **(l'impératif)** is used to give a command or a directive and to make requests.

For information on reflexive verbs and the use of pronouns in the imperative, see 17.5 and 18.2.

33.1 The imperative of most verbs is formed like the **tu, nous** and **vous** forms of the present indicative tense (without the corresponding subject pronouns). In the verbs of the first conjugation (**-er** verbs), however, the second person singular (**tu**) loses the final **s:**

donner *(to give)*		**finir** *(to finish)*		**vendre** *(to sell)*	
Donne. *(infml.)*	*Give.*	Finis. *(infml.)*	*Finish.*	Vends. *(infml.)*	*Sell.*
Donnez.	*Give.*	Finissez.	*Finish.*	Vendez.	*Sell.*
Donnons.	*Let's give.*	Finissons.	*Let's finish.*	Vendons.	*Let's sell.*

Traversons le pont.	Let's cross the bridge.
Choisissez un chapeau.	Choose a hat.
Attends une minute.	Wait a minute.

33.2 IMPERATIVES OF ÊTRE AND AVOIR:

être *(to be)*		avoir *(to have)*	
Sois. *(infml.)*	*Be.*	**Aie.** *(infml.)*	*Have.*
Soyez.	*Be.*	**Ayez.**	*Have.*
Soyons.	*Let's be.*	**Ayons.**	*Let's have.*

| Sois à l'heure. | Be on time. |
| Ayons plus de patience. | Let's be more patient. |

For other verbs that have irregular imperative forms, see the verb charts at the end of this summary.

33.3 THE NEGATIVE FORM OF THE IMPERATIVE:

The negative form of the imperative is formed in the same way as in the present indicative by placing **ne** before the verb and **pas** after.

| Ne dansez pas! | Don't dance! |
| Ne parle pas! | Don't speak! |

34. VERBS FOLLOWED BY THE INFINITIVE

34.1 Many verbs can be followed by the infinitive without a preceding preposition:

Je vais parler à Jean.	I am going to talk to Jean.
J'aime parler français.	I like to speak French.
Je ne sais pas danser.	I don't know how to dance.
Il faut acheter des clous.	We have to buy nails.

34.2 There are a good amount of verbs, however, that require the preposition **à** before the infinitive:

J'apprends à parler français.	*I am learning to speak French.*
Je l'aiderai à le faire.	*I'll help him do it.*
Il commence à s'inquiéter.	*He is starting to get worried.*

34.3 Some verbs must be followed by **de** plus the infinitive:

Il leur a demandé de fermer la porte.	*He asked them to shut the door.*
Elle a décidé de faire un voyage.	*She decided to take a trip.*

35. THE SUBJUNCTIVE

The indicative makes a simple statement; the subjunctive indicates a certain attitude or mood toward the statement—uncertainty, desire, emotion, etc. The subjunctive is used in subordinate clauses when the statement is unreal, doubtful, indefinite, subject to some condition, or is affected by will or emotion.

The verbs in the subjunctive are generally used in a dependent clause introduced by the word **que/qu'** *(that)*. When the independent part of the sentence contains any of the above emotions, uncertainties or other subjunctive conditions, the verb in the dependent clause is in the subjunctive.

Only two subjunctive tenses are used in everyday French: the present and past. The imperfect and pluperfect mostly appear in literature.

35.1 PRESENT SUBJUNCTIVE:

a. Drop the **-ent** of the third person plural present indicative and add **-e, -es, -e, -ions, -iez, -ent.** For irregular stems in the present subjunctive, see the verb charts following the summary.

parler *(to speak)*	finir *(to finish)*	vendre *(to sell)*
je parle	je finisse	je vende
tu parles	tu finisses	tu vendes
il parle	il finisse	il vende
nous parlions	nous finissions	nous vendions
vous parliez	vous finissiez	vous vendiez
ils parlent	ils finissent	ils vendent

Je veux que tu viennes avec moi.   *I want you to come with me.*

b. The irregular verbs **avoir** and **être**:

avoir *(to have)*	être *(to be)*
j'aie	je sois
tu aies	tu sois
il ait	il soit
nous ayons	nous soyons
vous ayez	vous soyez
ils aient	ils soient

35.2 IMPERFECT SUBJUNCTIVE:

As noted above, the imperfect and the pluperfect subjunctive are not used today in conversational French. They do, however, appear in literature.

To form the imperfect subjunctive, drop the ending of the first person singular of the past definite (simple past) and add **-sse, -sses, -t, -ssions, -ssiez, -ssent**, putting a circumflex (ˆ) over the last vowel of the third person singular:

donner *(to give)*	finir *(to finish)*	vendre *(to sell)*
je donnasse	je finisse	je vendisse
tu donnasses	tu finisses	tu vendisses
il donnât	il finît	il vendît
nous donnassions	nous finissions	nous vendissions
vous donnassiez	vous finissiez	vous vendissiez
ils donnassent	ils finissent	ils vendissent

35.3 PAST SUBJUNCTIVE:

The past subjunctive is used when the action in the subordinate clause has taken place before the action in the main clause.

Add the past participle to the present subjunctive of **avoir** (or **être**):

avoir (+ donner [*to give*])	être (+ aller [*to go*])
j'aie donné	je sois allé
tu aies donné	tu sois allé
etc.	etc.

Il est dommage qu'il n'ait pas obtenu plus de voix.

It's a shame he didn't get more votes.

35.4 Pluperfect Subjunctive (see note in 35.2 on the imperfect and pluperfect subjunctive):

Add the past participle to the imperfect subjunctive of **avoir** (or **être**):

avoir (+ donner)	être (+ aller)
j'eusse donné	je fusse allé
etc.	etc.

35.5 Infinitive vs. subjunctive

In order for the subjunctive to be used, the subjects of the independent or main clause and the dependent or subordinate clause <u>must</u> be different. If they are the same, the infinitive is used.

Subjunctive	**Je veux que tu sois là.**	*I want you to be there.*
Infinitive	**Je veux être là.**	*I want to be there.*

35.6 Uses of the subjunctive:

a. After verbs of command, request, permission, etc.:
Je tiens à ce que vous y alliez. *I insist on your going there.*

b. After expressions of approval and disapproval, necessity, etc.:
Il n'est que juste que vous le lui disiez. *It's only fair that you tell him that.*

Il faut que vous fassiez cela. *You have to do that.*

c. After verbs of emotion (desire, regret, fear, joy, etc.):

Je voudrais bien que vous veniez avec nous. — *I'd like you to come with us.*

Je regrette que vous ne puissiez pas venir. — *I'm sorry you can't come.*

d. After expressions of doubt, uncertainty, denial:

Je doute que j'y aille. — *I doubt that I'll go there.*

Il est possible qu'il ne puisse pas venir. — *It's possible that he may not be able to come.*

e. In relative clauses after expression like **il faut**:

Il me faut quelqu'un qui fasse cela. — *I need someone to do that.*

f. In adverbial clauses after certain conjunctions denoting purpose, time, concessions, etc.:

Je viendrai à moins qu'il ne pleuve. — *I'll come unless it rains.*

Asseyez-vous en attendant que ce soit prêt. — *Sit down until it's ready.*

g. In utterances expressing a wish or command:

Qu'ils s'en aillent! — *Let them go away!*

Dieu vous bénisse! — *God bless you!*

Vive la France! — *Long live France!*

36. FORMS OF THE REGULAR VERBS

A. CLASSES I, II, III

Infinitive	Pres. & Past Participles	Present Indicative	Present Subjunctive*	Past (passé composé)	Past Subjunctive	Imperfect Indicative
-er ending **parler** (to speak)	parlant parlé	parl + e es e ons ez ent	parl + e es e ions iez ent	j'ai + parlé tu as il a nous avons vous avez ils ont	que j'aie + parlé que tu aies qu'il ait que nous ayons que vous ayez qu'ils aient	parl + ais ais ait ions iez aient
-ir ending **finir** (to finish)	finissant fini	fin + is is it issons issez issent	finiss + e es e ions iez ent	j'ai + fini tu as il a nous avons vous avez ils ont	que j'aie + fini que tu aies qu'il ait que nous ayons que vous ayez qu'ils aient	finiss + ais ais ait ions iez aient
-re ending **vendre** (to sell)	vendant vendu	vend + s s - ons ez ent	vend + e es e ions iez ent	j'ai + vendu tu as il a nous avons vous avez ils ont	que j'aie + vendu que tu aies qu'il ait que nous ayons que vous ayez qu'ils aient	vend + ais ais ait ions iez aient

* Like the past subjunctive, the present subjunctive verb is generally preceded by **que** or **qu'** + the appropriate pronoun, as in **Il faut que je parte** and **Je veux qu'il quitte la maison.**

Past Perfect	Future	Future Perfect	Conditional	Conditional Perfect	Imperative
j'avais + parlé	parler + ai	j'aurai + parlé	parler + ais	j'aurais + parlé	
tu avais	as	tu auras	ais	tu aurais	parle
il avait	a	il aura	ait	il aurait	
nous avions	ons	nous aurons	ions	nous aurions	parlons
vous aviez	ez	vous aurez	iez	vous auriez	
ils avaient	ont	ils auront	aient	ils auraient	parlez
j'avais + fini	finir + ai	j'aurai + fini	finir + ais	j'aurais + fini	
tu avais	as	tu auras	ais	tu aurais	finis
il avait	a	il aura	ait	il aurait	
nous avions	ons	nous aurons	ions	nous aurions	finissons
vous aviez	ez	vous aurez	iez	vous auriez	finissez
ils avaient	ont	ils auront	aient	ils auraient	
j'avais + vendu	vendr + ai	j'aurai + vendu	vendr + ais	j'aurais + vendu	
tu avais	as	tu auras	ais	tu aurais	vends
il avait	a	il aura	ait	il aurait	
nous avions	ons	nous aurons	ions	nous aurions	vendons
vous aviez	ez	vous aurez	iez	vous auriez	vendez
ils avaient	ont	ils auront	aient	ils auraient	

B. VERBS ENDING IN -CER AND -GER

Infinitive	Pres. & Past Participles	Present Indicative	Present Subjunctive	Past (passé composé)	Past Subjunctive	Imperfect Indicative
placer[1] (to place)	*plaçant*[3] placé	place places place *plaçons* placez placent	place places place placions placiez placent	j'ai + placé tu as il a nous avons vous avez ils ont	que j'aie + placé que tu aies qu'il ait que nous ayons que vous ayez qu'ils aient	*plaçais* *plaçais* *plaçait* placions placiez *plaçaient*
manger[2] (to eat)	*mangeant* mangé	mange manges mange *mangeons* mangez mangent	mange manges mange mangions mangiez mangent	j'ai + mangé tu as il a nous avons vous avez ils ont	que j'aie + mangé que tu aies qu'il ait que nous ayons que vous ayez qu'ils aient	*mangeais* *mangeais* *mangeait* mangions mangiez *mangeaient*

[1] Similarly conjugated: **commencer, lancer**, etc.

[2] Similarly conjugated: **plonger, ranger, arranger**, etc.

[3] All spelling changes in verb forms will be italicized in this section.

	Past Perfect	Future	Future Perfect	Conditional	Conditional Perfect	Imperative
	j'avais + placé	placer + ai	j'aurai + placé	placer + ais	j'aurais + placé	
	tu avais	as	tu auras	ais	tu aurais	place
	il avait	a	il aura	ait	il aurait	
	nous avions	ons	nous aurons	ions	nous aurions	*plaçons*
	vous aviez	ez	vous aurez	iez	vous auriez	placez
	ils avaient	ont	ils auront	aient	ils auraient	
	j'avais + mangé	manger + ai	j'aurai + mangé	manger + ais	j'aurais + mangé	
	tu avais	as	tu auras	ais	tu aurais	mange
	il avait	a	il aura	ait	il aurait	
	nous avions	ons	nous aurons	ions	nous aurions	*mangeons*
	vous aviez	ez	vous aurez	iez	vous auriez	mangez
	ils avaient	ont	ils auront	aient	ils auraient	

C. VERBS ENDING IN -ER WITH CHANGES IN THE STEM

Infinitive	Pres. & Past Participles	Present Indicative	Present Subjunctive	Past (passé composé)	Past Subjunctive	Imperfect Indicative
acheter[1] (to buy)	achetant acheté	*achète achètes achète* achetons achetez *achètent*	*achète achètes achète* achetions achetiez *achètent*	j'ai + acheté tu as il a nous avons vous avez ils ont	que j'aie + acheté que tu aies qu'il ait que nous ayons que vous ayez qu'ils aient	achet + ais ais ait ions iez aient
appeler[2] (to call)	appelant appelé	*appelle appelles appelle* appelons appelez *appellent*	*appelle appelles appelle* appelions appeliez *appellent*	j'ai + appelé tu as il a nous avons vous avez ils ont	que j'aie + appelé que tu aies qu'il ait que nous ayons que vous ayez qu'ils aient	appel + ais ais ait ions iez aient
payer[3]† (to pay)	payant payé	*paie paies paie* payons payez *paient*	*paie paies paie* payions payiez *paient*	j'ai + payé tu as il a nous avons vous avez ils ont	que j'aie + payé que tu aies qu'il ait que nous ayons que vous ayez qu'ils aient	pay + ais ais ait ions iez aient
préférer[4] (to prefer)	préférant préféré	*préfère** préfères préfère* préférons préférez *préfèrent*	*préfère préfères préfère* préférions préfériez *préfèrent*	j'ai + préféré tu as il a nous avons vous avez ils ont	que tu aies que tu aies qu'il ait que nous ayons que vous ayez qu'ils aient	préfér + ais ais ait ions iez aient

[1] Verbs like acheter: mener, amener, emmener, se promener, lever, se lever, élever

[2] Verbs like appeler: se rappeler, jeter

[3] Verbs like payer: essayer, employer, ennuyer, essuyer, nettoyer (See note below.)

[4] Verbs like préférer: espérer, répéter, célébrer, considérer, suggérer, protéger

† Verbs ending in -ayer may use i or y in the present (except for nous and vous forms), the future, and the conditional, as in payer, essayer. Verbs ending in -oyer, -uyer change y to i (as in essuyer, ennuyer, employer, nettoyer). These changes are indicated by the use of italics.

** Note the change from é to è in the je, tu, il/elle/on, and ils forms of verbs like préférer.

Past Perfect	Future	Future Perfect	Conditional	Conditional Perfect	Imperative
j'avais + acheté	*acheter* + ai	j'aurai + acheté	*achèter* + ais	j'aurais + acheté	
tu avais	as	tu auras	ais	tu aurais	*achète*
il avait	a	il aura	ait	il aurait	
nous avions	ons	nous aurons	ions	nous aurions	achetons
vous aviez	ez	vous aurez	iez	vous auriez	achetez
ils avaient	ont	ils auront	aient	ils auraient	
j'avais + appelé	*appeller* + ai	j'aurai + appelé	*appeller* + ais	j'aurais + appelé	
tu avais	as	tu auras	ais	tu aurais	*appelle*
il avait	a	il aura	ait	il aurait	
nous avions	ons	nous aurons	ions	nous aurions	appelons
vous aviez	ez	vous aurez	iez	vous auriez	appelez
ils avaient	ont	ils auront	aient	ils auraient	
j'avais + payé	*paier/payer* + ai	j'aurai + payé	*paier/payer* + ais	j'aurais + payé	
tu avais	as	tu auras	ais	tu aurais	*paie*
il avait	a	il aura	ait	il aurait	
nous avions	ons	nous aurons	ions	nous aurions	payons
vous aviez	ez	vous aurez	iez	vous auriez	payez
ils avaient	ont	ils auront	aient	ils auraient	
j'avais + préféré	préférer + ai	j'aurai + préféré	préfér + ais	j'aurais + préféré	
tu avais	as	tu auras	ais	tu aurais	*préfère*
il avait	a	il aura	ait	il aurait	
nous avions	ons	nous aurons	ions	nous aurions	préférons
vous aviez	ez	vous aurez	iez	vous auriez	préférez
ils avaient	ont	ils auront	aient	ils auraient	

D. VERBS ENDING IN -OIR

Infinitive	Pres. & Past Participles	Present Indicative	Present Subjunctive	Past (passé composé)	Past Subjunctive	Imperfect Indicative
recevoir[1] (to receive)	recevant reçu	reçois reçois reçoit recevons recevez reçoivent	reçoive reçoives reçoive recevions receviez reçoivent	j'ai + reçu tu as il a nous avons vous avez ils ont	que j'aie + reçu que tu aies qu'il ait que nous ayons que vous ayez qu'ils aient	recev + ais ais ait ions iez aient

[1] Verbs like recevoir: devoir (dois, doive, dû).

Past Perfect	Future	Future Perfect	Conditional	Conditional Perfect	Imperative
j'avais + *reçu*	*recevr* + ai	j'aurai + *reçu*	*recevr* + ais	j'aurais + *reçu*	
tu avais	as	tu auras	ais	tu aurais	*reçois*
il avait	a	il aura	ait	il aurait	
nous avions	ons	nous aurons	ions	nous aurions	recevons
vous aviez	ez	vous aurez	iez	vous auriez	recevez
ils avaient	ont	ils auront	aient	ils auraient	

E. VERBS ENDING IN -NDRE

Infinitive	Pres. & Past Participles	Present Indicative	Present Subjunctive	Past (passé composé)	Past Subjunctive	Imperfect Indicative
craindre[1] (to fear)	craignant	crains	craigne	j'ai + craint	que j'aie + craint	craign + ais
	craint	crains	craignes	tu as	que tu aies	ais
		craint	craigne	il a	qu'il ait	ait
		craignons	craignions	nous avons	que nous ayons	ions
		craignez	craigniez	vous avez	que vous ayez	iez
		craignent	craignent	ils ont	qu'ils aient	aient
éteindre[2] (to extinguish)	éteignant	éteins	éteigne	j'ai + éteint	que j'aie + éteint	éteign + ais
	éteint	éteins	éteignes	tu as	que tu aies	ais
		éteint	éteigne	il a	qu'il ait	ait
		éteignons	éteignions	nous avons	que nous ayons	ions
		éteignez	éteigniez	vous avez	que vous ayez	iez
		éteignent	éteignent	ils ont	qu'ils aient	aient

[1] Verbs like craindre: **plaindre** *(to pity)*. The reflexive form, **se plaindre**, means *to complain*, and in the compound tenses is conjugated with **être**.

[2] Verbs like éteindre: **peindre** *(to paint)*; teindre *(to dye)*.

Past Perfect	Future	Future Perfect	Conditional	Conditional Perfect	Imperative
j'avais + *craint*	*craindr* + ai	j'aurai + *craint*	*craindr* + ais	j'aurais + *craint*	
tu avais	as	tu auras	ais	tu aurais	*crains*
il avait	a	il aura	ait	il aurait	
nous avions	ons	nous aurons	ions	nous aurions	*craignons*
vous aviez	ez	vous aurez	iez	vous auriez	*craignez*
ils avaient	ont	ils auront	aient	ils auraient	
j'avais + *éteint*	*éteindr* + ai	j'aurai + *éteint*	*éteindr* + ais	j'aurais + *éteint*	
tu avais	as	tu auras	ais	tu aurais	*éteint*
il avait	a	il aura	ait	il aurait	
nous avions	ons	nous aurons	ions	nous aurions	*éteignons*
vous aviez	ez	vous aurez	iez	vous auriez	*éteignez*
ils avaient	ont	ils auront	aient	ils auraient	

F. COMPOUND TENSES OF VERBS CONJUGATED WITH ÊTRE

Past (passé composé)	Past subjunctive	Past Perfect	Future Perfect	Conditional Perfect
je suis allé(e)	que je sois allé(e)	j'étais allé(e)	je serai allé(e)	je serais allé(e)
tu es allé(e)	que tu sois allé(e)	tu étais allé(e)	tu seras allé(e)	tu serais allé(e)
il est allé	qu'il soit allé	il était allé	il sera allé	il serait allé
elle est allée	qu'elle soit allée	elle était allée	elle sera allée	elle serait allée
nous sommes allé(e)s	que nous soyons allé(e)s	nous étions allé(e)s	nous serons allé(e)s	nous serions allé(e)s
vous êtes allé(e)(s)	que vous soyez allé(e)(s)	vous étiez allé(e)(s)	vous serez allé(e)(s)	vous seriez allé(e)(s)
ils sont allés	qu'ils soient allés	ils étaient allés	ils seront allés	ils seraient allés
elles sont allées	qu'elles soient allées	elles étaient allées	elles seront allées	elles seraient allées

G. COMPOUND TENSES OF REFLEXIVE VERBS (ALL REFLEXIVE VERBS ARE CONJUGATED WITH **ÊTRE)**

Past (passé composé)	Past subjunctive	Past Perfect	Future Perfect	Conditional Perfect
je me suis levé(e)	que je me sois levé(e)	je m'étais levé(e)	je me serai levé(e)	je me serais levé(e)
tu t'es levé(e)	que tu te sois levé(e)	tu t'étais levé(e)	tu te seras levé(e)	tu te serais levé(e)
il s'est levé	qu'il se soit levé	il s'était levé	il se sera levé	il se serait levé
elle s'est levée	qu'elle se soit levée	elle s'était levée	elle se sera levée	elle se serait levée
nous nous sommes levé(e)s	que nous nous soyons levé(e)s	nous nous étions levé(e)s	nous nous serons levé(e)s	nous nous serions levé(e)s
vous vous êtes levé(e)(s)	que vous vous soyez levé(e)(s)	vous vous étiez levé(e)(s)	vous vous serez levé(e)(s)	vous vous seriez levé(e)(s)
ils se sont levés	qu'ils se soient levés	ils s'étaient levés	ils se seront levés	ils se seraient levés
elles se sont levées	qu'elles se soient levées	elles s'étaient levées	elles se seront levées	elles se seraient levées

H. INFREQUENTLY USED AND "LITERARY" TENSES (CLASSES I, II, III)

Past Definite[1†]			Past Anterior[2]			Imperfect Subjunctive[3]		
parlai	finis	perdis	eus parlé	eus fini	eus perdu	parlasse	finisse	perdisse
parlas	finis	perdis	eus parlé	eus fini	eus perdu	parlasses	finisses	perdisses
parla	finit	perdit	eut parlé	eut fini	eut perdu	parlât	finît	perdît
parlâmes	finîmes	perdîmes	eûmes parlé	eûmes fini	eûmes perdu	parlassions	finissions	perdissions
parlâtes	finîtes	perdîtes	eûtes parlé	eûtes fini	eûtes perdu	parlassiez	finissiez	perdissiez
parlèrent	finirent	perdirent	eurent parlé	eurent fini	eurent perdu	parlassent	finissent	perdissent

[1] Used in formal narrative only. In informal conversation and writing, use the past tense (**j'ai parlé,** etc.).

[2] Used in literary style only, after **quand, lorsque, après que,** and **dès que** for an event that happened just before another event. Example: **Après qu'il eut dîné, il sortit.** (*As soon as he had eaten, he went out.*) This tense is infrequently found in ordinary conversation, but is used fairly often in literary works.

[3] *That I spoke, that I might speak,* etc.

† All other regular verbs use either **-er, -ir,** or **-re** endings, depending on the conjugation to which they belong. The past definite forms of irregular verbs must be memorized.

Past Perfect Subjunctive[4]

que j'eusse parlé	que j'eusse fini	que j'eusse perdu
que tu eusses parlé	que tu eusses fini	que tu eusses perdu
qu'il eût parlé	qu'il eût perdu	qu'il eût fini
que nous eussions parlé	que nous eussions fini	que nous eussions perdu
que vous eussiez parlé	que vous eussiez fini	que vous eussiez perdu
qu'ils eussent parlé	qu'ils eussent fini	qu'ils eussent perdu

[4] *That I had spoken, that I might have spoken,* etc. A predominantly literary tense.

37. FREQUENTLY USED IRREGULAR VERBS

The correct auxiliary verb is indicated in italics below each verb. For compound tenses, use the appropriate form of the auxiliary verb + past participle.

Infinitive	Pres. & Past Participles	Present Indicative	Present Subjunctive	Imperfect Indicative	Future	Conditional	Imperative
acquérir *avoir* (to acquire)	acquérant acquis	acquiers acquiers acquiert acquérons acquérez acquièrent	acquière acquières acquière acquérions acquériez acquièrent	acquér + ais ais ait ions iez aient	acquerr + ai as a ons ez ont	acquerr + ais ais ait ions iez aient	acquiers acquérons acquérez
aller *être* (to go)	allant allé(e)(s)	vais vas va allons allez vont	aille ailles aille allions alliez aillent	all + ais ais ait ions iez aient	ir + ai as a ons ez ont	ir + ais ais ait ions iez aient	va allons allez
(s')asseoir† *être* (to sit [down])	asseyant assis(e)(s)	assieds assieds assied asseyons asseyez asseyent	asseye asseyes asseye asseyions asseyiez asseyent	assey + ais ais ait ions iez aient	asseyer + ai or as assiér a or ons assoir ez ont	asseyer + ais or ais assiér ait or ions assoir iez aient	assieds-toi asseyons-nous asseyez-vous

Infinitive	Pres. & Past Participles	Present Indicative	Present Subjunctive	Imperfect Indicative	Future	Conditional	Imperative
avoir *avoir* (to have)	ayant eu	ai as a avons avez ont	aie aies ait ayons ayez aient	av + ais ais ait ions iez aient	aur + ai as a ons ez ont	aur + ais ais ait ions iez aient	aie ayons ayez
battre *avoir* (to beat)	battant battu	bats bats bat battons battez battent	batte battes batte battions battiez battent	batt + ais ais ait ions iez aient	battr + ai as a ons ez ont	battr + ais ais ait ions iez aient	bats battons battez

† There is a variant form of the conjugation of **s'asseoir** based on the present participle **assoyant** and first person singular **assois**, but it is rather archaic and is rarely used. There are also two variant forms for the future stem: **assiér-** and **assoir-**. **Assiér-** is the form most frequently used.

Infinitive	Pres. & Past Participles	Present Indicative	Present Subjunctive	Imperfect Indicative	Future	Conditional	Imperative
boire *avoir* (to drink)	buvant bu	bois bois boit buvons buvez boivent	boive boives boive buvions buviez boivent	buv + ais ais ait ions iez aient	boir + ai as a ons ez ont	boir + ais ais ait ions iez aient	bois buvons buvez
conclure *avoir* (to conclude)	concluant conclu	conclus conclus conclut concluons concluez concluent	conclue conclues conclue concluions concluiez concluent	conclu + ais ais ait ions iez aient	conclur + ai as a ons ez ont	conclur + ais ais ait ions iez aient	conclus concluons concluez
conduire *avoir* (to drive, to lead)	conduisant conduit	conduis conduis conduit conduisons conduisez conduisent	conduise conduises conduise conduisions conduisiez conduisent	conduis + ais ais ait ions iez aient	conduir + ai as a ons ez ont	conduir + ais ais ait ions iez aient	conduis conduisons conduisez
connaître *avoir* (to know)	connaissant connu	connais connais connaît connaissons connaissez connaissent	connaisse connaisses connaisse connaissions connaissiez connaissent	connaiss + ais ais ait ions iez aient	connaîtr + ai as a ons ez ont	connaîtr + ais ais ait ions iez aient	connais connaissons connaissez

Infinitive	Pres. & Past Participles	Present Indicative	Present Subjunctive	Imperfect Indicative	Future	Conditional	Imperative
courir *avoir* (to run)	courant couru	cours cours court courons courez courent	coure coures coure courions couriez courent	cour + ais ais ait ions iez aient	courr + ai as a ons ez ont	courr + ais ais ait ions iez aient	cours courons courez
croire *avoir* (to believe)	croyant cru	crois crois croit croyons croyez croient	croie croies croie croyions croyiez croient	croy + ais ais ait ions iez aient	croir + ai as a ons ez ont	croir + ais ais ait ions iez aient	crois croyons croyez
cueillir *avoir* (to gather, to pick)	cueillant cueilli	cueille cueilles cueille cueillons cueillez cueillent	cueille cueilles cueille cueillions cueilliez cueillent	cueill + ais ais ait ions iez aient	cueiller + ai as a ons ez ont	cueiller + ais ais ait ions iez aient	cueille cueillons cueillez
devoir *avoir* (to owe, ought)	devant dû	dois dois doit devons devez doivent	doive doives doive devions deviez doivent	dev + ais ais ait ions iez aient	devr + ai as a ons ez ont	devr + ais ais ait ions iez aient	*not used*

Infinitive	Pres. & Past Participles	Present Indicative	Present Subjunctive	Imperfect Indicative	Future	Conditional	Imperative
dire *avoir* (to say, to tell)	disant dit	dis dis dit disons dites disent	dise dises dise disions disiez disent	dis + ais ais ait ions iez aient	dir + ai as a ons ez ont	dir + ais ais ait ions iez aient	dis disons dites
dormir *avoir* (to sleep)	dormant dormi	dors dors dort dormons dormez dorment	dorme dormes dorme dormions dormiez dorment	dorm + ais ais ait ions iez aient	dormir + ai as a ons ez ont	dormir + ais ais ait ions iez aient	dors dormons dormez
écrire *avoir* (to write)	écrivant écrit	écris écris écrit écrivons écrivez écrivent	écrive écrives écrive écrivions écriviez écrivent	écriv + ais ais ait ions iez aient	écrir + ai as a ons ez ont	écrir + ais ais ait ions iez aient	écris écrivons écrivezs
envoyer *avoir* (to send)	envoyant envoyé	envoie envoies envoie envoyons envoyez envoient	envoie envoies envoie envoyions envoyiez envoient	envoy + ais ais ait ions iez aient	enverr + ai as a ons ez ont	enverr + ais ais ait ions iez aient	envoie envoyons envoyez

Infinitive	Pres. & Past Participles	Present Indicative	Present Subjunctive	Imperfect Indicative	Future	Conditional	Imperative
être *avoir* (to be)	étant été	suis es est sommes êtes sont	sois sois soit soyons soyez soient	ét + ais ais ait ions iez aient	ser + ai as a ons ez ont	ser + ais ais ait ions iez aient	sois soyons soyez
faillir[†] *avoir* (to fail)	faillant failli	*not used*	*not used*	*not used*	faillir + ai as a ons ez ont	faillir + ais ais ait ions iez aient	*not used*
faire *avoir* (to do, to make)	faisant fait	fais fais fait faisons faites font	fasse fasses fasse fassions fassiez fassent	fais + ais ais ait ions iez aient	fer + ai as a ons ez ont	fer + ais ais ait ions iez aient	fais faisons faites
falloir *avoir* (to be necessary, must [used only with **il**]	*no pres. part.* fallu	il faut	il faille	il fallait	il faudra	il faudrait	*not used*

[†] Used in such expressions as **Il a failli tomber** *(He nearly fell [lit., he failed to fall])*.

Infinitive	Pres. & Past Participles	Present Indicative	Present Subjunctive	Imperfect Indicative	Future	Conditional	Imperative
fuir *avoir* (to flee)	fuyant fui	fuis fuis fuit fuyons fuyez fuient	fuie fuies fuie fuyions fuyiez fuient	fuy + ais ais ait ions iez aient	fuir + ai as a ons ez ont	fuir + ais ais ait ions iez aient	fuis fuyons fuyez
haïr *avoir* (to hate)	haïssant haï	hais hais haït haïssons haïssez haïssent	haïsse haïsses haïsse haïssions haïssiez haïssent	haïss + ais ais ait ions iez aient	haïr + ai as a ons ez ont	haïr + ais ais ait ions iez aient	haïs haïssons haïssez
lire *avoir* (to read)	lisant lu	lis lis lit lisons lisez lisent	lise lises lise lisions lisiez lisent	lis + ais ais ait ions iez aient	lir + ai as a ons ez ont	lir + ais ais ait ions iez aient	lis lisons lisez
mettre *avoir* (to put, to place)	mettant mis	mets mets met mettons mettez mettent	mette mettes mette mettions mettiez mettent	mett + ais ais ait ions iez aient	mettr + ai as a ons ez ont	mettr + ais ais ait ions iez aient	mets mettons mettez

Infinitive	Pres. & Past Participles	Present Indicative	Present Subjunctive	Imperfect Indicative	Future	Conditional	Imperative
mourir *être*	mourant mort(e)(s)	meurs meurs meurt mourons mourez meurent	meure meures meure mourions mouriez meurent	mour + ais ais ait ions iez aient	mourr + ai as a ons ez ont	mourr + ais ais ait ions iez aient	 meurs mourons mourez
mouvoir[†] *avoir* (to move)	mouvant mû	meus meus meut mouvons mouvez meuvent	meuve meuves meuve mouvions mouviez meuvent	mouv + ais ais ait ions iez aient	mouvr + ai as a ons ez ont	mouvr + ais ais ait ions iez aient	 meus mouvons mouvez
naître *être* (to be born)	naissant né(e)(s)	nais nais naît naissons naissez naissent	naisse naisses naisse naissions naissiez naissent	naiss + ais ais ait ions iez aient	naîtr + ai as a ons ez ont	naîtr + ais ais ait ions iez aient	 nais naissons naissez
ouvrir *avoir* (to open)	ouvrant ouvert	ouvre ouvres ouvre ouvrons ouvrez ouvrent	ouvre ouvres ouvre ouvrions ouvriez ouvrent	ouvr + ais ais ait ions iez aient	ouvrir + ai as a ons ez ont	ouvrir + ais ais ait ions iez aient	 ouvre ouvrons ouvrez

[†] **Mouvoir** is seldom used except in compounds like **émouvoir** (*to move [emotionally]*).

Infinitive	Pres. & Past Participles	Present Indicative	Present Subjunctive	Imperfect Indicative	Future	Conditional	Imperative
partir *être* (to leave, to depart)	partant parti(e)(s)	pars pars part partons partez partent	parte partes parte partions partiez partent	part + ais ais ait ions iez aient	partir + ai as a ons ez ont	partir + ais ais ait ions iez aient	pars partons partez
plaire *avoir* (to please, to be pleasing to)	plaisant plu	plais plais plaît plaisons plaisez plaisent	plaise plaises plaise plaisions plaisiez plaisent	plais + ais ais ait ions iez aient	plair + ai as a ons ez ont	plair + ais ais ait ions iez aient	plais plaisons plaisez
pleuvoir *avoir* (to rain [used only with il])	pleuvant plu	il pleut	il pleuve	il pleuvait	il pleuvra	il pleuvrait	*not used*
pouvoir[†] *avoir* (to be able to, can)	pouvant pu	peux (puis)[†] peux peut pouvons pouvez peuvent	puisse puisses puisse puissions puissiez puissent	pouv + ais ais ait ions iez aient	pourr + ai as a ons ez ont	pourr + ais ais ait ions iez aient	*not used*

[†] The interrogative of **pouvoir** in the first person singular is always **Puis-je?**

Infinitive	Pres. & Past Participles	Present Indicative	Present Subjunctive	Imperfect Indicative	Future	Conditional	Imperative
prendre *avoir* (to take)	prenant pris	prends prends prend prenons prenez prennent	prenne prennes prenne prenions preniez prennent	pren + ais ais ait ions iez aient	prendr + ai as a ons ez ont	prendr + ais ais ait ions iez aient	prends prenons prenez
résoudre *avoir* (to resolve)	résolvant résolu	résous résous résout résolvons résolvez résolvent	résolve résolves résolve résolvions résolviez résolvent	résolv + ais ais ait ions iez aient	résoudr + ai as a ons ez ont	résoudr + ais ais ait ions iez aient	résous résolvons résolvez
rire *avoir* (to laugh)	riant ri	ris ris rit rions riez rient	rie ries rie riions riiez rient	ri + ais ais ait ions iez aient	rir + ai as a ons ez ont	rir + ais ais ait ions iez aient	ris rions riez
savoir *avoir* (to know)	sachant su	sais sais sait savons savez savent	sache saches sache sachions sachiez sachent	sav + ais ais ait ions iez aient	saur + ai as a ons ez ont	saur + ais ais ait ions iez aient	sache sachons sachez

Infinitive	Pres. & Past Participles	Present Indicative	Present Subjunctive	Imperfect Indicative	Future	Conditional	Imperative
suffire *avoir* (to be enough, to suffice)	suffisant suffi	suffis suffis suffit suffisons suffisez suffisent	suffise suffises suffise suffisions suffisiez suffisent	suffis + ais ais ait ions iez aient	suffir + ai as a ons ez ont	suffir + ais ais ait ions iez aient	suffis suffisons suffisez
suivre *avoir* (to follow)	suivant suivi	suis suis suit suivons suivez suivent	suive suives suive suivions suiviez suivent	suiv + ais ais ait ions iez aient	suivr + ai as a ons ez ont	suivr + ais ais ait ions iez aient	suis suivons suivez
(se) taire *être* (to be quiet, to say nothing)	taisant tu(e)(s)	tais tais tait taisons taisez taisent	taise taises taise taisions taisiez taisent	tais + ais ais ait ions iez aient	tair + ai as a ons ez ont	tair + ais ais ait ions iez aient	tais-toi taisons-nous taisez-vous
tenir *avoir* (to hold, to keep)	tenant tenu	tiens tiens tient tenons tenez tiennent	tienne tiennes tienne tenions teniez tiennent	ten + ais ais ait ions iez aient	tiendr + ai as a ons ez ont	tiendr + ais ais ait ions iez aient	tiens tenons tenez

Infinitive	Pres. & Past Participles	Present Indicative	Present Subjunctive	Imperfect Indicative	Future	Conditional	Imperative
vaincre *avoir* (to conquer)	vainquant vaincu	vaincs vaincs vainc vainquons vainquez vainquent	vainque vainques vainque vainquions vainquiez vainquent	vainqu + ais ais ait ions iez aient	vaincr + ai as a ons ez ont	vaincr + ais ais ait ions iez aient	vaincs vainquons vainquez
valoir *avoir* (to be worth)	valant valu	vaux vaux vaut valons valez valent	vaille vailles vaille valions valiez vaillent	val + ais ais ait ions iez aient	vaudr + ai as a ons ez ont	vaudr + ais ais ait ions iez aient	vaux† valons valez
venir *être* (to come)	venant venu(e)(s)	viens viens vient venons venez viennent	vienne viennes vienne venions veniez viennent	ven + ais ais ait ions iez aient	viendr + ai as a ons ez ont	viendr + ais ais ait ions iez aient	viens venons venez
vivre *avoir* (to live)	vivant vécu	vis vis vit vivons vivez vivent	vive vives vive vivions viviez vivent	viv + ais ais ait ions iez aient	vivr + ai as a ons ez ont	vivr + ais ais ait ions iez aient	vis vivons vivez

† The imperative of **valoir** is not often used.